# Singapore

# WORLD BIBLIOGRAPHICAL SERIES

General Editors:

Robert G. Neville (Executive Editor)

John J. Horton                    Ian Wallace

Hans H. Wellisch        Ralph Lee Woodward, Jr.

**John J. Horton** is Deputy Librarian of the University of Bradford and currently Chairman of its Academic Board of Studies in Social Sciences. He has maintained a longstanding interest in the discipline of area studies and its associated bibliographical problems, with special reference to European Studies. In particular he has published in the field of Icelandic and of Yugoslav studies, including the two relevant volumes in the World Bibliographical Series.

**Ian Wallace** is Professor of Modern Languages at Loughborough University of Technology. A graduate of Oxford in French and German, he also studied in Tübingen. Heidelberg and Lausanne before taking teaching posts at universities in the USA, Scotland and England. He specializes in East German affairs, especially literature and culture, on which he has published numerous articles and books. In 1979 he founded the journal *GDR Monitor*, which he continues to edit.

**Hans H. Wellisch** is Professor emeritus at the College of Library and Information Services, University of Maryland. He was President of the American Society of Indexers and was a member of the International Federation for Documentation. He is the author of numerous articles and several books on indexing and abstracting, and has published *The Conversion of Scripts* and *Indexing and Abstracting: an International Bibliography*. He also contributes frequently to *Journal of the American Society for Information Science*, *The Indexer* and other professional journals.

**Ralph Lee Woodward, Jr.** is Chairman of the Department of History at Tulane University, New Orleans, where he has been Professor of History since 1970. He is the author of *Central America, a Nation Divided*, 2nd ed. (1985), as well as several monographs and more than sixty scholarly articles on modern Latin America. He has also compiled volumes in the World Bibliographical Series on *Belize* (1980), *Nicaragua* (1983), and *El Salvador* (forthcoming). Dr. Woodward edited the Central American section of the *Research Guide to Central America and the Caribbean* (1985) and is currently editor of the Central American history section of the *Handbook of Latin American Studies*.

VOLUME 95

# Singapore

Stella R. Quah
Jon S. T. Quah
*Compilers*

## CLIO PRESS
OXFORD, ENGLAND · SANTA BARBARA, CALIFORNIA
DENVER, COLORADO

© Copyright 1988 by Clio Press Ltd.

All rights reserved. No part of this publication may be reproduced, stored in any retrieval system, or transmitted in any form or by any means, electronic, mechanical, photocopying or otherwise, without the prior permission in writing of the publishers.

British Library Cataloguing in Publication Data

Quah, Stella R.
Singapore. —— (World Bibliographical Series; 95).
I. Singapore. Bibliographies
I. Title  II. Quah, Jon S.T.
016.9595'7

ISBN 1–85109–071–1



Clio Press Ltd.,
55 St. Thomas' Street,
Oxford OX1 1JG, England.

ABC-Clio Information Services,
Riviera Campus, 2040 Alameda Padre Serra,
Santa Barbara, CA 93103, USA.



Designed by Bernard Crossland.
Typeset by Columns Design and Production Services, Reading, England.
Printed and bound in Great Britain by
Billing and Sons Ltd., Worcester.

# THE WORLD BIBLIOGRAPHICAL SERIES

This series, which is principally designed for the English speaker, will eventually cover every country in the world, each in a separate volume comprising annotated entries on works dealing with its history, geography, economy and politics; and with its people, their culture, customs, religion and social organization. Attention will also be paid to current living conditions – housing, education, newspapers, clothing, etc. – that are all too often ignored in standard bibliographies; and to those particular aspects relevant to individual countries. Each volume seeks to achieve, by use of careful selectivity and critical assessment of the literature, an expression of the country and an appreciation of its nature and national aspirations, to guide the reader towards an understanding of its importance. The keynote of the series is to provide, in a uniform format, an interpretation of each country that will express its culture, its place in the world, and the qualities and background that make it unique. The views expressed in individual volumes, however, are not necessarily those of the publisher.

## VOLUMES IN THE SERIES

# Contents

# Contents

# Introduction

Singapore has been described in numerous ways by insiders and outsiders, but some of the most common labels given are island-republic, city-state, global city, crossroads of the world, garden city, and one of the little dragons of the East. All these labels are appropriate, as will be appreciated shortly.

Physically, Singapore comprises the main island measuring 570.4 square kilometres and about fifty-seven islets, which add another 51.3 square kilometres to the total land area. Singapore is located between latitudes 1°09-1°29 degrees North and longitudes 103°38-104°06 degrees East, about 136.8 kilometres north of the Equator. Given its location in the Torrid Zone and the fact that there are no major mountains, the climate tends to be uniformly hot and humid with an average daily temperature of 26.6 degrees centigrade, ranging between 23.8 and 30.7 degrees centigrade.

In terms of distance, Singapore's closest neighbours are Malaysia to the north (the shortest distance between Singapore and Peninsular Malaysia is just 640 metres across the Strait of Johor) and east (the Malaysian states of Sabah and Sarawak) and Indonesia to the south.

According to figures for June 1986 in *Singapore facts and pictures 1987*, the population of Singapore was slightly more than two and one-half million, of which 76.3 per cent were Chinese, 15 per cent Malay, 6.4 per cent Indian, and 2.3 per cent were persons from Eurasian and other ethnic groups. This is just one of the dimensions of heterogeneity in the country. The population is also rather diverse in terms of religion and language. All the major world religions are represented in this small island, viz., Islam, Christianity, Buddhism, Hinduism, and a number of other religious groups. People speak English, Mandarin, Malay, and Tamil in addition to a large number of Chinese, Indian, and other dialects. It is thus common for the average Singaporean to be able to communicate in more than one language or dialect; perhaps the only monolingual people may be found among the thousands of tourists visiting Singapore each day.

To be able to function as a nation in the midst of such diversity, the state has taken a secular position, and the constitution guarantees freedom of religion and equality for all citizens irrespective of sex, religion, or ethnicity. The principle of freedom of worship is evident to the visitor in the numerous temples, mosques, churches, and shrines of all religious persuasions that dot the land. The language issue is represented in the recognition of Mandarin, Malay, Tamil, and English as official languages since the time when Singapore became a republic. Furthermore, there is a bilingual educational policy whereby school students are trained to be proficient in their mother tongue and English. There are, however, plans to proceed with a system of using only English as the medium of instruction in schools. The National University of Singapore and all tertiary educational institutions use only English as their medium of instruction. English is also the *de facto* language of state administration. There is a multilingual mass media; television, radio, and newspapers use one, some, or all of the four official languages.

Singapore was a British colony for nearly 140 years and attained internal self-government peacefully in June 1959. Ten political parties and thirty-four independent candidates contested the fifty-one seats in the 1959 general election. The People's Action Party (PAP) won forty-three of the fifty-one seats, and Lee Kuan Yew became the first Prime Minister of Singapore, as he was the leader of the PAP. For a brief period, (1963-65), Singapore merged with Malaysia as a federation. Since 9 August 1965, however, Singapore has been an independent republic.

As a former British colony, Singapore experienced the British judicial and political systems and retained most of the features of both systems upon gaining independence. Accordingly, Singapore's political system may be classified as a parliamentary democracy fashioned after the British model. As stated in the constitution, the president is the head of state and is elected for a four-year term by the unicameral parliament, which consists of seventy-nine members elected from single-member constituencies by a simple majority vote. However, this system may be modified. There is now a government proposal before a select parliamentary committee for the setting up of a system of team members of parliament, suggesting that certain pre-assigned electoral constituencies, or Group Representation Constituencies, may elect a team of three candidates instead of a single candidate. Parliament has a maximum term of five years, unless it is dissolved earlier by the president. The latter also appoints the Prime Minister as head of the government on the basis of a majority vote of the parliament. The Prime Minister and fourteen other ministers constitute the Cabinet, which is the supreme policy-making body of the government. However, while the Cabinet has the general direction and control of the government, it is collectively responsible to Parliament, which is the supreme legislative authority in the country.

Elections are free, fair, and held regularly. General elections are usually held within three months of the dissolution of Parliament. In practice, general elections have been held about once every four years from 1959 to 1984. There are twenty registered political parties in Singapore since 1950 (*Singapore facts and pictures 1987*, p. 30). To prevent political parties from unduly influencing the voters in a general election, voting was made compulsory after the May 1959 general election. The PAP's record in all the past seven general elections is impressive. The PAP won thirty-seven out of fifty-one seats in the 1963 election, all fifty-eight seats in the 1968 election with fifty-one seats uncontested, all sixty-five seats in the 1972 election with eight seats uncontested, all sixty-nine seats in the 1976 election with sixteen seats uncontested, all seventy-five seats in the 1980 election with thirty-seven seats returned unopposed and seventy-seven of the seventy-nine seats in the 1984 election with thirty seats uncontested and two seats won by the opposition parties, one each by the Workers' Party and the Singapore Democratic Party. The 1984 election was particularly significant because, for the first time since 1963, two opposition parties were able to succeed, albeit in small measure, in their contest for votes against the PAP. Currently, only one of the two opposition members remains in Parliament, namely Chiam See Tong, chairman of the Singapore Democratic Party, who was elected to Parliament for the first time in 1984. The Workers' Party Member of Parliament, J. B. Jeyaratnam, who had first entered Parliament when he won the Anson by-election in October 1981, had to step down in November 1986 after he lost his appeal against conviction for making a false declaration regarding his party's accounts and was fined S$5,000.

In view of the racial, linguistic, and religious diversity of the population, any incumbent government in Singapore must formulate and implement policies which will encourage and

promote harmony among the various ethnic groups. Another
obligation of the ruling government in this plural society is to
ensure that both public and private organizations in Singapore
are fair and impartial in their treatment of their clientele and
personnel, regardless of race, language, or religion. Not surpris-
ingly, there is a Presidential Council for Minority Rights, which
examines bills presented in Parliament to ensure that the rights of
the different minority groups in Singapore are not endangered.

In addition to Prime Minister Lee Kuan Yew, the current
Cabinet consists of fourteen other members: the Senior Minister
(Prime Minister's Office), S. Rajaratnam; the First Deputy Prime
Minister and Minister for Defence, Goh Chok Tong; the Second
Deputy Prime Minister, Ong Teng Cheong; the Minister for Law,
E. W. Barker; the Minister for Foreign Affairs and Minister for
National Development, S. Dhanabalan; the Minister for Educa-
tion, Tony Tan Keng Yam (PhD); the Minister for the
Environment, Ahmad Mattar (PhD); the Minister for Communi-
cations and Information and Second Minister for Defence
[Policy], Yeo Ning Hong (PhD); the Minister for Home Affairs
and Second Minister for Law, S. Jayakumar; the Minister for
Finance, Richard Hu Tsu Tau (PhD); the Minister for Labour,
Lee Yock Suan; the Minister for Community Development and
Second Minister for Foreign Affairs, Wong Kan Seng; the
Minister for Trade and Industry and Second Minister for Defence
[Services], Lee Hsien Loong (Brigadier-General, Reservist); and
the Acting Minister for Health, Yeo Cheow Tong.

The judicial system comprises the Supreme Court and the
Subordinate Courts. The Supreme Court consists of the High
Court, the Court of Appeal, the Court of Criminal Appeal, a
registrar, a deputy registrar, a senior assistant registrar, and
assistant registrars in charge of administrative and judicial
matters. The President, on advice of the Prime Minister, appoints
the Chief Justice and the other seven judges of the Supreme
Court. The Subordinate Courts include district, magistrates',
juvenile, and coroner's courts; the Small Claims Tribunal; and
registrars and deputy registrars. The Judicial Committee of the
Privy Council, whose proceedings are conducted in the United
Kingdom, is the final appellate court in Singapore.

With an export-oriented economy and negligible natural
resources, Singapore's economy is highly vulnerable to international fluctuations. The economy has experienced a recovery
from the 1985 recession: in 1986, there was a 1.9 per cent
economic growth in real terms and an expansion of the

manufacturing, transport and communications sectors. Tourist arrivals passed the three million mark in the same year. The economy recovered even further in 1987 when it grew by 8.8 per cent. Basic standard of living indicators point to a relatively comfortable life in Singapore. According to *Singapore facts and pictures 1987* (p. 36), in 1986 the per capita Gross National Product was S$14,435 [US$1 = S$2.05]; annual electricity consumption per capita was 3,664.0 kWh; water consumption per person for the year was 103,044 litres; there was one television set for every five persons; one telephone for every two persons; one public bus for every 299 persons; one taxi for every 242 persons; one doctor for every 930 persons; one nurse for every 302 persons; and one hospital bed for every 259 persons.

More importantly, home ownership is increasing consistently: by 1986, eighty-five per cent of the population were living in public housing apartments, most of them as owners. Indeed, the public housing programme has been remarkably successful. As a shortage of housing was a serious social problem, the British colonial government ordered and collected reports from various special housing commissions from 1907 to 1947. The common denominator in those reports was the finding that overcrowding and unsanitary housing conditions required prompt government action. In 1927, the colonial government created the Singapore Improvement Trust (SIT) as a planning authority in charge of implementing the General Improvement Plan. However, very little was actually accomplished by the SIT as far as housing was concerned. The last colonial Housing Committee, appointed in 1947 to seek solutions to the acute housing shortage, recommended the building of 4,336 units to accommodate about 36,000 people for the period 1948 to 1950. The SIT did not meet the stated goal and could complete only 2,359 housing units during that period. Similarly, the goal of 19,395 units was set for the period 1955-59, and again the SIT built only 10,978 units.

When the PAP government took office under internal self-government in 1959, they 'inherited' a serious housing problem. The government abolished the SIT and created the Housing and Development Board (HDB) to deal specifically with the housing building programme. The Housing and Development Act of 1960 gives the Minister for National Development the power to administer the low-cost housing programme, which includes the clearance of slums (completed some years ago) and the erection, conversion, improvement, and extension of any building for sale, lease, rental, or other purposes. Operating under the portfolio of the Minister for National Development, the HDB, as a statutory board, has completed five Five-Year Building Programmes. In 1986, HDB completed 38,097 dwelling units and had 51,990 more units under construction during the same year. Under the Home Ownership Scheme launched in 1964, the HDB has sold 427,755 apartments, according to figures as of 31 December 1986 (*Singapore facts and pictures 1987*, p. 109). The sixth Five-Year Building Programme, 1986-90, is now in progress.

The success in public housing is just one item in the list of Singapore's accomplishments. Similar impressive results have been obtained in curbing population growth; controlling once endemic communicable diseases; organizing the flow of traffic, making the small island's airline, Singapore Airlines, one of the top air carriers in the world in terms of efficiency and service; turning the swampy areas, the dirty, rat-infested back lanes, and the old congested neighbourhoods into a clean garden city; and, overall, transforming a small-scale entrepôt economy into a high-technology-based economy competing aggressively and success-fully with such countries as South Korea, Taiwan, and Hong Kong – the other little dragons – in the world market.

All these aspects and more of the history and life of Singapore and its people are described, analysed, praised, and criticized in the books and articles contained in this bibliography. A final word must be said about the details of the bibliography.

*The bibliography*

There were several guidelines set for this project in terms of the scope of the work included, the time period covered, the maximum number of entries, and the language and accessibility of the material. We set out to include works dealing with Singapore as the only, or the major, topic, and have selected publications concerned with some thirty-four subject areas (see chapter headings); material produced by Singaporeans on other topics has been excluded.

It would not have been feasible to have included all of the publications on Singapore in one volume and, moreover, we wanted to direct readers to the most recent works. Accordingly, a maximum number of 750 entries was decided upon, with most of the works being published between 1980 and 1988. However, earlier publications of special significance have been included, particularly concerning the areas of history and politics. We followed the publishers' policy on covering, wherever possible, only publications in the English language. In addition, in order to inform readers about material that can be easily obtained in book shops and libraries, all unpublished items such as theses, dissertations, academic exercises, and mimeographed material of restricted circulation have been excluded.

To the above restrictions of topic, time, space, language, and accessibility, we must add the aspect of selection. We have used our personal judgement in selecting publications providing the most interesting, comprehensive, reliable, and unique information on Singapore. Nonetheless, despite our best efforts to cover the ground as thoroughly as possible, there will inevitably be some omissions. However, we are confident that the vast majority of the significant publications on Singapore that fall within the above guidelines are to be found in this volume.

The books, journal articles, and other publications included in this bibliography provide specific details on the lives, work, recreation, beliefs, attitudes, hopes, and aspirations of Singaporeans. It is hoped that the reader will find the information not only useful but also intriguing, and that he or she will decide to pay a visit to this fascinating nation.

## Acknowledgements

In the course of searching for published material on Singapore many people were contacted and interviewed, either as authors, or as sources of information on further sources. We wish to express our gratitude to all those who helped by providing information, or facilitating access to books and articles. We are very grateful to the authors (too many to be listed here) who kindly provided us with copies of their publications and patiently answered all our queries. The Librarians at the National University of Singapore (NUS), particularly those at the Reference Department, provided kind, cheerful, and efficient assistance in conducting the computer searches without which this project would have taken much longer to complete. Last, but definitely not least, we are indebted to Dr. Robert G. Neville, Executive Editor of the World Bibliographical Series at Clio Press, for his professional advice and comments on the original manuscript and for his patience and understanding.

*Stella R. Quah*
*Jon S. T. Quah*
*Singapore, May 1988*

# The Country and Its People

1 **Singapore in Southeast Asia: an economic and political appraisal.**
Iain Buchanan. London: G. Bell, 1971. 331p.
This volume includes eight chapters which provide an overview of important aspects of the country as they appeared in the early 1970s. The first three chapters cover, in chronological order, the economic development of Singapore and the subjects of other chapters are: ethnic and linguistic diversity; socioeconomic disparities; the problem of poverty; Singapore in Southeast Asia; and political power in a city-state. There is a list of references and an index.

2 **The development progress of Hong Kong and Singapore.**
Theodore Geiger, Frances M. Geiger. Hong Kong: Macmillan, 1975. 239p. bibliog.
This book was first published in the United States under the title *Tales of two city-states* in 1973. The authors compare and discuss the 'macro-economic management and development policies' of the two city-states in ten chapters organized in three parts. The first part deals with an overview of development progress and policies and the Chinese sociocultural background. The second part is on Hong Kong and includes its change from entrepôt to manufacturing, economic prospects, fruits of economic growth, and government structure and policies. The third part deals with Singapore in terms of challenges and responses, the economy and its prospects, Singapore's search for the good life, and government structure and politics. There are four appendixes and an index.

3 **Our heritage and beyond: a collection of essays on Singapore, its past, present and future.**
Edited by S. Jayakumar. Singapore: Singapore National Trade Unions Congress (NTUC), 1982. 173p.
As a Member of Parliament (currently also Minister with two portfolios, Law and Home Affairs), Jayakumar offers an interesting collection of fourteen essays

1

discussing matters of social policy concerning education, the economy, health care, public housing, the trade unions, foreign policy, defence, and welfare. The special feature of this book is that most of the chapter contributors are policy-makers themselves, including the Prime Minister, six other cabinet members, members of parliament, and heads of statutory boards or corporations.

## 4 A salute to Singapore.
Anthony Lawrence. Singapore: Times of Singapore, 1984. 284p.

This book celebrates the 25th anniversary of Singapore's self-rule. A carefully selected group of forty-one well-known photographers from all over the world was given an assignment to capture the achievements of Singapore during the past twenty-five years. The outcome, this book, was considered 'a superb effort' by the President of the Republic. This remarkable collection of photographs is indeed one of the best introductions to the country and its people today.

## 5 Singapore – a decade of independnece.
Edited by Charles Ng, T. P. B. Menon. Singapore: Alumni International Singapore, 1975. 127p.

Presents papers by Singaporean intellectuals on the early pioneers, the young Singaporean, morality, urban transport, the arts, population control, shipping, scientific technological infrastructure, and Singapore at the United Nations.

## 6 1907 handbook to Singapore.
G. M. Reith. Singapore: Oxford University Press, 1985. 3rd ed.

This handbook was first published in 1892 and a second edition appeared fifteen years later. This third edition is mostly of historical interest; although the author's aim was to provide a guide for travellers to Singapore, his description of details no longer found in the Republic adds to the historical material on Singapore.

## 7 Singapore: towards the year 2000.
Edited by Saw Swee-Hock, R. S. Bhathal. Singapore: Singapore Association for the Advancement of Science, 1981. 163p.

A collection of twelve papers by political leaders and intellectuals. The essays deal with political development, the emerging administrative state, population growth, political parties and trade unions, the environment, technological changes, energy conservation, medicine, the fine arts, cultural change and social values, and the prospects for this creative society.

## 8 Trends in Singapore. Proceedings and background paper.
Edited by Seah Chee Meow. Singapore: Singapore University Press; Institute of Southeast Asian Studies, 1975. 153p.

A collection of papers presented in a seminar of the same title organized by the Institute of Southeast Asian Studies. It deals with the challenges to security and stability and various views on Singapore's politics and economics.

9  **Straits Times Annual.**
   Times Periodicals, Pte. Ltd.   Singapore: Times Periodicals, (annual).
This yearly magazine includes feature articles on various aspects of life in
Singapore and of general interest such as poetry, photography, and essays on
historical, social, and other aspects. The reader may find one main problem with
this publication: nearly one half of the total number of pages are dedicated to
advertisements.

10  **Singapore, its successes and future.**
    K. G. Tregonning.   Singapore: J. M. Sasson, 1980. 32p.
For a reader in need of a brief description of the most salient aspects of
Singapore, this booklet will be useful. It contains colour photographs and deals
with eleven subjects of development in Singapore: the airline, the government,
industry, public housing, tourism, the university, finance, banking, and the stock
exchange. The author presents his views on these subjects in an anecdotal style,
sparing the reader the trouble of reading numerical data, charts and tables. The
booklet may be a good start for the reader who is completely unfamiliar with
Singapore and wants to have a bird's-eye view of the nation at the beginning of
the 1980s. However, for a more precise and up-to-date description of Singapore's
development, including reliable statistics, the reader is referred to the sections of
this bibliography on statistics and population, and government publications such
as *Singapore facts & pictures.*

11  **Singapore.**
    Ines Vente, Rolf E. Vente.   Singapore: MPH, 1979. 196p.
This book is a conversation piece, providing a pictorial view of life in Singapore.
The good quality colour photographs were taken by Ines Vente, while Rolf Vente
wrote the accompanying text. The latter was kept at a minimum, simply giving
brief background information for every photograph. It appears that the authors
did not want to distract the reader's attention from the colours and textures of
landscapes and faces depicted in the photographs.

12  **Area handbook for Singapore.**
    Nena Vreeland (et al.).   Washington, DC: American University,
    1977. 210p. bibliog. (Foreign Area Studies).
A useful but outdated handbook on Singapore. The nine chapters in the book
deal with the general character of the society, geography, population, and labour
force, historical setting, social organization and values, political setting, political
process, character and structure of the economy, foreign trade and finance, and
armed forces and internal security.

13  **Singapore: twenty-five years of development.**
    Edited by You Poh Seng, Lim Chong Yah.   Singapore: Nan Yang
    Xing Zhou Lianhe Zaobao, 1984. 392p.
This volume of fifteen essays was written by economists, political scientists, and
sociologists from the National University of Singapore to commemorate the
celebration of Singapore's twenty-five years of nation-building. In the introduc-

3

**The Country and Its People**

tory chapter, Lim Chong Yah describes the physical, demographic, economic, social, and political transformation in Singapore from 1959 to 1984. The four chapters in Part I deal with the patterns of economic structure, changing patterns of foreign trade and investment, the fiscal system, and money, banking, and finance. Part II focuses on population and manpower topics and has four chapters on population trends, human resources development, labour-management relations, and productivity trends. Political and social topics are discussed in Part III, which also has four chapters on political change and continuity, public enterprises, the public bureaucracy, and social change and planning. 'ASEAN economic cooperation and Singapore' is the only chapter in Part IV. The concluding chapter by Ow Chin Hock compares the economic and social conditions of Singapore between the 1950s and the early 1980s.

# Geography
# and Tourism

14 **Singapore's river, a living legacy.**
   Linda Berry.   Singapore: Eastern Universities Press, 1982. 92p.
   map.
A collection of charming photographs of river scenes and people, accompanied by
an account of the history of human settlements along the Singapore River aimed
at the general reader. The author's principal objective is to describe the features
of the landscape and the riverside-dwellers.

15 **Study of lightning deaths in Singapore.**
   T. C. Chao, J. E. Pakiam, J. Chia.   *Singapore Medical Journal*,
   vol. 22, no. 3 (1981), p. 150-57.
A study of deaths caused by lightning during the period 1956 to 1979, including
the circumstances leading to death, the mode of death, and post-mortem results.
The authors' conclusion includes some preventative advice.

16 **The Straits of Malacca and Singapore: navigational, resource, and
   environmental considerations.**
   Chia Lin Sien.   In: *Southeast Asian seas: frontiers for development.*
   Edited by Chia Lin Sien, Colin MacAndrews. Singapore: McGraw-
   Hill, 1981, p. 239-63.
A review of the legal and political aspects of the management of resources of the
region including the influence of the superpowers and the adoption of the Traffic
Separation Scheme (TSS), the navigational features of the Straits, and the need
for a monitoring system to implement the TSS.

17   **Utilization and management of Singapore's coastal zone.**
Chia Lin Sien.   In: *Proceedings of MAB/COMAR Regional
Seminar on Man's Impact on Coastal and Estuarine Ecosystems.*
Edited by Toshiro Saeki. Tokyo: MAB Coordinating Committee of
Japan and Japan National Commission for UNESCO, 1985,
p. 13-16.

The paper describes the transformation of the coastal zone in Singapore and the
role played by government agencies in the planning and implementation of coastal
zone use and management projects.

18   **Culture shock. Singapore and Malaysia.**
JoAnn Craig.   Singapore: Times Books International, 1979. 217p.

Described as an example of 'practical anthropology studies' (in the foreword),
and 'a survival kit for expatriates' and 'a vast eye-opener' for world travellers (by
two reviewers), the book discusses in seven chapters various cultural differences
that may, if not understood and accepted, cause conflict, insult, or embarrassment
to both the visitor and his or her local hosts in Singapore and Malaysia. The first
two chapters deal with some general aspects of cultural differences, courtesies,
and customs. Chapters 3 to 5 discuss separately the Chinese, Malay, and Indian
communities and their customs. The last two chapters focus on the visitor's
cultural shock and provide some guidelines of behaviour for expatriates.

19   **Impressions of Singapore.**
Geoffrey Dutton.   Singapore: Times Books International, 1981.
152p. maps.

Primarily a traveller's book which describes in engaging prose various aspects of
interest to actual or potential visitors, including some episodes in Singapore's
history and details of daily life among some Singapore communities. Colour
photographs help to convey an invitation to the reader to visit Singapore.

20   **Geographic analysis of Singapore's population.**
John W. Humphrey.   Singapore: Department of Statistics, 1985.
195p. maps. (Census Monograph no. 5).

The latest volume of a monograph series, commissioned and published by the
Department of Statistics, on specific themes based on the population figures of the
1980 Census of Population. The other monographs in the series cover
demography, language, and housing themes. Humphrey presents a detailed
analysis of seven aspects of the geography of Singapore's population: the
historical patterns in colonial and modern Singapore; the population distribution
in 1980; the current demographic characteristics; literacy, education, and
economic characteristics; housing and household patterns; and a projection of
future patterns of population growth and distribution. Twenty-eight tables, 59
maps, and 4 charts provide further information.

21  **Lightning fatalities in Singapore.**
    J. E. Pakiam, T. C. Chao, J. Chia.  *Meteorological Magazine*,
    vol. 110 (1981), p. 175-87.

A detailed description and analysis of statistics on deaths caused by lightning
covering data since 1922. The authors report on the variation of these figures in
terms of sex, month, diurnal variation, location, and other relevant aspects. See
also 'Study of lightning deaths in Singapore' by T. C. Chao, J. E. Pakiam, and
J. Chia in this section.

22  **Singapore landscape: a historical overview of housing change.**
    Siew-Eng Teo, Victor R. Savage.  *Singapore Journal of Tropical
    Geography*, vol. 6, no. 1 (1985), p. 48-63.

A description of the continuous transformation that Singapore's landscape has
undergone since 1819 when Sir Thomas Stamford Raffles established Singapore as
a British colony. The main emphasis of the paper is on the historical development
of housing.

23  **Some aspects of applied coastal geomorphology in Singapore.**
    Wong Poh Poh.  In: *Proceedings of First International Conference
    on Geomorphology, Abstracts of Papers*. Edited by T. Spencer.
    Manchester: University of Manchester, 1985. Abstract 655.

A study of the physical features of major beaches in Singapore, identifying and
describing three types of beaches.

7

# Flora and Fauna

**24  Fungi in the coastal waters of Singapore.**

V. Balakrisna, T. K. Tan, G. Lim.   *Journal of the Singapore National Academy of Science*, vol. 10 (1983), p. 1-3.

A report of the findings from a survey of fungi in seven coastal sites in Singapore, describing and discussing the nineteen species identified in the study. See also the article by T. K. Tan and G. Linn in this section.

**25  Living with plants. A gardening guide for Singapore and Malaysia.**

Amy Ede, John Ede.   Singapore: MPH Publications, 1980. 83p.

A charming combination of advice and colour photographs, designed to help the budding gardener, by two of the most successful gardeners in Singapore (the Edes specialize in the cultivation of orchids). The book is divided into two sections dealing with outdoor, and indoor gardening, respectively. The Edes had two main collaborators: Norma O. Miraflor, who edited the text, and Alan Lee, who took the photographs.

**26  Butterflies of West Malaysia and Singapore.**

W. A. Fleming.   Singapore: Longman Malaysia, 1975. 2 vols.

A fine collection of colour plates of butterflies organized as a catalogue, or guide, with scientific names and other relevant information briefly presented for each type or species.

**27  A guide to the wild flowers of Singapore.**

Foo Tok Shiew.   Singapore: Singapore Science Centre, 1985. 160p.

A pocketbook, ideal for the active explorer, including brief but informative descriptions of local wild flowers and colour photographs.

28 **Birds of Singapore.**
Christopher Hails. Singapore: Times Editions, 1987. 168p. maps.
Hails divides his study into six sections dealing with the environmental features of the island and additional sections telling where the birds are found, their habitats, and practices. He includes a species checklist, a glossary, and an index. There are numerous diagrams, illustrations, and maps.

29 **Coral reefs of Malaysia and Singapore.**
Lisette Henrey. Singapore: Longman Malaysia, 1982. 81p.
This volume is part of the series entitled Malaysia Nature Handbooks edited by M. W. F. Tweedie. Henrey describes the coral community and reef animals and provides guidelines for the exploration of the reef. The book includes an index and two appendixes with sources of information and a description of an emergency medical kit.

30 **Mosses of Singapore and Malaysia.**
Anne Johnson. Singapore: Singapore University Press, 1980. 126p.
A detailed description of a large number of mosses, illustrated by drawings.

31 **Orders and families of Malayan seed plants.**
H. Keng. Singapore: Singapore University Press, 1983. 3rd ed. 500p.
A textbook presenting a concise but comprehensive treatise of the flora of the Malay Peninsula and Singapore first published in 1969 and reprinted several times.

32 **Annotated list of seed plants of Singapore (X).**
H. Keng. *Gardens Bulletin*, vol. 39 (1986), p. 67-95.
This is the latest installment published (Part XI is in press) of a detailed list of seed plants in Singapore. Part I appeared in vol. 26 (1973), p. 233-37 and dealt with gymnosperms, enumerating seven families and thirty-two species.

33 **A guide to shrimps, prawns, lobsters, and crabs of Malaysia and Singapore.**
Compiled by Donald L. Lovett. Selangor, Malaysia: Faculty of Fisheries and Marine Science, August 1981. 156p. (Occasional Publication no. 2).
A professional publication including a description of various species of crustacea in the region and providing detailed diagrams of their anatomy, scientific names, references, and a systematic index.

34 **Heinemann guide to common epiphytic ferns of Malaysia and Singapore.**
Audrey Piggot. Singapore: Heinemann Educational Books, 1979. 26p.

A brief but useful description of the fern flora typical of the rain forest vegetation in the region. See also the work of Wee Yeow Chin in this section.

35 **Plants and flowers of Singapore.**
Ivan Polunin. Singapore: Times Editions, 1987. 160p. bibliog.

This is the most recent, and one of the best, books on the flora of Singapore. Polunin brings his vast experience as a naturalist and contributor to the *National Geographic* magazine and the Time-Life series into this study. The narrative is engaging and the abundant colour photographs of Singapore's flora are among the best ever published. The book is a testimony to the reputation of Singapore as a 'garden city'. Polunin provides a background on the original setting and vegetation, and discusses man's influence including agricultural activity; the urban survivors; ornamental plants and gardening; the Botanic Gardens; and the greening of Singapore. There is also a discussion of species, a glossary, and an index.

36 **Fungi in the fresh waters of Singapore.**
T. K. Tan, G. Lim. *Journal of the Singapore National Academy of Science*, vol. 13 (1984), p. 185-91.

A report of findings from a survey of fungi in water samples collected from reservoirs, rivers, a lake, a pond and canals in Singapore. The genera and species found are described. See also the article by V. Balakrisna, T. K. Tan, and G. Lim in this section.

37 **Seaweeds of Singapore.**
Teo Lee Wei, Wee Yeow Chin. Singapore: Singapore University Press, 1983. 123p. bibliog.

The authors, both botanists, offer a careful and expert study of seaweeds in Singapore. Diagrams, a glossary, and an index are included.

38 **Singapore green: a history and guide to the Botanic Gardens.**
Bonnie Tinsley. Singapore: Times Books International, 1983. 139p.

In this description of Singapore's oldest national park, Tinsley provides a brief history of the gardens from 1819. She then takes the reader for a stroll through the gardens, an illusion encouraged not only by her vivid prose but also by numerous colour photographs, most of which were taken by the author and her husband.

39 **Mangrove ecosystem in Singapore.**
Wee Yeow Chin. In: *Proceedings of the Symposium on Mangrove Forest Ecosystem Productivity in Southeast Asia.* Bogor, Indonesia: Biotrop, 1983, p. 93-98. (Special Publication no. 17).

A succinct historical account of the evolution and changes in mangrove vegetation in Singapore, a description of the small secondary mangrove areas that have survived the threat of urban development, and an appeal for the preservation of nature reserves.

40 **A guide to ferns in Singapore.**
Wee Yeow Chin. Singapore: Singapore Centre, 1983. 72p.

A pictorial description of the different species of ferns. See also the work by Audrey Piggott in this section.

41 **The role of nature reserves in an urban Singapore.**
Wee Yeow Chin. *Malayan Naturalist*, vol. 37, no. 3 (1984), p. 17-20.

Describes the open and recreational spaces available to Singapore's urban population, noting that there is still much to be done to bring apartment dwellers closer to nature, primarily by creating more parks.

42 **Common ferns and fern-allies of Singapore.**
Wee Yeow Chin. Singapore: Malayan Nature Society (Singapore Branch), 1984. 84p.

Compared to his *Guide to ferns in Singapore* (q.v.) published in 1983, Wee presents in this book a more detailed and sober study. The illustrations, plates, and photographs are very useful. An earlier study on the same subject was conducted by Anne Johnson and published in 1959 in the *Malayan Nature Journal* and appeared again in 1977 as a second edition published by the Singapore University Press.

43 **The greening of Singapore: past, present and future.**
Wee Yeow Chin. In: *Proceedings of the 3rd Symposium on Our Environment March 27-29, 1984.* Edited by L. L. Koh, C. S. Hew. Singapore: National University of Singapore, Faculty of Science, 1985, p. 326-31.

A description and discussion of the official efforts to implement the concept of a 'garden city' in Singapore. Three phases of the task are identified: the first phase, initiated in 1967, sought to line all roads with trees; the second phase focused on improving and adding colour; and the third and current phase concentrates on quality. The author suggests guidelines for future development.

11

44  **Tropical ferns as garden and house plants.**
Wee Yeow Chin.   In: *Golden gardening – fifty years of the Singapore Gardening Society*. Edited by Anne Tofield. Singapore: Singapore Gardening Society, 1985, p. 51-55.

A description of the local wild ferns that have horticultural potential, their growing areas, planting material, and guidelines for planting and collecting them.

45  **The city and the forest. Plant life in urban Singapore.**
Wee Yeow Chin, Richard Corlett.   Singapore: Singapore University Press, 1986. 186p. bibliog.

Both authors are members of the Department of Botany, National University of Singapore. They present a serious and careful analysis of the symbiotic link between the urban environment and what is left of the tropical rain forest in Singapore. The book has an index.

46  **Singapore's fabulous Jurong Bird Park.**
Winston Williams.   Singapore: Jurong Bird Park, 1983. 66p.

A guide for visitors to the park, including colour photographs of the exhibits and explanatory captions. For a careful study of birds of Singapore see the work by Christopher Hails in this section.

# History

47  **Singapore 1941-1942.**
Louis Allen.  London: Davis-Poynter, 1977. 343p. bibliog.
This is one of many books written about the 'worst military disaster in British history' i.e., the fall of Singapore to the Japanese during the Second World War. Allen attempts a serious analysis and documentation throughout the twelve chapters. There are also four appendixes with further information and an index. *Defeat in Malaya. The fall of Singapore*, by Arthur Swinson, (New York: Ballantine Books, 1969, 160p.) is concerned with the same period. It is an account of the Japanese campaign in Malaya from 1941 to 1942, the main goal of which was to take Malaya and Singapore. The volume includes a brief bibliography.

48  **An anecdotal history of old times in Singapore 1819-1867.**
Charles Burton Buckley.  Singapore: Oxford University Press, 1984. 790p.
This is the first edition by Oxford University Press of Buckley's book by the same title, originally published in 1902 in Singapore by Fraser and Neave Ltd. Buckley's account of old times in Singapore is well-documented by numerous and lengthy quotations, or full transcripts of relevant historical documents, and is based on his own experience of nearly fifty years of residence in Singapore. This 1984 edition includes a brief but interesting introduction by another renowned historian, C. M. Turnbull.

49  **The Singapore story. From Raffles to Lee Kuan Yew.**
Noel Barber.  Glasgow: Fontana, 1978. 224p. bibliog.
As a personal account of the growth of Singapore, written in an easy anecdotal style, the work is more journalistic than scholarly. The story covers four periods: 'the unknown island', 1819-1941; 'the end of the myth', 1941-45; 'the road to independence', 1945-65; and 'an experiment in living', 1965-78. There is a short list of books consulted and an index. Another work of interest is Noel Barber's *A*

*sinister twilight. The fall of Singapore 1942* (Boston, Massachusetts: Houghton Mifflin, 1968, 364p.). This volume is journalistic reconstruction of the Japanese attack (and subsequent siege and occupation) on Singapore from the viewpoint of the British and local civilian population. The 12 chapters are organized into three parts, dealing with the situation before, during and after, the Japanese attack. There is a bibliography and an index.

## 50 Social and economic history of modern Singapore.
Curriculum Development Institute of Singapore (CDIS). Singapore: Longman, 1984. 266p. maps.

This volume was written by CDIS as a history course textbook for lower secondary school students, reflecting the needs and requirements of the new history syllabus designed by the Ministry of Education. There are two volumes. The first one covers the period 1819 to 1900 and the second one deals with developments from 1901 to 1965. The work is well illustrated, and foreign readers may find it useful as an introduction to Singapore's history before independence.

## 51 Singapore: struggle for success.
John Drysdale. Singapore: Times Books International, 1984. 506p. 2 maps. bibliog.

This detailed history of Singapore from after the Japanese surrender in 1946 until its attainment of independence in August 1965 is described carefully by the author, who has taken three and a half years to complete the book. Using a wide variety of sources, including interviews with prominent leaders of the People's Action Party (PAP), Drysdale has described in detail their struggle with the British colonial government to attain self-government, their battle with the communists, and their fight for racial equality during their two-year sojourn in Malaysia.

## 52 Raffles. The story of Singapore.
Raymond Flower. Singapore: Eastern Universities Press, 1984. 374p.

This is a very readable history book. Its attractive format, clarity of style, and the abundance of high quality photographs, are three of its best features. There are four parts dedicated to the 'Founders' the 'Pioneers' the 'Myth-makers' and the 'agony and the fruition'. Part One covers five chapters on ancient times in Singapore, Penang, and Sir Thomas Stamford Raffles and his arrival in Singapore. Part Two deals with the early years of Singapore under the British, including the Chinese secret societies, the Straits Chinese, and 'daily life in the 1850s'. Part Three continues a narration of life in Singapore until the eve of the Japanese attack in 1941. The chapters in Part Four discuss the modern period of Singapore's development.

## 53 The Singapore saga. Part one.
F. J. George. Singapore: Society of Singapore Writers, 1985. 438p.

Covers the historical period ranging from Sir Thomas Stamford Raffles's landing in Singapore to the attainment of independence in 1965. Includes numerous photographs and an index.

54 **The strategic illusion: the Singapore strategy and the defence of Australia and New Zealand, 1919-1942.**

Ian Hamill. Singapore: Singapore University Press, 1981. 406p.

Analyses the Singapore strategy and the construction of its naval base in the context of the overall British defence policy during the colonial era. There is a critical assessment of the British assumption of its capacity to defend the empire.

55 **Pioneers of Singapore. A catalogue of oral history interviews.**

Lam Bee Goh. Singapore: Archives and Oral History Department, 1984. 171p.

Covers the interviews with seventy-three persons conducted as part of the Pioneers of Singapore Project, which is one of two pioneer oral history projects of the Archives and Oral History Department. Each entry includes the name of the interviewee, the archives' reference number, the interviewee's date of birth and occupation, the duration of interview, language or dialect used, and pagination and language of the transcript.

56 **The historiography of Singapore.**

Edwin Lee. In: *Singapore studies: critical surveys of the humanities and social sciences.* Edited by Basant K. Kapur. Singapore: Singapore University Press, 1986, p. 1-31.

An excellent survey of research done on the history of Singapore from 1819 to 1965 when Singapore attained independence. The major works on the economic, social, diplomatic, military, administrative and political history of Singapore are reviewed in this chapter.

57 **When Singapore was Syonan-to.**

Low Ngiong Ing. Singapore: Eastern Universities Press, 1973. 134p.

This book began as a privately printed and distributed book entitled *This Singapore* (1947) and was written with the collaboration of Cheng Hui Ming, Assistant to the Secretary for Chinese Affairs in Singapore after the Japanese occupation. The present version is an expanded form of the 1947 book and presents a personal account of life in Singapore during the Japanese occupation.

58 **The magic dragon. The story of Singapore.**

Donald Moore. Bungay, England: Richard Clay (Chaucer Press), 1975. 252p.

An interpretation of Singapore's history in an attempt to explain Singapore's success as a new nation.

59 **The fall of Singapore. Great true stories of World War Two.**

Frank Owen. London: Pan Books, 1962. 206p. maps.

A provocative complementary reading to erudite historical studies of the same event. The writer warns that 'this is an angry story' of what some people have described as Britain's worst military disaster in modern history. There are several maps and an index. See also Ivan Simmon's book in this section.

60 **City of the lion.**
J. Norman Parmer. *Wilson Quarterly*, vol. 7, no. 5 (Winter 1983),
p. 48-65.
Parmer, a historian, offers an interesting description of Singapore's colonial past
and its distinguishing features from the time of Sir Thomas Stamford Raffles to
the end of the Japanese occupation in 1945.

61 **Singapore: a popular history 1819-1960.**
H. F. Pearson. Singapore: Eastern University Press, 1961. 166p.
bibliog.
A historical account from the perspective of 'the social lives of the people who
lived in it'. There is an index.

62 **Singapore 150 years. 150th anniversary of the founding of
Singapore.**
Edited by Mubin Sheppard. Singapore: Malaysian Branch of the
Royal Asiatic Society (MBRAS), 1973. 317p.
A collection of twenty-nine papers by historians and historical documents
arranged into two parts. Part 1 deals with ancient Singapore. The papers in Part 2
cover the period from the founding of Singapore to the 1870s. All the papers
appeared before, individually, in various issues of the *Journal of the Malaysian
Branch of the Royal Asiatic Society* and were specially selected and reprinted for
this commemorative publication.

63 **Syonan – my story. The Japanese occupation of Singapore.**
Mamoru Shinozaki. Singapore: Asia Pacific Press, 1975. 123p.
The most important contribution of this book is the particular angle of analysis
offered by the author. Shinozaki was a Director of Education and later the Head
of the Welfare Department in the Japanese occupation government. He offers his
version of the Japanese administration's impact upon the local population and his
efforts at minimizing the hardship suffered by the local residents.

64 **Singapore. Too little, too late. Some aspects of the Malayan disaster
in 1942.**
Ivan Simmon. Kuala Lumpur: University of Malaya Cooperative
Bookstore, 1981. 165p. maps.
The first edition of this book was published in 1970 by Lee Cooper Ltd. of
London. The author, a former British forces chief engineer assigned to the
Malaya Command, decided 'to write my own version', given his disagreement
with official British accounts and the fact that his own reports were disregarded by
the British military authorities. His story is presented in sixteen brief chapters,
which include maps and several photographs. There is an index.

65 **A portrait of Malaysia and Singapore.**
Tan Ding Eing.   Singapore: Oxford University Press, 1975. 266p.
maps.
A history textbook covering seventeen main themes, including the Malacca
sultanate, the Malay powers, and the Johore empire and their relations with
foreign powers, mainly the Portuguese and the British on the one hand and Siam
(now Thailand) on the other. The modern period is discussed by focusing on the
constitutional and political development of Singapore and Malaysia.

66 **Your Chinese roots. The overseas Chinese story.**
Thomas Tsu-wee Tan.   Singapore: Times Books International,
1986. 263p. maps.
This interesting analysis of overseas Chinese communities is presented in twelve
chapters organized in four parts: an introduction; a description of the flow of
Chinese immigrants to America, Australia, New Zealand, and Britain; the efforts
to transplant the Chinese community through the setting up of associations in the
host countries; and a final part on guidelines to trace Chinese origins. While the
general focus is on overseas Chinese, the book has two specific sections on
Singapore. The first of these sections (p. 58-72) deals with Singapore as a major
destination and the characteristics of the early immigrants. The second section
(p. 110-30) describes the features of Chinese community organization in
Singapore.

67 **A history of modern Malaysia and Singapore.**
K. G. Tregonning.   Singapore: Eastern Universities Press, 1972.
298p. bibliog.
A history textbook which was addressed to students taking the Cambridge-
General Certificate of Education examination. It begins with a chapter on the
non-Islamic background and ends with the separation of Singapore from Malaysia
in 1965. There is an index.

68 **A history of Singapore 1819-1975.**
C. M. Turnbull.   Kuala Lumpur: Oxford University Press, 1977.
384p. bibliog.
This is one of the best studies of Singapore's history. The author deals with the
period from 1819 to 1975 and organizes the presentation into nine chapters: the
foundations of the settlement, 1819-26; the little colony, 1826-67; the best period
of the empire, 1867-1914; the consequences of the First World War, 1914-41; the
Second World War, 1941-42 and 1942-45; the postwar period, 1945-55; the road
to independence, 1955-65; and the first decade of independence, 1965-75. There is
a very useful bibliography and an index.

69 **Singapore then and now.**
Ray Tyers.   Singapore: University Education Press, 1976. 260p.
An interesting collection of photographs with detailed captions, covering various
sites of Singapore such as Empress Place, the Singapore River, Collyer and
Raffles Quays, and Serangoon Road, among others.

70 **Scholar, banker, gentleman, soldier. The reminiscences of Dr Yap Pheng Gek.**
Yap Pheng Gek.   Singapore: Times Books International, 1982. 122p.

This book, published under the auspices of the Institute of Southeast Asian Studies, offers an anecdotal history of Singapore. Yap presents, in this small volume, a personalized glimpse of life in Singapore during the first three quarters of this century. The author narrates the story of his life in an engaging prose, providing his own views not only on social and family life but also on the economic and political developments he witnessed and participated in as a member of the local educated Chinese élite of colonial Singapore.

71 **Political development in Singapore 1945-1955.**
Yeo Kim Wah.   Singapore: Singapore University Press, 1973. 320p. bibliog.

Perhaps the most comprehensive and thorough study of a selected period of political development in Singapore, this book was considered to be one of the two best non-fiction books in English by the Singapore Book Development Council in 1976. This study describes the origins of the independence movement in eight chapters dealing with historical background, the political parties involved, the citizenship-language controversy, students politics, labour politics, and the electoral experiment. There is an index.

# Population

72 **Public policy and population change in Singapore.**
Edited by Peter S. J. Chen, James T. Fawcett. New York:
Population Council, 1979. 275p.
A collection of fifteen papers by various academics, government officials, and
medical doctors describing the success of the family planning programme
implemented by the Singapore government in the mid-1960s. Fawcett wrote the
introductory chapter on Singapore's population policies, and he and Chen wrote
their appraisal of the Singapore experience in the concluding chapter. The rest of
the chapters are organized into three parts dealing with the context of Singapore's
population policies, the effects of population policies, and population aspects of
development policies.

73 **Singapore: rapid fertility transition in a compact society.**
James T. Fawcett, Siew-Ean Khoo. *Population and Development
Review*, vol. 6, no. 4 (1980), p. 549-79.
A brief historical background of Singapore emphasizing the urban nature of its
environment and its rapid economic and social development from the 1960s
onwards, illustrated by figures showing the decline in population growth. After
reviewing the wide educational and occupational opportunities available and data
on people's attitudes towards procreation, the authors conclude that the
government's successful approach to population policies could be emulated by
other countries.

74 **Demographic trends in Singapore.**
Saw Swee Hock. Singapore: Department of Statistics, 1981. 75p.
(Census Monograph no. 1).
The Singapore Department of Statistics commissioned experts to conduct detailed
analyses of various aspects of the census data collected in the 1980 Population

Census of Singapore. The analyses were to be published as a monograph series and this work is the first monograph in the series. It provides a succinct study of population changes in Singapore including figures from 1871 and covering basic demographic aspects such as vital statistics, ethnic group, sex ratio, age cohorts, literacy, educational qualifications, occupation, and residential and citizenship status. The last of the volume's five chapters deals with population projections up to the year 2000.

75 **Population projections for Singapore, 1980-2070.**
Saw Swee Hock. Singapore: Institute of Southeast Asian Studies, 1983. 32p.
A brief but useful statistical analysis of the total male and female population figures and the possible trends of growth based on two different assumptions.

76 **Singapore.**
Saw Swee Hock. In: *Population policies in Asian countries: contemporary targets, measures and effects.* Edited by Hermann Schubnell. Hong Kong: Drager Foundation, 1984, p. 118-54.
A detailed historical account of population trends in Singapore from 1947 to 1982, with figures illustrating changes in growth, ethnic and gender composition, language group, age structure, and other important characteristics.

77 **Population trends, problems and policies in Singapore.**
Saw Swee Hock. In: *Singapore: twenty-five years of development.* Edited by You Poh Seng, Lim Chong Yah. Singapore: Nan Yang Xing Zhou Lianhe Zaobao, 1984, p. 141-64.
Following the book's main theme, this chapter covers the trend in population growth for the twenty-five-year period from 1959 to 1984. In addition to population figures illustrating changes, the author also discusses the national family planning programme and its various policies.

78 **Alternative paths to future population growth in Singapore.**
Saw Swee Hock. *New Zealand Population Review*, vol. 11, no. 1 (1985), p. 19-34.
Based on two separate assumptions, namely, maintaining fertility at replacement level and keeping fertility below replacement level, two alternative paths are suggested by the author. His discussion of each alternative is fully illustrated with figures.

79 **Singapore: new population policies for more balanced procreation.**
Saw Swee Hock. *Contemporary Southeast Asia*, vol. 7, no. 2 (1985), p. 92-101.
A clear and detailed description of the population policies introduced in Singapore in 1984 to correct some imbalances in population growth.

80 **Dynamics of ageing in Singapore's population.**
Saw Swee Hock. *Annals of the Academy of Medicine Singapore*, vol. 14, no. 4 (1985), p. 711-13.

An examination of the demographic trends in terms of two main factors of change, namely, fertility and mortality, concluding that fertility decline is the most important determinant of an ageing population.

# Ethnic Groups

81 **The cultural logic of Singapore's 'multiracialism'.**
Geoffrey Benjamin. In: *Singapore: society in transition.* Edited by
Riaz Hassan. Kuala Lumpur: Oxford University Press, 1976,
p. 115-33. (East Asian Social Science Monographs).

Examines the Singapore government's emphasis on preserving the Republic's
multiethnic character and working against ethnic discrimination. The author also
considers multiracialism as a cultural system, and discusses it in the context of the
anthropoligical concepts of race, culture, and language. Comparing Singapore to
other countries, Benjamin concludes that ethnicity is a social fact closely linked to
the process of nation-building.

82 **Social change and the Chinese in Singapore.**
Cheng Lim-keak. Singapore: Singapore University Press, 1985.
235p.

Contains nine chapters dealing with the various types of registered Chinese
associations in Singapore and their economic role. This work provides an
interesting description of the characteristics of Chinese trade and other economic
activities from the colonial period until 1982.

83 **Ethnicity and nationality in Singapore.**
Chew Sock Foon. Athens, Ohio: Ohio University Monographs in
International Studies. 1987. 229p. bibliog. (Southeast Asia Series
no. 78).

This study has six chapters dealing with a review of the literature, a description of
the Singapore case, and the patterns of ethnic and national identification. The
book is a revised version of the author's PhD dissertation. In her description of
the organization of the study, she indicates that the central data base for her study
is a 1970 national sample survey of adult Singapore citizens, the Singapore

National Identity Survey (SNIS). The SNIS was conducted by two sociologists, one American, John A. MacDougall, and one Singaporean, Chiew Seen Kong, and was the basis for Chiew's M.Soc.Sc. thesis completed in 1971 at the University of Singapore. Unfortunately, Chew Sock Foon does not acknowledge in her bibliography or footnotes the original study conducted by Chiew and his subsequent publications on the subject (see Chiew Seen Kong's other publications in this section).

84  **Ethnicity and national integration: the evolution of a multi-ethnic society.**
Chiew Seen Kong.   In: *Singapore development policies and trends.*
Edited by Peter S. J. Chen. Singapore: Oxford University Press,
1983, p. 29-64.
A survey of cultural pluralism and political turmoil; the formation of Singapore as a plural society; ethnic boundaries in colonial Singapore; subethnic divisions; a Singapore model of structural and cultural integration including education and language; and ethnic tolerance and national identity.

85  **Straits Chinese society. Studies in the sociology of the Baba communities of Malaysia and Singapore.**
John Clammer.   Singapore: Singapore University Press, 1980.
168p.
An anthropological analysis of the Straits Chinese or 'Babas', one of the Chinese subgroups in Singapore. Clammer provides some historical background and notes on the development of this cultural group. Given the close historical links between Singapore and Malaysia, another relevant book on the subject was written by Cheo Kim Ban with the title *A Baba wedding* in 1983. It describes with colourful photographs the details of the traditional wedding ceremony among the Babas in Malacca, Malaysia.

86  **Religion and language among Singapore Indians.**
John Clammer.   In: *Proceedings of the Conference on Tamil Language and Literature in Singapore.* Edited by K. Anbalagan.
Singapore: Tamil Language Society, 1981, p. 139-48.
A description of the religious and linguistic characteristics of Singaporeans of Indian descent, their internal differences in terms of ancestral origin and their response to external religious movements.

87  **The institutionalization of ethnicity in Singapore.**
John Clammer.   *Ethnic and Racial Studies*, vol. 5, no. 2 (April 1982), p. 127-39.
The personal views of an anthropologist on the ethnic pluralism of Singapore, emphasizing the prevalence of ethnic identity among the three main cultural groups, i.e., Malay, Indians, and particularly Chinese. This paper is a slightly modified version of a chapter by the same author, entitled 'Chinese ethnicity and political culture in Singapore' in *The Chinese in Southeast Asia. Vol. 2. Identity, culture and politics* (1981), edited by L. A. P. Gosling. Singapore: Maruzen Asia; Ann Arbor, Michigan: Center for South and Southeast Asian Studies.

88 **Chinese ethnicity and political culture in Singapore.**
John R. Clammer. In: *The Chinese in Southeast Asia*. Edited by
L. A. Peter Gosling, Linda C. Y. Lim. Singapore: Maruzen Asia,
1983, p. 266-84.

Problems of political and economic activity and ethnic identity among
Singaporean Chinese are discussed in the context of the multicultural environment in Singapore.

89 **The roots of Malay literature in English.**
Dudley de Souza. *Solidarity*, vol. 101 (1984), p. 37-44.

The author describes the main historical events that served as obstacles, or
incentives, to the expression of Malay literature in English and discusses the
identity problems faced by Malay writers who used English as a medium of
expression.

90 **A Nonya mosaic.**
Gwee Thian Hock. Singapore: Times Books International, 1985.
154p.

An interesting biography of a Straits Chinese family narrated by the son, who
focuses on his mother as the central character of the book. A good source of
anecdotal information for readers interested in the domestic life of Singaporeans
in general and the 'Babas', or Straits Chinese, in particular during the first half of
this century.

91 **Language and identity: the case of the Chinese in Singapore.**
Eddie C. Y. Kuo. In: *Chinese culture and mental health*. Edited by
Tseng Wen-Sheng, David Y. H. Wu. New York: Academic Press,
1985, p. 181-92.

Discusses the close links between language, group identity, and self-identity and
presents the case of Singaporean Chinese with multiple and overlapping identities
in the context of language policies and the importance of mother tongues.

92 **Ethnicity and fertility in Singapore.**
Eddie C. Y. Kuo, Chiew Seen Kong. Singapore: Institute of
Southeast Asian Studies, 1984. 183p. (Research Notes and Dis-
cussions Paper no.48).

A report of the Singapore study which was part of the Ethnicity and Fertility in
Southeast Asia Project sponsored by the International Development Research
Centre and the Institute of Southeast Asian Studies, involving five other
countries. This report presents the main ethnic differences found in fertility,
fertility preferences, family planning, and nuptiality among the three main ethnic
groups in Singapore, namely, Chinese, Malays, and Indians.

93   **Chinese society in nineteenth century Singapore.**
Lee Poh Ping.   Kuala Lumpur: Oxford University Press, 1978.
139p. bibliog. index.

Describes the mercantile Chinese class formed in Singapore during the 19th century. The study is presented in six chapters. The first chapter discusses the approach used by the writer to conduct his historical analysis. Chapter 2 deals with the free trade society and the gambier and pepper society. Chapter 3 describes the social and political organization of the two societies. Chapter 4 looks at the confrontation between the two societies. Chapter 5 discusses the British intervention in the Malay peninsula and Singapore. Chapter 6 focuses on the structure of the Chinese mercantile class after intervention.

94   **Minority literature among the ethnic Chinese.**
Liaw Yock Fang.   *Solidarity*, vol. 101 (1984), p. 33-36.

A brief but interesting analysis of the development of modern Malay literature. The author identifies three stages of its development following important historical events such as the end of the Second World War, the end of the colonial period, and the separation of Malaysia and Singapore. However, the author does not explain the discrepancy between the term 'ethnic Chinese' in the title and the exclusive focus on Malay writers in the text of his article.

95   **History of the Chinese clan associations in Singapore.**
Edited by Lim How Seng, Lim Guan Hock, Kua Bak Lim.
Singapore: National Archives, 1986. 147p.

In 1985, clan associations in Singapore formed the Singapore Federation of Chinese Clan Associations. One of the first tasks of the Federation was to record the historical development of Chinese clans in Singapore, and this volume is the outcome of such a commitment. A research team was specially appointed to collect relevant material from the National Archives and many other private and official sources and documents. The book has eight chapters dealing with Chinese migration: early immigrant society, the 'bang' structure of the Chinese community in Singapore, the associations and Chinese education, the spirit of mutual help, cultural activities, the change from overseas Chinese to citizen, and the prospects of a new era and new directions. As nearly ninety per cent of the contents consists of photographs, this book serves as an interesting supplement to historical studies of the Chinese community in Singapore such as *Social change and the Chinese in Singapore* by Cheng Lim-keak or *A social history of the Chinese in Singapore and Malaya, 1800-1911* by Yen Ching-hwang (see these items elsewhere in this section).

96   **Subcommunal participation and leadership cohesiveness of the Chinese in nineteenth century Singapore.**
Mak Lau Fong.   *Modern Asian Studies*, vol. 17, no. 3 (1983),
p. 437-53.

Two main aspects are analysed in this paper: the differences in communal group participation among various Chinese dialect group organizations and the leadership cohesiveness among the communal group leaders. The possible influence of secret societies and nepotism practices is also discussed.

97   The relevance of caste in the study of Singapore Indians.
     A. Mani.   *Review of Southeast Asian Studies*, vol. 5, nos. 1-4
     (1975), p. 29-48.
A detailed discussion of the issue, presented in three sections: a historical
background on the caste system in India; the relevance of the 'varna-model' (the
assumption that the hierarchy of caste is clear and immutable) in the study of
Singaporean Indians; and the features of caste in Singapore.

98   Unity and disunity in Singapore Indian community – some issues.
     A. Mani.   In: *Proceedings of Third Tamil Youth Seminar*. Edited
     by Theynmozhi Somasundram. Singapore: Tamils Representative
     Council, 1984, p. 25-35.
As a sociologist, the author focuses on the concept of community and discusses
the problems of maintaining a feeling of community among Singapore Indians in
comparison to the efforts made by the Chinese and Malay communities in
Singapore.

99   The history of Jews in Singapore 1830-1945.
     Eze Nathan.   Singapore: Herbilu Editorial & Marketing Services,
     1986. 212p. appendixes.
Nathan was born in Singapore in 1906. This is his personal account of the history
of his own community. The fourteen chapters of this book cover a description of
the early history of the Jewish community; its pattern of development; the
outcome and implications of the Second World War including the Japanese
occupation of Singapore; and the community's internment and exodus.

100  We remember. Cameos of pioneer life.
     Yvonne Quahe.   Singapore: Landmark Books, 1986. 186p.
This is the outcome of an oral history project undertaken by Quahe who recorded
and collated the stories of about forty Chinese immigrants who came to Singapore
in search of fortune and happiness during the period 1900 to 1939. She personally
interviewed some of them and the rest participated in interviews conducted by the
Oral History Department, Singapore. The book has seven chapters dealing, in a
rough chronological sequence, with the travel plans, the arrival, and variations in
the personal fortunes of the immigrants as they struggled to settle and earn a
living in the new land. Photographs of early immigrants and scenes of Singapore
and China add a note of realism to the narration.

101  The position of the Indian community in Singapore: an economic
     profile.
     G. Shantakumar.   *Singapore Indian Chamber of Commerce
     Economic Bulletin*. vol. 24, no. 1 (1984), p. 1-4.
An analysis of the demographic, economic, educational, and occupational
characteristics of Singaporeans of Indian descent vis-à-vis the total population.
The Indian community has advanced considerably in the past decade in terms of
its economic standing, and by improving the educational qualifications of

Singaporean Indians in the lower income group, this group will be able to increase its occupational and economic status.

102  **Singapore's little India. Past, present and future.**
Sharon Siddique, Nirmala Puru Shotam.  Singapore: Institute of
Southeast Asian Studies, 1982. 174p.
This book presents an interesting study of a subgroup within the Indian community in Singapore. It describes the physical setting and daily lives of Indians living in the area of Serangoon Road known as 'Little India'. After dealing with the main features of the Indian community in Singapore, the authors discuss the historical background of the area, its present condition and characteristics and speculate about its future as an ethnic enclave. The presentation is supplemented by colour photographs, building plans, and sketches of architectural designs of typical houses in the area.

103  **Malays and modernization. A sociological interpretation.**
Tham Seong Chee.  Singapore: Singapore University Press, 1977.
319p. bibliog. index.
This study focuses on the Malay population in Singapore and Malaysia and discusses some aspects of their development. These aspects are: the Malay institutions; historical and contemporary occupational patterns; education and socioeconomic motivation; the Malay élites; the impact of literary élites; modernization and religious reform; ideology, politics, and entrepreneurial development; and economic modernization.

104  **Mental health in Singapore and its relation to Chinese culture.**
Tsoi Wing Foo.  In: *Chinese culture and mental health*. Edited by
Tseng Weng-sheng, David Wu. New York: Academic Press, 1985,
p. 229-49.
A description of various cultural characteristics of the Chinese Singaporeans that the author sees as significant in the study of their mental health status. In addition to some 'culture-related' syndromes, Tsoi discusses schizophrenia, neurosis, suicide, and other mental health problems.

105  **Socio-economic problems of the Malays in Singapore.**
Wan Hussin Zoohri.  *Sojourn Social Issues in Southeast Asia*,
vol. 2, no. 2 (1987), p. 178-208.
As a Member of Parliament in Singapore, the author is well-acquainted with this topic and provides a useful description of the current situation. He focuses on educational attainment, occupational status, and home ownership among the Singaporean Malays, providing first a historical account of the poverty and slow educational progress of the Malays in contrast to the growing prosperity of non-Malays. He then describes in detail the development efforts of the Malay community through organizations such as the Singapore Malay Teachers' Union (KGMS), the Council for the Education of Muslim Children (MENDAKI), the Singapore Muslim Trust Fund (DANAMIS), the Singapore Malay-Muslim Economic Congress (KEMAS), the Malay Affairs Bureau (MAB), as well as the

government's economic, educational, and religious assistance to the Malay community, including the provision for the administration of Muslim law and the setting up of the Muslim Religious Council of Singapore (MUIS).

106  **Ethnicity, language and intergroup relations in Malaysia and Singapore: a social psychological analysis.**
C. Ward, M. Hewstone.  *Journal of Multi-cultural and Multi-lingual Development*, vol. 6, nos. 3-4 (1985), p. 271-96.

A comparison of Malaysia and Singapore in terms of their approaches to multiculturalism and nation-building, focusing on the social identity, ethnic group stereotypes, social distance, language, and other aspects of two ethnic groups, i.e., the Malay and the Chinese communities in these two countries.

107  **An illustrated cycle of Chinese festivities in Malaysia and Singapore.**
C. S. Wong.  Singapore: Malaysia Publishing House, 1987. 237p. bibliog. index.

This is a beautifully illustrated book describing in detail the history behind each of a long cycle of Chinese festivals and which considers their importance and provides an account of Chinese celebrations. The book is divided into three parts: the first part introduces the Chinese calendar for Malaysia and Singapore and explains the twelve animal symbols. Part two deals with the Chinese New Year celebrations in nine chapters. Part three covers the traditional festivals in seven chapters. An epilogue, explanatory notes, and a section on Chinese traditions and beliefs are included. While the text is very interesting, a great deal of the attraction of this publication rests on the excellent photographs by Ronni Pinsler, a talented Singapore-born photographer and researcher.

108  **Traditional Chinese concepts of food and medicine in Singapore.**
David Y. H. Wu.  Singapore: Institute of Southeast Asian Studies, 1979. 31p. (Occasional Paper no. 55).

An examination of the opinions of a group of Chinese university students on the 'heating' and 'cooling' properties of vaious types of food, drinks, and traditional Chinese medicines.

109  **The fetish of relationships: Chinese business transactions in Singapore.**
Yao Souchou.  *Sojourn Social Issues in Southeast Asia*, vol. 2, no. 1 (1987), p. 89-111.

A detailed description of the author's observations of a Chinese foundry firm in Singapore, collected over a six-month period. Aspects such as face-to-face relations, internal organization, customer relations, and management style are discussed in terms of Chinese cultural values and beliefs.

110   **Ethnic boundaries and structural differentiation: an anthropological analysis of the Straits Chinese in nineteenth century Singapore.**
Yao Souchou.   *Sojourn Social Issues in Southeast Asia*, vol. 2, no. 2 (1987), p. 209-30.

The author compares the official objectives and regulations of two Chinese associations in Singapore, namely, the Kheng Tek Whay, which was the first association created by the Straits Chinese in Singapore in 1831, and the Straits Chinese British Association (SCBA), established in 1900. The differences in political and social orientation and philosophy of these two organizations are examined. The term 'Straits Chinese' refers to 19th-century Chinese settlers who 'through marriage with local Malay women or through cultural adaptation . . . produced a kind of Sino-Malay synthesis' also referred to as Baba or Peranakan culture.

111   **A social history of the Chinese in Singapore and Malaya, 1800-1911.**
Yen Ching-hwang.   Singapore: Oxford University Press, 1986.
433p. bibliog. index. glossary.

The author analyses the early Chinese community 'from within', clarifying that the community's relations with the British are omitted. There are nine chapters covering the historical formation of the Chinese community, its dialect and clan organizations, secret societies and social structures, class structure and social mobility, social division and social conflict, social problems and control mechanisms, culture and education, and a concluding chapter.

# Languages and Dialects

112    **Language and society in Singapore.**
Edited by Evangelos A. Afendras, Eddie C. Y. Kuo.    Singapore: Singapore University Press, 1980. 300p. bibliog.

A collection of papers by linguists and some social scientists on theoretical and descriptive aspects of language and society in Singapore. The papers are arranged in five parts containing eleven chapters covering sociolinguistic classification of the community, religion, mass media and schooling, and language policy.

113    **Language and culture in a multi-ethnic society: a Singapore strategy.**
Chan Heng Chee.    *Ilmu Masyarakat* (Malaysian Social Science Association Publication), no. 5 (1984), p. 62-70.

The article describes how a 'highly volatile political issue' such as language was defused by the Singapore government's language policy on bilingualism, and what the author sees as the cultural consequences of such policy.

114    **Certain lexical features of Singapore Mandarin.**
Chen Chung Yu.    In: *New papers on Chinese language use.*
Edited by Beverly Hong. Canberra: Australian National University, 1984, p. 93-104.

A description of the special features found in the use of Mandarin among Singaporeans, the most salient of which is, according to the author, a 'strong Southern influence.'

115   **The language of survival.**
Shirley Chew.   In: *Singapore: society in transition.* Edited by Riaz
Hassan. Kuala Lumpur: Oxford University Press, 1976, p. 149-54.
(East Asian Social Science Monographs).
A brief analysis of government pronouncements from 1959 to 1975 concerning the
languages of education, primarily English and Chinese.

116   **The English language in Singapore.**
Edited by William Crewe.   Singapore: Eastern Universities Press,
1977. 208p.
Ten informative chapters on important aspects of the linguistics and socio-
linguistics of English language use in Singapore. Of the ten chapters, eight were
contributed by academics and experts on the subject, including the chapter that
Crewe wrote himself.

117   **A study of the development of language among pre-school children
in Singapore with particular reference to English.**
Joseph A. Foley.   In: *On TESOL '84: a brave new world for
TESOL.* Edited by P. Larson, E. L. Judd, D. S. Messerschmitt.
Washington, DC: Georgetown University, 1985, p. 29-44.
After a brief historical description of the development of the English language in
Singapore from 1970 to 1980, the author reviews and discusses school syllabuses
in primary schools in the light of his findings from a small-scale study on preschool
children.

118   **A sociolinguistic profile.**
Eddie C. Y. Kuo.   In: *Singapore: society in transition.* Edited by
Riaz Hassan. Kuala Lumpur: Oxford University Press, 1976.
p. 134-148. (East Asian Social Science Monograph).
This paper deals with the linguistic features of Singapore; the changing status of
major languages; ethnicity, language, and communicability; and other issues
related to language.

119   **Language policy and nation-building in a multi-ethnic society: the
case of Singapore model.**
Eddie C. Y. Kuo.   In: *Cultural identity and modernisation in
Asian countries: proceedings of Kokugakuin University Centennial
Symposium.* Edited by the Institute for Japanese Culture and
Classics. Tokyo: Kokugakuin University, 1983, p. 94-101.
The author focuses on the discussion on the multilingualism policy followed by
the Singapore government and argues that such a policy has diffused ethnic
tension, promoted national identity, and served as a link between tradition and
modernity.

## Languages and Dialects

120 **Language and social mobility in Singapore.**
Eddie C. Y. Kuo. In: *Language and inequality.* Edited by
N. Wolfson, J. Manes. Berlin, GFR: Mouton, 1985, p. 337-54.
Two main aspects are discussed: the language-related government policies and
statistics on language use and literacy, and school enrolment. English is found to
be closely related to educational achievement and social mobility.

121 **Language in the family domain in Singapore: an analysis of the 1980
census statistics.**
Eddie C. Y. Kuo. *Singapore Journal of Education,* vol. 7, no. 1
(1985), p. 27-39.
The author describes and analyses the principal household language, languages
spoken at home, home language retention and shift, and the link between home
language and social class.

122 **Language across the university curriculum.**
Lee Kok Cheong. In: *Proceedings of Seminar on Language
across the Curriculum.* Edited by SEAMEO (Southeast Asian
Ministers of Education Organization). Singapore: Regional English
Language Centre, 1985, p. 22-26.
The discussion is based on the analysis of the curriculum and methods of
instruction at the National University of Singapore, and the author offers his
views and suggestions on problems and possible solutions to improve the standard
of English in tertiary education.

123 **The introduction of hanyu pinyin to both Singapore and Malaysia.**
S. C. Loo. In: *Proceedings of the First International Symposium
on Teaching Chinese as a Foreign Language.* Kuala Lumpur:
Nanyang Shang Bao, 1985, p. 1-8.
The term 'hanyu' pinyin refers to one of the romanized versions of Mandarin
(intended to replace the use of Chinese characters). This paper describes the
author's views on the teaching of hanyu pinyin based on his experience in training
teachers.

124 **Promotion of Mandarin – the Singapore experience.**
S. C. Loo. In: *Proceedings of the Symposium on Teaching and
Testing of Spoken Modern Standard Chinese.* Singapore: Lian He
Zao Bao, 1985, p. 1-8.
A description of the efforts in promoting Mandarin over other Chinese dialects in
Singapore before and after Singapore became a republic in 1965.

125 **Changes in Tamil language acquisition and usage in Singapore: a case of subtractive bilingualism.**
A. Mani, S. Gopinanthan. *Southeast Asian Journal of Social Science*, vol. 11, no. 1 (1983), p. 104-17.
The authors focus on Tamil as an accepted 'language of intra-group communication' among Singaporeans of Indian origin and discuss its linguistic trends; its shifts in status; aspects of Tamil literacy, speech, and comprehension; its use within the family; and the possible loss in the common use of Tamil.

126 **Language policy and social transformation in contemporary Singapore.**
Charles Pendley. *Southeast Asian Journal of Social Science*, vol. 11, no. 2 (1983), p. 46-58.
After reviewing briefly the social implications of economic development and the features of the dominant ideology in Singapore, the author discusses several aspects of language policy such as the functional division between English as a practical language and mother tongues for cultural identity; the policy of bilingualism; and the Mandarin campaign.

127 **Social class, ethnicity and language choice: language use in major shopping areas in Singapore.**
John Platt. *Southeast Asian Journal of Social Science*, vol. 13, no. 1 (1985), p. 61-81.
A detailed report of the planning, method, and findings of a language study conducted by the author in four commercial areas in Singapore. It was found that while certain preferences in language choice existed in each of the four areas, other factors such as age, ethnicity, and social class were also important.

128 **The English of Singapore and Malaysia.**
R. K. Tongue. Singapore: Eastern University Press, 1979. rev. ed. 127p.
The first edition of this book appeared in 1974. This revised edition includes the author's insights in to the changes in the use of English since 1974. Eight aspects of the language are discussed: pronunciation; grammar; vocabulary; common phrases and expressions; idioms and slang; stylistic, social, and cultural features of the use of English; English in public notices; and some frequent substandard forms of English. There is also an index of words used in the examples.

# Religion

129  **Thaipusam in Singapore: religious individualism in a hierarchical culture.**
Lawrence A. Babb.   In: *Studies in ASEAN sociology. Urban society and social change.* Edited by Peter S. J. Chen, Hans-Dieter Evers. Singapore: Chopman Enterprises, 1978, p. 277-96.

A detailed description of the various ritual phases and features of Thaipusam, a Hindu religious festival, as it is celebrated in Singapore.

130  **Chinese temples in Singapore.**
Leon Comber.   Singapore: Eastern Universities Press, 1958. 110p. bibliog.

An interesting description of the external symbols of religion among the Chinese in the 1950s. The author provides his interpretation of worship among the Chinese, including a discussion of Confucianism, Taoism and Buddhism, before focusing on the original purpose of the book, namely, a guide to Chinese temples. There are two indexes; one lists Chinese and English names and the other is a general index.

131  **Forever beginning II. One hundred years of Methodism in Singapore.**
Compiled and edited by Theodore R. Doraisamy.   Singapore: The Methodist Church in Singapore, 1986. 144p.

This volume follows *Forever beginning*, the centennial celebration volume published in 1985 and dealing with the details of the celebration and some of the history of the congregation. A more detailed account is presented in volume 2, which deals with evangelism, the ministry, missions, education, social concerns of the church, and other organizational matters involving women, adults, and youth. There is an index and numerous photographs are included.

34

132 **Evangelism in Singapore. A research analysis among Baptists.**
David Finnell.    Singapore: Singapore Baptist Book Store, 1986.
130p. bibliog.

The study focuses on English-speaking youth, English-speaking adults, Mandarin
speakers, bilingual youth, and bilingual adults. For each group, Finnell discusses
various aspects of religious life such as personal and group evangelism,
institutional channels of conversion, human channels of conversion, church
awareness and attraction, reasons for joining the Baptist church, and other
relevant matters.

133 **Growing churches Singapore style. Ministry in an urban context.**
Keith Hinton.    Singapore: Overseas Missionary Fellowship, 1985.
234p. bibliog.

This analysis of church growth is presented in three parts. The first part deals with
contextual factors influencing church growth including historical development, the
second presents the institutional factors influencing church growth, and the final
part discusses strategies for growing churches. A glossary and an index are
included.

134 **Hinduism in Singapore. A guide to the Hindu temples of Singapore.**
Jean-Pierre Mialaret.    Singapore: Donald Moore for Asia Pacific
Press, 1969. 72p.

Urban redevelopment has drastically changed the face of Singapore, and the
description presented by Mialaret in 1969 must be appreciated as a useful
historical piece. The author provides a guide to the Hindu temples after offering a
brief description of the basic aspects of Hindu religion, its principal deities, and
festivals. He also includes an index of main temples and an index of Hindu names
and words.

135 **The administration of Islam in Singapore.**
Sharon Siddique.    In: *Islam and society in Southeast Asia*. Edited
by Taufik Abdullah, Sharon Siddique. Singapore: Institute of
Southeast Asian Studies, 1986, p. 315-31.

Discusses briefly the main features of the historical development of Islam in
Singapore, the changes that took place after the Second World War, and the
'present realities' of Islam as an ideology in which Islam has become 'a vehicle'
for community development among Muslims in Singapore. For the specific legal
aspects of Islam, the author relies a great deal on the study of Islamic law by
Professor Ahmad Ibrahim, which appears in the section 'The Constitution and the
Legal System'.

136 **Muslim society, higher education and development: the case of Singapore.**
Sharon Siddique, Yang Razali Kassim. In: *Muslim society, higher education and development in Southeast Asia.* Edited by Sharom Ahmat, Sharon Siddique. Singapore: Institute of Southeast Asian Studies, 1987, p. 128-76.

Deals with a problem often discussed in the social science literature of the region, namely, the socioeconomic position of the Malays in the general context of Singapore society as well as in the context of the Muslim community in Singapore. The authors follow a chronological approach in their description of the Malay and Muslim communities.

137 **In his good time. The story of the church in Singapore 1819-1978.**
Bobby E. K. Sng. Singapore: Graduates' Christian Fellowship, 1980. 343p. bibliog.

A historical account of the development of the Protestant church presented in nine chapters. The topics discussed in these chapters are the various stages from 1819 to 1840; 1841 to 1880; the new frontiers, 1881 to 1900; expansion and uncertainty, 1901 to 1940; disruption and reconstruction, 1941 to 1948; a vibrant new world, 1949 to 1964; nationhood and spiritual renewal, 1965 to 1978; and a final chapter on retrospect and prospects. There is an index.

138 **Religious switching in Singapore. A study of religious mobility.**
Joseph B. Tamney, Riaz Hassan. Singapore: Select Books; Bedford Park, Australia; Flinders University of South Australia, 1987. 63p. bibliog. (Asian Studies Monograph 3).

The authors discuss some official statistics on religion and data collected by other researchers. There are four appendixes with additional information.

139 **Religion and modernization. A study of changing rituals among Singapore's Chinese, Malays and Indians.**
Tham Seong Chee. Singapore: Graham Brash, 1985. 198p. bibliog.

Based on a survey report completed by the author under the auspices of UNESCO in 1982. The topics covered include cultural and religious rites for pregnancy, childbirth, puberty, betrothal, marriage, funerals, culturally defined 'contamination' and 'pollution', and other rituals.

140 **The building of a dream.**
David W. F. Wong. Singapore: Christian Life Publishers, 1986. 158p.

A collection of articles appearing in a religious bulletin concerning the efforts of a Christian group to build a church in Singapore. The snippets of news cover the period from 1978 to 1985 and describe the group's growth and activities.

# Social Conditions

## Social strata

141 **Fishermen in flats.**
Chew Soo Beng. Melbourne: Monash University Centre of
Southeast Asian Studies, 1982. 151p. (Monash Papers on Southeast
Asia no. 9).
The author introduces this book as 'a study of how a fishing village was lost to
development.' He narrates the story in eight chapters, beginning with a brief
description of Singapore's public housing programme and a few main features of
the Malay community in Singapore. The other chapters deal with a description of
the fishing village where the study was conducted and the views of his informants
on resettlement and the problems of adjustment they faced.

142 **Extraordinary beliefs among students in Singapore and Canada.**
Laura P. Otis, Eddie C. Y. Kuo. *Journal of Psychology*, vol. 116
(1987), p. 215-26.
The term 'extraordinary beliefs' is defined by the authors as beliefs dealing with
traditional religion, luck, fortune-telling, psychic phenomena, spirits, and strange
sightings. The data were collected from 113 Canadian and 75 Singaporean
university students.

143 **Balancing autonomy and control: the case of professionals in
Singapore.**
Stella R. Quah. Cambridge, Massachusetts: Massachusetts
Institute of Technology, Center for International Studies, 1984.
147p.
Analyses the role of four professions in Singapore's historical and economic
development as well as Singapore's nation-building efforts. The four professions

37

selected are medicine, architecture, law, and engineering. The author provides statistical data to illustrate the development of these professions and deals with such development in four sections, namely, a discussion of relevant sociological concepts in the analysis of the professions, the main historical features of the four professions, the role of these professions in national development, and a concluding section on the basic features of the role of professionals in Singapore.

144 **Income inequality in Singapore. Impact of economic growth and structural change 1966-1975.**
V. V. Bhanoji Rao, M. Ramakrishnan. Singapore: Singapore University Press, 1980. 161p. bibliog.

A detailed discussion of income distribution during a ten-year period. There are six chapters dealing with economic growth; changes in income distribution; taxation, public housing, and real income inequality; and implications for development policy. Three appendixes provide further figures.

145 **Élites and national development in Singapore.**
K. E. Shaw, Peter S. J. Chen, Lee Sheng-Yi, George G. Thomson. Tokyo: Institute of Developing Economies, 1977. 116p.

Six chapters analysing various aspects of groups in power or groups occupying top positions in Singapore. The first chapter is a general discussion of the concept of the power élite; the second chapter deals briefly with business élites; the third chapter is a more substantial analysis, with figures, of the developmental or bureaucratic élite and its role in the process of modernization; the fourth chapter focuses on professionals and intellectuals; the fifth chapter deals with the political élite; and the final chapter, entitled 'Comments and discussions', is a transcription of dialogues between a Japanese group and the chapter authors.

# Family and women

146 **Notes on the mobilization of women into the economy and politics of Singapore.**
Chan Heng Chee. In: *Political and social change in Singapore.* Edited by Wu Teh-yao. Singapore: Institute of Southeast Asian Studies, (Nov. 1975), p. 13-35. (Southeast Asian Perspectives no. 3).

An interesting and informative discussion of the role of women in Singapore as an outcome of the changing political ideology of the nation from 1955 to 1975. The issues covered are: ideals, ideology, and women's roles in the 1950s; ideals and ideology in the 1970s; and the extent of economic and political mobilization of women.

147 **Culture and fertility: the case of Singapore.**
Chang Chen Tung, Ong Jin Hui, Peter S. J. Chen. Singapore:
Institute of Southeast Asian Studies, 1980. 95p. (Research Notes
and Discussion Papers no. 21).
An overview of the social aspects of population growth and population control in
Singapore, based on population figures. The authors demonstrate the difference
in fertility patterns among the main ethnic groups in Singapore.

148 **The dilemma of parenthood. A study of the value of children in
Singapore.**
Peter S. J. Chen, Eddie C. Y. Kuo, Betty J. Chung. Singapore:
Maruzen Asia, 1982. 120p.
Based on the Singapore data from a multinational study entitled 'The Value of
Children' and involving seven countries in addition to Singapore. The opinions of
a random sample of Singaporean parents on the value and cost of sons and
daughters are examined as well as the relationship between values and cost on the
one hand and family relations, the status of women, fertility behaviour, and
population policies on the other.

149 **The dynamics of child-rearing decisions. The Singapore experience.**
Betty J. Chung, Peter S. J. Chen, Eddie C. Y. Kuo, Nirmala
Srirekam Purushotam. Singapore: Maruzen Asia, 1981. 91p.
Presents some of the Singapore findings from a larger cross-national project on
'The Value of Children' involving Indonesia, South Korea, Taiwan, the
Philippines, Thailand, Turkey, and the United States. This book deals with the
results of in-depth interviews with a selected group of people on their motivations
and decisions concerning parenthood and number of children.

150 **Handbook for women.**
Family Planning Association of Singapore. Singapore: Family
Planning Association of Singapore, 1981. 77p.
Provides some opinions on women's roles, education, career and employment
opportunities, laws relating to women, sex education, and family planning.
Includes a list of support services and agencies for women in Singapore. See also
the *Directory of social services* (q.v.) for a more comprehensive list of social
services. A related publication dedicated to women is *Labour pains. Coming to
grips with sexual inequality* by a group named 'After-5 Collective' and published
in Singapore in 1984 by Asiapac. In contrast with the handbook, *Labour pains* is a
humorous description of the role of women in Singapore.

151 **The contemporary family in Singapore.**
Edited by Eddie C. Y. Kuo, Aline K. Wong. Singapore:
Singapore University Press, 1979. 306p. bibliog.
Twelve chapters, five of which the editors wrote alone or with others, on various
sociological aspects of the family as an institution in Singapore. The papers deal
with basic aspects of the study of family in Singapore, the urban kinship network,

**Social Conditions.** Family and women

women's status, daughters of working mothers, social change and the Malay family, nuptiality patterns, divorce, ethnic intermarriage, caste and marriage among the Singapore Indians, the national family planning programme, marriage counselling, and the family and the law.

152 **Survey on family life.**
Family Services Development, Ministry of Community Development. Singapore: Straits Times Press, May 1987. 145p.

The Family Services Development Branch commissioned this survey, which covers three main aspects of the family in Singapore: family values, family activities and general family life, and husband-wife responsibilities. Three-fourths of this report are tables with figures on these aspects of family life.

153 **Report on national survey on married women, their role in the family and society.**
Ministry of Social Affairs, Research Branch. Singapore: Ministry of Social Affairs, 1984. 219p.

Provides a great deal of information on the views of a sample of Singaporean married women between fifteen and sixty-four years of age on subjects such as employment, reasons for working, children's education, childcare, and care of the aged. As one of the main purposes of this publication is to provide statistics, the appendixes with figures constitute about a third of the total length of the book.

154 **Sex-role socialization in a transitional society.**
Stella R. Quah. *International Journal of Sociology of the Family*, vol. 10, no. 2 (1980), p. 213-31.

A discussion of the status of women in Singapore focusing on the influence of family and school upon young girls' perceptions of male and female roles in society. The paper is divided into three sections: an explanation of sex-role stereotypes and the influence of socialization, a demonstration of how sex-role stereotypes are learned and reinforced during the first grades of elementary school in Singapore, and a discussion of how sex-role stereotypes contribute to the situation of conflicting demands faced by working women in Singapore.

155 **Impact of policy on the family: can the family be strengthened by legislation?**
Stella R. Quah. *Southeast Asian Journal of Social Science*, vol. 9, nos. 1-2 (1981), p.33-53.

Examines the influence of government policies on family life in Singapore. The discussion is presented in three parts: an explanation of the meaning of family and family policy, an analysis of specific policies that affect the family in Singapore directly and indirectly, and the lessons that may be learned by other countries from the experience of Singapore concerning family policy.

156 **Between two worlds: modern wives in a traditional setting.**
Stella R. Quah.   Singapore: Institute of Southeast Asian Studies,
1988. 66p.

This study deals with the aspects of delayed motherhood, perceptions of
marriage, marital satisfaction, and the conflicting pressures of traditional and
modern values which women have to face in a rapidly changing Asian society such
as Singapore. The monograph presents and discusses the opinions and attitudes
on marriage held by Singapore women who married later and waited longer to
have their first child than most of their contemporaries.

157 **Women's work: factory, family and social class in an industrialising
order.**
Janet Salaff, Aline Wong.   In: *Women in the urban and industrial
workforce: Southeast and East Asia.* Edited by Gavin W. Jones.
Canberra: Australian National University, Development Studies
Centre, 1984, p. 189-214.

Deals with Singapore's female labour force, women's efforts to adjust to job
demands, and changes in the role of their families as sources of support prompted
by economic development and the advance of industrialization.

158 **Teenage marriages in Singapore.**
J. S. H. Tay, W. C. L. Yip.   *Singapore Medical Journal*, vol. 25,
no. 4 (1984), p. 216-24.

The data discussed are from the 1980 Population Census. The authors analyse the
figures in terms of ethnicity, level of education, religion, and other aspects.

159 **Economic development and women's place: women in Singapore.**
Aline K. Wong.   London: Change International Reports, 1980.
20p. maps. (Change International Reports no. 1).

Summarizes the main characteristics of the role of women in the Singapore
economy. The discussion is based on the author's research and findings from
other sources.

160 **Women's work and family life: the case of electronics workers in
Singapore.**
Aline K. Wong, Ko Yiu Chung.   East Lansing, Michigan:
Michigan State University, 1984. 37p. (Women in International
Development Working Paper Series no. 64).

A report and discussion of findings from a study of a small sample of ten single
and ten married female factory workers in the electronics industry. The authors
discuss various aspects such as job commitment, job security, and social and
cultural values of the women involved in the study.

161 **Divorce in Singapore.**
    Aline K. Wong, Eddie C. Y. Kuo.   Singapore: Graham Brash,
    1983. 113p. bibliog.
'.n abbreviated report of a study commissioned by the Singapore Ministry of
Social Affairs. It includes an analysis of divorce statistics from 1960 to 1981 as
well as the findings from a survey of non-Muslim divorced individuals. The first
chapter describes the objectives and methodology of the study; chapter 2 deals
with the trend of divorce from 1960 to 1981; chapters 3 and 4 are based on a
documentary analysis of non-Muslim divorces and centered on divorce patterns
and social factors affecting divorce; and chapters 5 to 8 present the data from a
survey of non-Muslim divorcees, including their family background, marital
problems, the actual divorce situation, divorce problems, and divorce adjustment.
The study includes 56 tables with divorce figures.

# Social problems

162 **Crime patterns and socio-legal responsibility.**
    Michael Chai, Ong Jin Hui.   *Police Life Annual 77*, 1977.
    p. 37-41.
An analysis of crime statistics from 1967 to 1977 and the corresponding activities
of law-enforcement agencies. The paper covers the sharp drop in robberies,
sociological factors in crime trends, the role of the public, police response, and
social change and social control in the future.

163 **Meeting family needs.**
    Ngiam Tee Liang.   *Social Dimension*, 1 (1988), p. 4-9.
A discussion of approaches to help families in Singapore, from the perspective of
social work. Ngiam, the current President of the Singapore Association of Social
Workers (SASW), presents and discusses findings from surveys on family life in
Singapore and make some recommendations. The journal is the official
publication of the SASW.

164 **Homicide in Singapore.**
    Kua Ee Heok, A. F. Yuan, A. L. Ang.   *Medicine, Science and
    Law* (Journal of the British Academy of Forensic Sciences),
    vol. 25, no. 1 (1985), p. 26-28.
A study of seventy-five homicide defendants, eight of whom showed evidence of
mental abnormalities. A comparison between the 'normal' and 'abnormal'
defendants is made in terms of age, weapons used, relation to victims, and other
aspects.

165 **Inhalant abuse in Singapore.**
Ong Teck Hong. *International Journal of Addictions*, 21, 8
(1986), p. 955-960.
A useful description of this recent social problem among teenagers including the
methods and substances used, places frequented by the addicts, and personal
characteristics such as their ethnic, educational and residential background. Ong
also offers his views on the probable causes of this youth problem and makes
some recommendations.

166 **Drug dependence and drug abuse in Singapore.**
Edited by Kua Ee Heok, Tsoi Wing Foo. Singapore: Heinemann
Asia, 1986. 58p. bibliog.
As the editors indicate, this book aims at educating the public. Both the editors
and the other five contributors are medical doctors, two of whom are specialists in
psychiatry and one in psychology. The nine brief chapters deal with an
introduction to the problem of drug abuse, a historical overview, heroin and
opiate abuse, glue-sniffing, and abuse of alcohol, sedatives and hypnotics,
marijuana, amphetamines, LSD, and cocaine. There is also a glossary of terms,
an index, and a list of six books for further reading on the general topic of
substance abuse.

167 **Mechanisms of conflict reduction among Chinese secret societies in
Singapore and Malaysia.**
Mak Lau Fong. In: *Studies in ASEAN sociology. Urban society
and social change.* Edited by Peter S. J. Chen, Hans-Dieter Evers.
Singapore: Chopman Enterprises, 1978, p. 227-44.
The chapter is divided into four sections. In the first section, the author describes
briefly the historical development of Chinese secret societies. The second section
deals with the societies' communal and social involvement. The third section
discusses the possible reasons for their survival or why some societies out-lived
others. The final section lists briefly some implications of the findings.

168 **The sociology of secret societies.**
Mak Lau Fong. Kuala Lumpur: Oxford University Press, 1981.
178p. maps. bibliog.
This book deals with the emergence and survival of Chinese secret societies in
Singapore and Peninsular Malaysia. The discussion is presented in nine chapters.
After a general introduction to the study in chapter 1, the second chapter
discusses the concept of secret organizations, a typology of secret societies, and
the possible reasons for their emergence and survival. Chapter 3 explores the
historical roots of Chinese secret societies. Chapter 4 discusses the patterns of
activity or occupations in which members were involved and the development of
such patterns from the early 19th century to the present. Chapter 5 focuses on the
changes in organizational structure of the societies over time. Chapter 6 describes
the principle of territorial demarcation, and the conflicts and solutions associated
with territorial claims. Chapter 7 focuses on conflict reduction through symbiotic
participation. Chapter 8 compares the patterns of activity found in the early
Straits Settlements period with those observed during the Japanese occupation of

Singapore and after the Second World War. The main conclusions of the study are presented in chapter 9. There are several diagrams, tables with figures, and an index.

### 169  Crime prevention, behaviour and attitudes of the public in Singapore.
Ong Jin Hui, Mak Lau Fong, Chang Chen Tung.  *Police Life Annual 82*, (1982), p. 32-41.

The findings from a survey conducted by the authors are presented and discussed. The paper deals with the general adequacy of crime prevention, sense of personal security, crime prevention in practice, general approaches to crime prevention, the crime prevention campaign, and the neighbourhood watch as an approach to crime prevention.

### 170  Friends in blue. The police and the public in Singapore.
Stella R. Quah, Jon S. T. Quah.   Singapore: Oxford University Press, 1987. 236p. bibliog.

This is a study on planned social change in the area of crime prevention. The authors analyse the attitudes and views of the public towards the police before and after the implementation of the Neighbourhood Police Post (NPP) system in Singapore. The first chapter presents a historical background of the NPP system; the second chapter gives an overview of the public's attitudes towards the police and crime; the next five chapters deal with sense of security, contact with police, satisfaction with police services, expectations of the police, and knowledge of police work. The study concludes with an assessment of the impact of the NPP system and identifies five lessons to be learnt from Singapore's experience for those countries interested in introducing a similar system. Detailed statistical data and further information are provided in five appendixes.

### 171  Singapore Anti-Narcotics Association 15th Annual Report 1986.
Singapore Anti-Narcotics Association (SANA).   Singapore: SANA, 1986. 78p.

SANA's annual report provides the reader with a current and detailed description of the aims and objectives of the organization, its board of management, its president's report, work completed on preventive education and aftercare support, the statement of accounts, and a set of appendixes listing SANA members, visitors, and conferences held concerning drug abuse.

### 172  Curbing drug abuse. The SAF experience.
Edited by Tai Foong Leong.   Singapore: Ministry of Defense and Federal Publications, 1981. 124p.

Discusses, in eleven chapters, some important aspects of the problem of drug abuse in Singapore: historical antecedents; a description of drug abuse and its effects; trends of drug abuse; profile of drug takers; drug abuse and military performance; policies, control, and enforcement measures; rehabilitation, education, and prevention; an evaluation of the work of the Singapore Armed Forces (SAF) in containing and preventing drug abuse; and SAF's future plans in this regard. These chapters were written by the editor and six other contributors, all of whom were SAF officers or officers from the Ministry of Defence.

173　**National anti-drug abuse campaign 83.**
　　Edited by K. V. Veloo.　Singapore: Singapore Anti-Narcotics
　　Association (SANA), 1983. 70p.

The purpose of this publication was to serve as a reference source for both the community leaders involved in the antidrug campaign and the public. It includes eleven brief papers on relevant aspects of drug abuse prevention and treatment in Singapore, including the objectives of drug prevention education, the current drug scene, commonly abused drugs, social considerations and consequences of drug abuse, the law versus the pusher, the addict and the law, treatment and rehabilitation of addicts, supervision of addicts, aftercare of addicts, and a paper on SANA. The final chapter describes the case stories of five drug addicts. The contributors are all officials of various government bodies involved in the prevention and treatment of drug abuse and members of SANA.

174　**Compensating victims of crime in Singapore.**
　　Yeo Meng Heong.　*Malaya Law Review*, vol. 26, no. 2 (1984),
　　p. 219-37.

A review and discussion of various rationale for crime victim compensation, comparing the situation in England and Singapore. The author presents some suggestions for improvement.

# Social values

175　**Singapore development policies and trends.**
　　Edited by Peter S. J. Chen.　Singapore: Oxford University Press,
　　1983. 384p. bibliog.

This book follows the same format of Riaz Hassan's 1976 study (in this section) dealing with important social, political, and economic aspects of development in Singapore. Fourteen scholars from the National University of Singapore contributed individual papers to this collection. The editor wrote the introduction. The other chapters deal with ethnicity, demography, the economy, trade unions and employment, public enterprise, wages, political leadership, public bureaucracy, industrial relations, education, communication, and international relations with the Association of Southeast Asian Nations (ASEAN), the European Economic Community (EEC), and East Asia. Contains an index and appendixes.

176　**National integration: the case of Singapore.**
　　Chiew Seen Kong.　In: *Studies in ASEAN sociology. Urban*
　　*society and social change.* Edited by Peter S. J. Chen, Hans-Dieter
　　Evers. Singapore: Chopman Enterprises, 1978, p. 130-46.

This chapter is based on data from a larger study on Singaporean national identity, the author's unpublished M.Soc.Sci thesis completed in 1971 at the University of Singapore. In this chapter, Chiew discusses the concepts of ethnic diversity and national integration, establishes some assumptions on their link in Singapore, and presents findings from his earlier study to demonstrate that national integration has increased and that people's attitudes and languages used in interethnic communication are related to national identity.

177 **Singapore: ideology, society, culture.**
John R. Clammer. Singapore: Chopman Enterprises, 1985. 169p.

A collection of essays the author has published individually elsewhere, or has presented in public talks or seminars over the years. He offers his views on several aspects of contemporary Singapore, namely, religion, culture, and problems of race, ethnicity, and language. Three of the five chapters of the book are dedicated to these subjects. The other two chapters are: the introduction, describing the anthropological perspective used by the author in his analysis, and the concluding chapter, dedicated to 'a structural overview of Singapore society.'

178 **Singapore: society in transition.**
Edited by Riaz Hassan. Kuala Lumpur: Oxford University Press, 1976. 371p. bibliog. (East Asian Social Science Monographs).

A collection of eighteen chapters written by researchers from the University of Singapore. The topics discussed in these chapters are: the economic system; the political system and political change; bureaucracy; education; the legal system; multiracialism; languages; religion; intermarriage; land use; public housing; demographic changes; the status of women and youth; economic growth, equity, and race; and a concluding discussion on the developmental process. The editor contributed two chapters on his own (housing and the conclusion) and one co-authored (on interethnic marriage). There is an index.

179 **Singapore: a disciplined society.**
Mollie Neville, Warwick Neville. Singapore: Heinemann Publishers, 1980. 46p. map.

A brief and general overview of the organized and disciplined social conditions in Singapore. The Nevilles discuss language, family, social relations, housing, and other aspects of life in Singapore. For a different treatment of the concept of social discipline see the work by Stella Quah on 'Social discipline in Singapore' in this section.

180 **Social discipline in Singapore: an alternative for the resolution of social problems.**
Stella R. Quah. *Journal of Southeast Asian Studies*, vol. 15, no. 2 (Sept. 1983), p. 266-89.

Discusses the viability of social discipline as an approach to the solution of social problems using the case of Singapore as an example. The three sections of the paper deal with the definitions of social discipline and democracy, the case of public housing and family planning as concrete examples, and a critical assessment of the combination of social discipline and democracy in Singapore.

181 **Adoption procedures in West Malaysia and Singapore.**
Yeo Meng Heong. *Malayan Law Journal*, vol. 2 (1984), p. lix-lxx.

A description and critical discussion of the statutory provisions for the adoption of children, covering problems such as eligibility for adoption, preconditions for adoption, and other relevant aspects.

# Social Services

## Health

182　**Safety, efficacy and quality of medicines.**
Edited by R. Alagaratnam, Matthew C. E. Gwee.　Singapore:
Singapore University Press, 1977. 141p.

A collection of papers presented at a symposium of the same title, organized by the departments of Pharmacy and Pharmacology of the University of Singapore. The eleven chapters deal with the scientific, clinical, and legislative aspects of medicines in Singapore.

183　**The impact of eugenic protection laws on fertility and logistics of successfully implementing policies – Singapore experience.**
G. Anandakumar, S. S. Ratnam.　*Singapore Journal of Obstetrics and Gynaecology*, vol. 15, no. 3 (1984), p. 132-46.

Despite the uncommon title, this article simply describes the efforts at family planning in Singapore, the history of private and official programmes, and the various effective population control policies introduced by the government since 1964. For more details on Singapore population control policy see items in the 'Population' section.

184　**Social policies, fertility and its influence on maternal and child health.**
S. Arulkumaran, S. S. Ratnam.　In: *Recent advances in international maternal and child health*. Edited by P. Jellife, E. Jeliffe.
Oxford: Oxford University Press, 1985, p. 27-37.

Singapore's experience is highlighted in this article to demonstrate how the improvement in socioeconomic conditions and effective population control policies can have a positive effect upon the health status of mothers and infants.

185   **Rising caesarean section rates in Singapore.**
      S. Arulkumaran, D. M. F. Gibb, R. L. Tambyraja, S. H. Heng,
      S. S. Ratnam.   *Singapore Journal of Obstetrics and Gynaecology*,
      vol. 16, no. 1 (1985), p. 5-14.

A study of childbirth statistics from 1980 to 1983 focusing on perinatal mortality, obstetric intervention rates, use of emergency caesarean operations, induced labour cases, and other aspects. The authors provide several suggestions to lower the rate of caesarean operations. See other papers on the topic in the same volume of this journal.

186   **Dermatomyositis and cancer in Singapore.**
      Chan Heng Leong.   *International Journal of Dermatology*, vol. 24
      (1985), p. 447-50.

A description of the medical observation of twelve patients suffering from dermatomyositis and observations on its link with cancer. The study is relevant to the study of cancer of the nose and throat among Asians of Chinese descent.

187   **Maternal-child hepatitis B virus transmission in Singapore.**
      S. H. Chan, K. L. Tan, K. T. Goh, C. Lim, F. H. M. Tsakok,
      C. J. Oon, S. S. Ratnam.   *International Journal of Epidemiology*,
      vol. 14, no. 1 (1985), p. 173-77.

A report of a two-year study conducted by experts from various fields of medicine including microbiology and obstetrics. The study compares the incidence of mother-infant transmission of hepatitis B among Chinese, Malay, and Indian mothers.

188   **Epidemiology of diabetes mellitus in Singapore: comparison with
      other ASEAN countries.**
      Cheah Jin Seng, Yeo Peng Boon, Thai Ah Chuan, K. F. Lui,
      K. W. Wang, Y. T. Tan, Y. K. Ng, B. Y. Tan.   *Annals of the
      Academy of Medicine, Singapore*, vol. 14, no. 2 (1985), p. 232-39.

A description of the most important features of Singaporean patients suffering from diabetes, particularly ethnicity, sex, age, weight, and diet. The Singapore figures are compared to those of the other ASEAN (Association of Southeast Asian Nations) members.

189   **Cardiopulmonary resuscitation at the Singapore General Hospital.**
      M. H. Choo, W. C. Tan, C. H. Oon, S. Quek, W. Tan,
      S. Wong.   *Annals of the Academy of Medicine, Singapore*,
      vol. 13, no. 3, (1984), p. 542-47.

Analysis of the use of cardiopulmonary resuscitation (CPR) shows that the public is not familiar with CPR and that such an effective technique is not commonly taught among medical doctors.

190   **A review of recent patterns of infant feeding in Singapore.**
J. J. Counsilman, O. A. C. Viegas.   *Tropical Biomedicine*, no. 2
(Nov. 1985), p. 161-65.
An interesting review and comparison of the findings from seven studies on infant
feeding practices in Singapore since 1951. The authors outline three main patterns
and discuss the influence of Westernization in the decline of breastfeeding.

191   **Cigarette smoking in Singapore.**
S. C. Emmanuel, A. J. Chen, A. Phe.   Singapore: Ministry of
Health, July 1986. 15p.
A review of the measures introduced by the government to discourage cigarette
smoking and an analysis of figures on smoking from three national surveys
conducted in 1974, 1976, and 1984. The three-pronged approach of education,
persuasion, and legislation have succeeded in lowering the proportion of smokers
from twenty-three per cent in 1978 to nineteen per cent in 1984.

192   **Utilization and expenditure on medical services in a local
community.**
N. P. Fong, K. H. Phua.   *Singapore Medical Journal*, vol. 26,
no. 2 (April 1985), p. 131-38.
The findings of a survey of 331 residents in a public housing estate in Singapore
are presented and discussed. The data on estimated number of visits to general
practitioners, hospital admissions, government- and employer-supported medical
benefits, and estimated household expenditure on health indicate that in this small
community people prefer to see private rather than government medical
practitioners; older people tend to be hospitalized more often; and most people
do not have extensive medical coverage.

193   **Epidemiological surveillance of communicable diseases in
Singapore.**
Goh Kee Tai.   Tokyo: Southeast Asian Medical Information
Center (SEAMIC) and International Medical Foundation of Japan
(IMF), 1983. 282p.
The thirteen chapters of this book present a detailed discussion of epidemiological
surveillance on malaria, dengue haemorrhagic fever, enteric fevers, diarrhoeal
diseases, viral hepatitis, zoonotic diseases, viral diseases, sexually transmitted
diseases, tuberculosis, and leprosy. The last two chapters deal with the national
childhood immunization programme and the system of quarantine services in
Singapore. The author is a medical doctor and head of the Quarantine and
Epidemiology Department, Ministry of the Environment, as well as secretary of
the Joint Coordinating Committee on Epidemic Diseases in Singapore.

194 **The role of Chinese traditional medical practice as a form of health care in Singapore. I. Preliminary study.**
Suzanne Chan Ho, Kwok Chan Lun, W. K. Cheng Hin Ng.
*American Journal of Chinese Medicine*, vol. 8, no. 1 (1980), p. 26-36.

A report of the findings from a study of 672 patient records from one of the major traditional Chinese medicine institutions in Singapore. The paper describes the characteristics of these patients in terms of age, ethnicity, sex, and the nature of health complaint.

195 **The role of Chinese traditional medical practice as a form of health care in Singapore. II. Some characteristics of providers.**
Suzanne Chan Ho, Kwok Chan Lun, W. K. Cheng Hin Ng.
*American Journal of Chinese Medicine*, vol. 11, no. 1 (1983), p. 16-23.

The findings from a study of the organization and services of 19 voluntary institutions providing Chinese traditional medical care are presented and discussed.

196 **The role of Chinese traditional medical practice as a form of health care in Singapore. III. Conditions, illness behaviour and medical preferences of patients of institutional clinics.**
Suzanne Chan Ho, Kwok Chan Lun, W. K. Cheng Hin Ng.
*Social Science and Medicine*, vol. 18 (1984), p. 745-52.

The findings of a survey of patients attending traditional Chinese medicine clinics in Singapore, describing their health complaints, preferred treatment, and how they deal with illness.

197 **Childhood obesity in Singapore children: epidemiologic review and anthropometric evaluation.**
T. F. Ho. Singapore: Singapore Paediatric Society, 1984. 46p.
(11th Haridas Memorial Lecture).

A detailed review and discussion of statistical data for the period 1974 to 1983, covering comparisons of school children in terms of age, school grade, ethnicity, sex, and other aspects. Suggests the use of an improved obesity classification system.

198   **Risk factors for ischaemic heart disease in the ethnic groups of Singapore.**
K. Hughes, P. P. B. Yeo, K. C. Lun, S. P. Sothy, K. W. Wang, L. Chan, A. C. Thai, K. F. Lui, W. O. Phoon, J. S. Cheah, P. Lim. In: *Proceedings of the International Epidemiological Association Xth Scientific Meeting.* Vancouver: University of British Columbia, 1984, p. 31.
A report of a study based on 3,000 randomly chosen adults from the three main ethnic groups and focusing on possible interrelations of specific risk factors. This paper deals with exercise, smoking, alcohol, blood pressure, cholesterol, and other aspects.

199   **Alcohol-related hospitalisation in Singapore.**
Kua Ee Heok. *Singapore Medical Journal*, vol. 27, no. 5 (1986), p. 392-95.
Sixty-two Chinese and Indian patients hospitalized because of alcohol-related problems were the subjects of a study reported in this paper. A comparison of the severity of alcohol dependence was made in terms of ethnicity, age, and sex.

200   **A cross-cultural study of alcohol dependence in Singapore.**
Kua Ee Heok. *British Journal of Addiction*, vol. 82 (1987), p. 1-3.
A group of 46 Indian and Chinese hospital patients admitted as alcoholics were studied. The Indian patients were found to have a more severe alcohol dependence, a longer history of alcohol drinking, and a family history of alcohol dependence more often than the Chinese patients.

201   **Homicide and mental illness in Singapore.**
Kua Ee Heok, A. L. Ang, A. F. Yuan. *Singapore Medical Journal*, vol. 25, no. 2 (1985), p. 61-63.
A brief report on figures showing that only one in ten homicides is committed by an insane person. For another version of this topic, see the paper written by the same authors on homicide in Singapore in the section on social conditions.

202   **Racial differences in peptic ulcer frequency in Singapre.**
J.Y. Kang, S.J. LaBrooy, I. Yap, R. Guan, K.P. Lim, M.V. Math, H.H. Tay. *Digestive Diseases and Sciences*, vol. 31 (Supplement, (1986), p. 825-28.
This report of a hospital study of 1,248 peptic ulcer patients and 2,023 general medicine patients over a four-year period demonstrates the influence of racial differences in the incidence of the peptic ulcer among Singaporeans of Chinese, Malay or Indian descent.

203 **Health care in old age.**
Edited by Kua Ee Heok, Ang Peng Chye, Anne Merriman.
Singapore: Gerontological Society, 1986. 156p.

Includes twenty-four brief chapters on important aspects of ageing such as nutrition, exercise, health assessment, various common health disorders in old age, physiotherapy, and services available to the elderly.

204 **A cross-cultural study of the possession-trance in Singapore.**
Kua Ee Heok, Sim Li-Ping, Chee Kuan-Tsee. *Australian and New Zealand Journal of Psychiatry*, vol. 20 (1986), p. 361-64.

The authors describe the symptoms and main characteristics of thirty-six young men who had a history of 'trance' and were referred to a psychiatrist for further evaluation during their compulsory military service medical examination. A follow-up of twenty-six of these men four years later indicated no evidence of mental illness.

205 **The role of Chinese traditional medical practice as a form of health care in Singapore. IV. Physicians in private practice.**
Kwok Chan Lun, Suzanne Chan Ho, W. K. Cheng Hin Ng.
*American Journal of Chinese Medicine*, vol. 11 (1983), p. 43-53.

Summarizes the findings from a study of fifty-five traditional Chinese physicians and their clinics conducted by the authors in 1980. The physicians' age, sex, level of education, dialect group, professional training, and some aspects of their medical practice are described.

206 **The practice of Chinese traditional medicine in Singapore.**
Kwok Chan Lun, Suzanne Chan Ho, W. K. Cheng Hing Ng.
*International Journal of Chinese Medicine*, vol. 1, no. 2 (1984),
p. 17-29.

This is another version of the study conducted by the authors in 1980 and reported in four instalments in other journals (refer to the corresponding items in this section). This paper presents highlights from the previous publications.

207 **Occupational lead exposure in various industrial sectors in Singapore: a collaborative study.**
S. F. Kwok, C. N. Ong, W. O. Phoon. In: *Proceedings of the 10th Asian Conference on Occupational Health.* Edited by Lai Chan See, Low Wong Fook, Lee Hin Peng, Ong Choon Nam.
Singapore: Asian Association of Occupational Medicine, 1984,
p. 491-95.

Two laboratories from the government and the university collaborated in this study conducted from 1978 to 1982 to identify the type and extent of lead exposure and absorption among 2,000 workers from seventeen different industrial and commercial sectors.

208    **Cancer incidence in Singapore by occupational groups.**
       Lee Hin Peng.    *Annals of the Academy of Medicine Singapore*,
       vol. 13, no. 2 (1984), p. 366-70.
The author analysed cancer registration records containing information on occupational status of the patient and was able to determine the occupational distribution of different types of cancer based on Chinese males' records for the period 1968 to 1977.

209    **The epidemiology of lung cancer in Singapore.**
       Lee Hin Peng.    *Annals of the Academy of Medicine Singapore*,
       vol. 14, no. 3 (1985), p. 485-90.
A useful and concise discussion of the characteristics of patients affected by lung cancer in Singapore between 1968 and 1977. Important aspects such as sex, ethnicity, and cigarette smoking are described and analysed. The highest lung cancer incidence was found among Chinese (particularly Hokkien and Teochew) males and cigarette smokers.

210    **Meningitis in Singapore infants and children.**
       P. S. Low, W. C. L. Yip, J. S. H. Tay, H. B. Wong.    *Journal of the Singapore Paediatric Society*, vol. 26, nos. 3 & 4 (1984),
       p. 150-54.
A report of a study of eighty-four children affected by the disease, including details of the course of illness and recovery.

211    **The scheme of charges for government medical services.**
       Ministry of Health.    Singapore: Ministry of Health, 1983. 48p.
A detailed description of medical fees, eligibility, and definitions, including a schedule of daily ward fees, outpatient fees, consultation and medical examination fees, dental treatment, X-ray examinations, laboratory examinations, radiotherapy, radioisotope studies, medical reports, implants, prostheses and appliances, and renal and other rehabilitation treatment.

212    **SATA bulletin.**
       Edited by B. P. Mozoomdar, N. C. Sen-Gupta, Mariam
       Thomas.    Singapore: Singapore Anti-Tuberculosis Association
       (SATA), June 1987. 48p.
Published twice annually (June and December), the bulletin includes brief articles on various aspects of health and illness such as nutritional supplements, common respiratory allergies, health hazards of smoking, and other information useful to the general public. SATA was established in 1946 and has been providing diagnostic and treatment services as well as collaborating actively with the TB Control Unit of the Ministry of Health in health campaigns.

213  **Development of hospital care and nursing in Singapore.**
Compiled and edited by Viji Mudeliar, C. R. S. Nair,
R. P. Norris.  Singapore: Ministry of Health, 1979. 118p. bibliog.

The editors and compilers were, at the time of publication, higher nursing officers
with the Ministry of Health. They provide a brief historical background of
hospitals and the nursing profession in Singapore from the time of Sir Thomas
Stamford Raffles. The book follows a chronological sequence with its six chapters
covering the 'early times' (1819-70); the 'beginnings' (1870-1900); 'footprints'
(1900-40); and the events during and after the Second World War, closing with a
chapter on the trend towards specialization. As the authors are not historians or
scholars, the discussion and bibliography are limited, but the book provides useful
details in the development of the nursing profession in Singapore. See also a
related study on the history of medicine and three other professions in Singapore
entitled *Balancing autonomy and control: the case of professionals in Singapore*
by Stella R. Quah in the section on social conditions.

214  *In vitro* **fertilisation in Singapore – the medical aspects.**
S.C. Ng.  In: *Proceedings of the First Regional Seminar on Legal
Medicine.* Singapore: Medico-Legal Society of Singapore, 1984,
p. 45-48.

*In vitro* fertilization is popularly known as the 'test-tube baby' procedure to help
childless couples. This paper is a description of the details and various aspects of
the *in vitro* fertilization programme in Singapore and an appeal for its
continuation within the appropriate legal framework to monitor its application.
See further details of the programme in *'Development of an in vitro fertilisation
progamme in Singapore'* by the same author and others in this section.

215  **Development of an** *in vitro* **fertilisation programme in Singapore.**
S. C. Ng, S. S. Ratnam, H. Y. Law, W. R. Edirisinghe,
C. M. Chia, M. Rauff, P. C. Wong, H. H. V. Goh,
C. Anandakumar, K. E. Leong, S. C. Yeoh.  *Singapore Journal
of Obstetrics and Gynaecology,* vol. 15, no. 2 (1984), p. 84-91.

A detailed description of how and when the *in vitro* fertilization programme was
set up in Singapore. Figures on patients attended are provided. For more details
on this programme see 'In vitro *fertilisation in Singapore – the medical aspects*'
by S. C. Ng in this section.

216  **Current situation on occupation health in Singapore.**
C. N. Ong.  In: *Occupational health in developing countries in
Asia.* Edited by W. O. Phoon, C. N. Ong. Tokyo: SEAMIC,
1985, p. 31-40.

The fast pace of development of occupational health in Singapore is described in
terms of public awareness, personnel involved, services offered, and research and
educational efforts. A useful description of research in this area of medicine in
Singapore is provided.

217 **Drug use among juveniles: control and rehabilitation.**
Ong Jin Hui. In: *Proceedings of the Fourth Asian-Pacific Conference on Juvenile Delinquency.* Tokyo: Keio University, 1985, p. 122-36.

A description of the official efforts to combat drug abuse in Singapore, including legislation, preventive measures, and rehabilitation and a comparison of adult and juvenile drug abusers, identifying main trends and problems.

218 **Epidemiology of viral hepatitis B in Singapore.**
C. J. Oon, L. Chan, K. T. Goh, S. H. Quak, K. L. Tan.
In: *Viral hepatitis and liver disease.* Edited by G. N. Vyas, J. L. Dienstag, J. H. Hoofnagle. Orlando, Florida: Grune & Stratton, 1984, p. 642-43.

A description of the process by which the disease is acquired in Singapore, based on studies conducted on various groups of patients. Figures are given on the proportion of people affected in various age groups and ethnic communities. See also p. 680 of the same book for a summary of Singapore's strategy to control hepatitis B infections.

219 **Twenty-year history of the Singapore Cancer Society.**
Phua Kai-Hong. In: *Two decades of concern.* Edited by Singapore Cancer Society. Singapore: Singapore Cancer Society, 1984, p. 5-8.

A historical account of the research, rehabilitation and community work, development, and programmes of the Singapore Cancer Society.

220 **Ageing: socio-economic implications for health care in Singapore.**
Phua Kai-Hong. *Annals of the Academy of Medicine Singapore* vol. 16, no. 1 (Jan. 1987), p. 15-23.

A discussion of demographic changes in Singapore and their effect on health services planning for the aged. The author emphasizes the need for innovative approaches in the organization and financing of health care for the aged.

221 **Saving for health.**
Phua Kai-Hong. *World Health Forum,* vol. 8 (1987), p. 38-41.

A summary of the main features of the Medisave Scheme, a compulsory savings programme geared to serve as medical insurance to pay for hospitalization and surgery. Under the scheme, three per cent of the employee's monthly salary is saved under the special Medisave account together with an equal amount provided by the employer.

222 **Accessibility of modern and traditional health services in Singapore.**
Stella R. Quah. *Social Science & Medicine*, vol. 11, no. 5 (1977),
p. 333-40.

The discussion of accessibility is approached in terms of the quantity of traditional
and modern services, the geographical distribution of such services, their cost for
the consumer, how well people are informed on these services; and how easy
people think it is to get those services.

223 **Health policy and traditional medicine in Singapore.**
Stella R. Quah. *Social Science & Medicine*, vol. 15A, no. 2
(1981), p. 149-56. bibliog.

An analysis of the development of traditional and modern medical services in
Singapore and the effect of government policy upon such development. The paper
provides tables with figures. For details on modern health services see, in the
section on statistics, the *Annual Statistics Bulletin 1985* published by the Ministry
of Health.

224 **Current research on oral contraception in Singapore.**
S. S. Ratnam, R. N. V. Prasad. *Singapore Journal of Obstetrics
and Gynaecology*, vol. 15, no. 1 (Supplement, 1984), p. 52-59.

A description of the research efforts at the University Department of Obstetrics
and Gynaecology and a discussion of the importance of further local research on
the medical aspects of contraception.

225 **Ethics of *in vitro* fertilization.**
S. S. Ratnam, S. C. Ng, A. H. Sathananthan. *Singapore Journal
of Obstetrics and Gynaecology*, vol. 16 (1985), p. 95-102.

The focus of this paper is Singapore's experience with an *in vitro* fertilization
programme and the religious and cultural aspects related to the ethnics of such a
medical procedure.

226 **The code of ethics on the sale of infant formula products in
Singapore.**
Sale of Infant Foods Ethics Committee Singapore (SIFECS).
Singapore: Ministry of Health, 1982. 16p.

As the SIFECS monitors the marketing practices of infant milk manufacturers,
this publication presents not only the code of ethics but also the guidelines on
basic marketing principles, advertising, and codes of conduct concerning the use
of infant formulas in hospitals, clinics, and homes.

227 **Increasing life expectancy in Singapore during 1969-1981.**
Saw Swee-Hock. *Singapore Medical Journal*, vol. 25, no. 3
(1984), p. 104-14.
A description and discussion of population figures calculated by the author to
examine changes in life expectancy over time and comparisons across ethnic
groups and sex. The analysis shows an increase on life expectancy for both males
and females in the total population.

228 **Cancer incidence in Singapore 1968-1977.**
K. Shanmugaratnam, H. P. Lee, N. E. Day. Lyon, France:
International Agency for Research on Cancer (IARC), 1983. 171p.
bibliog. (Scientific Publications no. 47).
The incidence, prevalence, and mortality figures concerning cancer are described
in a careful and systematic manner by the three authors. The first five chapters
provide basic information on Singapore, its modern medical services, cancer
mortality figures, and the Singapore Cancer Registry. Chapters 3 to 13 deal with
specific aspects of cancer victims such as ethnicity, language, migrant status, age,
type of cancer, and a commentary on cancer patterns. Ten appendixes provide
further details. In addition to IARC, two other organizations contributed to the
publication of this volume: the World Health Organization and the Singapore
Cancer Registry.

229 **Singapore's challenges in perinatal care.**
R. L. Tambyraja, S. Arulkumaran, O. A. C. Viegas,
Y. C. Wong, S. S. Ratnam. In: *Proceedings of the XVIII*
*Singapore-Malaysia Congress of Medicine Lectures & Symposia.*
Edited by Lee Hin Peng. Singapore: Singapore Medical Associ-
ation, 1984, p. 161-73.
This is a more detailed version of the paper on caesarean operations described
elsewhere in this section. This paper includes the findings from a ten-year study of
perinatal cases under the care of Singapore University physicians.

230 **Current problems in legal medicine.**
Edited by Tan Tiong Tee. Singapore: Medico-Legal Society of
Singapore, 1981. 125p.
A collection of papers presented at the Seminar on Legal Medicine organized by
the Medico-Legal Society of Singapore. Most of the papers are contributions from
physicians and lawyers; one paper is by a police officer and another by a family
counsellor. The scope of the papers ranges from the legal implications of medical
practice and the problems of informed consent to aspects of traffic accidents, drug
abuse, and transsexualism.

231  **Hospital mortality in a Singapore paediatric unit: a 20-year review (1964-1983).**
J. S. H. Tay, P. S. Low, W. C. L. Yip, H. B. Wong.  *Journal of the Singapore Paediatric Society*, vol. 27, nos. 1 & 2 (1985), p. 82-88.

The source of information is the weekly records of admissions and deaths of patients at the Department of Paediatrics of the National University of Singapore Faculty of Medicine. A succinct description of main causes of death and other details are provided.

232  **Psychosocial aspects of repeat abortions in Singapore – a preliminary report.**
Tsoi Wing Foo, S. S. Ratnam, G. E. Tay.  *Singapore Medical Journal*, vol. 25, no. 2 (1984), p. 116-21.

Describes the increasing rate of repeat abortions for the period 1975 to 1982 and discusses the findings of a study exploring possible reasons for this increase, including personality traits.

233  **Plastic surgery: facing the facts.**
George Wong.  Singapore: Times Books International, 1987. 96p.

As a plastic surgeon, the author is well qualified to write this informative and easy-to-read description and discussion of fifteen types of plastic surgery operations normally performed in Singapore. After defining the field of plastic surgery in the first chapter, Wong discusses in subsequent chapters operations involving face lifts, eyes, nose, ears, chin and neck, and breasts, 'spare tyres', scar removal, moles, warts, freckles, cysts and nodules, harelip, and cleft palate. There are three chapters on silicone and collagen injections, tattoos, and the use of lasers. The text is accompanied by diagrams and photographs. There is a glossary of terms and an appendix with the schedule of fees for the operations described, recommended by the Singapore Medical Association.

234  **Childhood immunisation.**
H. B. Wong.  *Journal of the Singapore Paediatric Society*, vol. 27, nos. 1 & 2 (1985), p. 7-19.

A useful description of the national childhood immunization programme in Singapore. The author discusses its cost-effectiveness, problems and advantages, the high rate of population compliance, and the general success of the programme.

235  **Prenatal diagnosis of genetic diseases in Singapore.**
H. B. Wong, R. L. Tambyraja.  *Singapore Journal of Obstetrics & Gynaecology*, vol. 16, no. 3 (1985), p. 119-24.

The results of analysis of Singapore figures on three types of genetic diseases (Mendelian monogenic, chromosomal, and multifactorial genetic diseases) are presented and discussed, and the diagnostic and follow-up procedures involving doctors and parents are described.

236   **Health fair at Teban Gardens: an innovative approach in health**
      **education and promotion in Singapore.**
      Y. Y. Yam, N. P. Fong.   *Singapore Community Health Bulletin*,
      vol. 25 (1984), p. 5-6.

A description and analysis of a health fair held in a public housing estate to
promote healthy life styles. The authors point out the positive aspects of such a
public health education programme and recommend that it be repeated in other
housing estates.

237   **The impact of immunisations on the promotion of child health in**
      **Singapore and current recommendations.**
      W. C. L. Yip.   In: *Proceedings of the 5th Asian Congress of*
      *Paediatrics, Pre-Congress Symposium on Social Paediatrics.* Edited
      by Perla D. Santos Ocampo. Kuala Lumpur: Association of
      Paediatric Societies of the Southeast Asian Region, 1985,
      p. 154-55.

Updates the information on Singapore's experience in child immunization. For
more details on the national immunization programme see other items on the
topic in this section.

# Housing

238   **High-rise, high-density living. SPC Convention 1983 selected**
      **papers.**
      Edited by Boey Yut Mei, Tan Sioe An, Aline K. Wong, Chong
      Chung Nee, Larry Ng, David Chan, Seow Mong Lin.   Singapore:
      Singapore Professional Centre, 1984. 237p.

A collection of thirty-three of the forty papers presented at the international
convention by the same title, organised by the Singapore Professional Centre
(SPC) and held in Singapore from 5th to 9th September 1983. The papers are
arranged into three sections. The first section deals with planning and design and
includes nine papers on housing policies, the concept of microcosmos,
environmental factors in housing design, the aspects of transport in high-density
living, and housing experiences in Hong Kong, Tokyo, Singapore, and Sri Lanka.
Part 2 covers fourteen papers on engineering and construction aspects of housing,
including the effect of technology, prefabrication, maintenance, fire safety, and
housing management. Part 3 focuses on 'user culture' and the flat dwellers and
includes ten papers on cross-cultural aspects, internal space, the urban
community, residents' organizations, and community services.

239 **Highrise residential prices 1971-82.**
Peter M. Brown. In: *Real estate review of Singapore.* Edited by
Marmix Enterprises. Singapore: Times Periodicals, 1984, p. 58-60.

The fluctuation in the cost of private apartments in Singapore is described and discussed. The author also makes a comparison of price trends in terms of district location.

240 **Residential property prices 1972-82.**
Peter M. Brown. In: *Real estate review of Singapore.* Edited by
Marmix Enterprises. Singapore: Times Periodicals, 1984, p. 74-79.

Deals with residential property prices applicable to low-rise dwellings in Singapore. An analysis of price trends is given according to the district location.

241 **Singapore – the housing experience.**
M. J. Greaves, Look Yep Sang, Tay Kay Poh. In: *Proceedings of
the Commonwealth Association of Surveyors and Land Economy.*
London: CASLE, 1985, p. 33-41.

Although this paper reviews Singapore's housing problems and their solutions in a historical manner, the authors offer their analysis from the perspective of housing management, as all three of them are building and estate management experts. (For sociological, architectural, economic, and administrative aspects of public housing in Singapore, see other items in this section.)

242 **Families in flats: a study of low income families in public housing.**
Riaz Hassan. Singapore: Singapore University Press, 1977. 249p.

A group of low-income families that underwent relocation as part of the nation-wide public housing programme serves as the basis for this study. The author describes their opinions and their economic and social situation as they adjust to life in high-rise apartments. (See other items on Singapore's public housing programme in this section.)

243 **Review of construction techniques and mechanisation in Singapore.**
Lim Teck Cheong, Lim Chong Nam, James Smith. *Professional
Builder*, vol. 1, no. 3 (1984), p. 25-29.

A study of the construction industry in Singapore over the past twenty years. Emphasis is given to the modernization of construction techniques and the use of mechanized equipment.

244 **Singapore's experience in public housing: some lessons for other
new states.**
Jon S. T. Quah. In: *Political and social change in Singapore.*
Edited by Wu Teh-yao. Singapore: Institute of Southeast Asian
Studies, (Nov. 1975), p. 113-54. (Southeast Asian Perspectives,
no. 3).

Deals with the success of the public housing programme in three sections: a description of the public housing programme from 1960 to 1974, the external and internal causes of the Housing and Development Board's (HDB) success, and the lessons that other Asian and African new states may learn. For an assessment of the housing programme ten years later see *Housing a nation* by A. Wong and S. H. K. Yeh in this section.

245 **Public housing.**
Jon S. T. Quah. In: *Government and politics of Singapore.*
Edited by Jon S. T. Quah, Chan Heng Chee, Seah Chee Meow.
Singapore: Oxford University Press, 1987, rev. ed., p. 233-58.
Public housing in Singapore is discussed in this chapter in terms of the Singapore Improvement Trust's (SIT) poor performance in public housing, the Housing and Development Board's (HDB) success in public housing, the reasons for the HDB's success, and the consequences of the HDB's public housing programme. The two main reasons for HDB's success are government support in terms of financial assistance and legislation for its public housing programme and the initiation of effective measures for solving implementation problems.

246 **An update on neighbourhood planning and design with reference to Singapore public housing.**
Thomas T. W. Tan, Kenson Kwok. *Planews*, vol. 11, no. 1 (Dec. 1986), p. 23-31.
The authors, sociologists working at the Systems and Research Department of the Housing and Development Board in Singapore, discuss the theoretical implications of the concept of neighbourhood and present relevant data from the Singapore population living in high-rise public housing. The data demonstrate the presence of two types of neighbourhood, the neighbourhood of convenience (providing physical facilities) and a smaller neighbourhood of friendship and social interaction.

247 **Housing a nation. 25 years of public housing in Singapore.**
Edited by Aline K. Wong, Stephen H. K. Yeh. Singapore: Housing and Development Board, 1985. 538p. maps.
A comprehensive description by the Housing and Development Board (HDB), of the complex job of providing low-cost housing. The book covers in fourteen chapters the areas of resource planning; physical planning and design; infrastructure; construction standards, technology, and safety; contracts management; housing policies and procedures; estate management; policies, process, and impact of resettlement, including a resettlement case study; characteristics and life style of families living in public housing apartments; and dimensions of community in public housing estates. The final chapter is an appraisal of the achievements of the HDB written by its chief executive officer, Liu Thai Ker. The other chapters are written by various teams of HDB experts. Aline Wong, one of the editors, was a co-author of the two chapters dealing with the residents' life style and community links. Seven appendixes provide further details.

248 **Public housing in Singapore. A multi-disciplinary study.**
    Edited by Stephen H. K. Yeh.   Singapore: Singapore University
    Press and Housing and Development Board, 1975. 439p. bibliog.

A collection of thirteen relevant papers on various aspects of housing in
Singapore including the public housing programme; the population's housing
conditions and housing needs up to the time of publication; an economic analysis
of the construction activity of the Housing and Development Board (HDB);
urban renewal; architectural design; estate management; public housing dwellers'
satisfaction with living conditions; industrial employment in HDB estates;
neighbourhoods, neighbouring practices, and neighbourliness in HDB estates;
and change in life styles among HDB apartment dwellers. The book also includes
two appendixes with the questionnaires used in the 1968 and 1973 household
surveys. Two earlier studies of relevance to interested readers are *50,000 up:
homes for the people* published in 1966 by the HDB in Singapore; and *Homes for
the people: A study of tenants' views on public housing in Singapore* by Stephen
H. K. Yeh published in 1972 by the Government Printing Office.

249 **Households and housing.**
    Stephen H. K. Yeh.   Singapore: Department of Statistics, 1984.
    106p. (Census Monograph no. 4).

Yeh, a sociologist, is one of the various professionals and experts commissioned
by the Singapore Department of Statistics to present a study on a specific theme
based on the figures from the 1980 Census of Population. This monograph focuses
on housing and is divided into two parts. The first part discusses households, their
pattern of growth from 1957 to 1980, the trends in household size, type of
household and tenancy, and projections in household formation from 1980 to
1990. The second part deals with the housing situation in 1980, progress in
housing, demand and supply, and urban planning. Two appendixes provide
detailed tables of the services and facilities found in new towns. See also Yeh's
earlier study on housing in the section on social services.

# Welfare

250 **Telecommunications and economic development in Singapore.**
    Chen Huey Tsyh, Eddie C. Y. Kuo.   *Telecommunications Policy*,
    vol. 9, no. 3 (Sept. 1985), p. 240-44.

An analysis of economic indicators and telephone figures from 1964 to 1982
confirms the presence of a link between higher economic development and
improved standards of social welfare on the one hand, and the increased
availability and use of telephones in Singapore on the other hand.

251 **Problems of the aged.**
Committee on the Problems of the Aged. Singapore: Ministry of
Health, February 1984. 54p.

This report is popularly known in Singapore as the Howe Yoon Chong Report.
Howe was the Minister for Health and chairman of the twelve-member committee
appointed by the Prime Minister to study the problems of the aged. The report
consists of six chapters dealing respectively with the description of a proposed
national policy for the elderly, employment, financial security, health and
recreational needs, social services and institutional care, and family relations.

252 **Cooperative societies in Singapore 1925-1985.**
R. O. Daniel. Singapore: Singapore National Co-operative
Federation, 1987. 150p.

A historical overview of the cooperative movement in Singapore and a list of the
various cooperative societies by sector, such as housing, credit, agriculture,
transport and others.

253 **Day care centre for the elderly in an urbanized city: a three-year
study in Singapore.**
Fong Ngan Phoon, S. Yong, S. Sin. In: *Proceedings of 3rd
Symposium on Our Environment March 27-29, 1984.* Edited by
Koh Lip Lin, Hew Choy Sin. Singapore: National University of
Singapore, Faculty of Science, 1985, p. 320-25.

The first day care centre for the aged ever set up in Singapore is the focus of
analysis in this study, which covers the period from 1980 to 1983. The authors
describe the most relevant characteristics of the elderly attending the centre, i.e.,
age, type of disability or health problem, sex, and other features.

254 **The aged – who cares? A souvenir handbook of the Gerontological
Society.**
Gerontological Society. Singapore: Gerontological Society, 1987.
81p.

A collection of brief essays written by the Gerontological Society members on
various aspects of old age under two general themes: problems of growing older
and working with the elderly.

255 **Suicide in the island of Singapore.**
E. H. Kua, Tsoi Wing Foo. *Acta Psychiatric Scandinavia,*
vol. 71, 1985, p. 227-29.

A brief discussion of the most salient features of the 230 recorded cases of suicide
in 1980 in Singapore. The authors found that most cases were elderly males, the
highest proportions were in the Indian and Chinese groups, and the most common
method of suicide was jumping from high-rise apartment buildings.

256 **Directory of community and social services for senior citizens.**
Ministry of Social Affairs, Community Development Section.
Singapore: Ministry of Social Affairs, 1984. 122p.

This directory is divided into four sections covering residential services, financial assistance and general relief, medical services, and community support services. In every section, each service is listed by name, address and telephone number, contact person, admission criteria, capacity (number of places available), and fees chargeable, if any.

257 **Handbook on services for the disabled.**
Ministry of Community Development. Singapore: Ministry of Community Development, 1987. 48p.

Provides detailed information on voluntary welfare organizations and government departments offering services to the handicapped. Every agency or service is listed and information is provided on person to contact, office hours, background, and specific services and activities.

258 **Child welfare development: the Singapore experience.**
Stella R. Quah. In: *Administration for child welfare.* Edited by T. N. Chaturvedi. New Delhi: Indian Institute of Public Administration, 1979, p. 283-95.

Compares two types of welfare services, case services and public social utilities, and argues that in most developing nations, including Singapore, the case services predominate while it is the public social utilities approach that is needed most. Figures are presented on the demand for child welfare services in Singapore compared to the supply.

259 **A survey on homes for the elderly in Singapore.**
Singapore Council of Social Service. Singapore: Singapore Council of Social Service, 1985. 69p.

After a general introduction on the care of the elderly and the objectives of the study, this report presents in three chapters the methodology of the study, the main findings, and the discussion and recommendations. Three appendixes provide more detailed figures on the findings.

260 **Directory of social services.**
Singapore Council of Social Service. Singapore: Singapore Council of Social Service, 1985. 3rd ed. 243p.

The first edition of this rather useful book was published in 1979. The directory is divided into four parts. The first part presents a simple and brief classification of Singapore's social services in terms of the type of recipients. The second part, which accounts for sixty-three per cent of the book, is a list of voluntary social and welfare organizations including name, address, telephone, person to contact, office hours, brief historical background, membership, and a description of the organization's services and activities. The third part is a list of government bodies providing social and welfare services. The final part is a set of three appendixes: a

Social Services. Welfare

list of community centres; hospitals and government clinics; and private paying and temple (free) homes for the aged. An index of areas of service is also provided.

261  **A manual on community work in Singapore.**
Edited by S. Vasoo.   Singapore: Singapore Council of Social Service, 1981. 69p.

An overview of the historical development of community work in Singapore, knowledge and practice of community work, and what is expected of a community worker at the personal and management levels. There are five chapters dealing with the historical background of community work in Singapore, community work theory and practice, community work agencies, and the development of volunteer manpower for community work. The final chapter presents the main conclusions. Three appendixes provide further details on the study, community work projects, and community-oriented agencies in Singapore. There is a list of references.

262  **Social policies for the disabled in Singapore.**
S. Vasoo.   *Social Dimension* (May-Aug. 1983), p. 11-13.

This periodical is published by the Singapore Association of Social Workers. The article reviews existing legislation and makes some recommendations for improvement.

263  **Neighbourhoods and precincts.**
S. Vasoo.   *Solidarity*, vol. 101 (1984), p. 17-26.

A description of the community organizations set up by the government to promote community participation in the social and political life of Singapore as well as to promote self-help at the neighbourhood level. The grassroots organizations discussed are community centres, Citizens' Consultative Committees, and Residents' Committees. Vasoo provides the historical background of these organizations, their development and reorganization, and the approaches used by community leaders and members of these organizations to carry out their tasks.

264  **Twenty-five years of social service.**
Edited by S. Vasoo, John Ang, Ng Guat Tin, Ngiam Tee Liang.
Singapore: Singapore Council of Social Service, 1983. 50p.

This is the silver jubilee publication of the council, describing its historical development, activities, main trends, and future development plans. It includes a section on the history and activities of the council, the 25th Board of Members, and several statements by government and council officials.

265    **The Singapore Council of Social Service – some thoughts on its role in the future.**
Ann Wee.    In: *Twenty-five years of social service*. Edited by
S. Vasoo, John Ang, Ng Guat Tin, Ngiam Tee Liang. Singapore:
Singapore Council of Social Service, 1983, p. 17-19.

As a member of the council's Board of Management and Head of the Department of Social Work, National University of Singapore, the author presents her views on the role played by the council during the early years of nation-building and the changing socioeconomic and demographic situation of the country where the council will need to consider the care of the elderly as a main priority.

# Politics

266 **The Singapore party system.**
Thomas J. Bellows. *Journal of Southeast Asian History*, Special
issue: Party Systems of Southeast Asia, vol. 8, no. 1 (Mar. 1967),
p. 122-38.
An informative article providing a political analysis and, as seen from the stand
point of the 1980s, a historical perspective of Singapore's political system when
the Republic was just two years old. Bellows reviews the economic factor, the
'ephemeral opposition', the party organization, the citizens' consultative committees, party leaders and appeals, and the impact of effective government.

267 **The People's Action Party of Singapore: emergence of a dominant
party system.**
Thomas J. Bellows. New Haven, Connecticut: Yale University,
1970. 195p. bibliog. (Southeast Asia Studies).
This monograph is based on the author's doctoral dissertation for Yale University
on the Singapore party system and is an attempt to explain the transformation of
the open and competitive party system into a dominant party system. The study
stretches from the inception of the People's Action Party (PAP) in November
1954 until the 1968 general election. Bellows examines the PAP's ideology, its
alliance with the communists, and its organization, among other aspects. There
are five appendixes.

268 **Big fish, small pond.**
Thomas J. Bellows. *Wilson Quarterly*, vol. 7, no.5 (Winter
1983), p. 66-82.
Focuses on the Prime Minister of Singapore, Lee Kuan Yew, and presents the
nation's development as Lee's masterpiece. Bellows suggests that, rather than a
nation, Singapore may be better understood 'as a system with Lee as the
governing intelligence.'

## Politics

### 269 The tiger and the Trojan horse.
Dennis Bloodworth. Singapore: Times Books International, 1986. 353p.

The publisher warns in the book jacket that 'this is not an academic study.' This feature needs to be kept in mind. The author is a well-known and successful novelist and journalist who took up the challenge of describing and commenting on the 'inside story' of the power struggle between the People's Action Party and the Communist United Front.

### 270 The dynamics of one party dominance. The PAP at the grass-roots.
Chan Heng Chee. Singapore: Singapore University Press, 1976. 272p. bibliog.

Focuses on the PAP's (People's Action Party) activities at the grassroots level in five of the fifty-eight electoral constituencies during the period from 1969 to 1971. The author describes and explains the PAP success in eight chapters. The first chapter introduces the research problem. The other chapters discuss a decade of PAP's rule; the settings, problems, and community activities and associations in the five selected constituencies; the party organization at the constituency level; non-party institutions; local issues; and the opposition. There are five appendixes which provide further information together with an index.

### 271 The political system and political change.
Chan Heng Chee. In: *Singapore: society in transition*. Edited by Riaz Hassan. Kuala Lumpur: Oxford University Press, 1976, p. 30-51. (East Asian Social Science Monographs).

In this balanced treatment of the political system in Singapore, the author describes the changes in the political system in terms of authority and accountability, the participation of the governed, and the distribution of economic and social goods.

### 272 A sensation of independence. A political biography of David Marshall.
Chan Heng Chee. Singapore: Oxford University Press, 1984. 260p.

Marshall, a Jewish Singaporean lawyer who was Chief Minister from 1955 to 1956 and a prominent political figure, is currently Singapore's ambassador to France. The publisher classifies this book as 'the first serious political biography and study of the era.' Indeed, Chan approached the study from two angles, the life of Marshall and the significant political events of Singapore's struggle for independence.

### 273 The role of parliamentary politicians in Singapore.
Chan Heng Chee. *Legislative Studies Quarterly*, vol. 1, no. 3 (Aug. 1976), p. 423-41.

Focuses on the roles and activities of parliamentary politicians at two levels, the national legislature and the constituency. The author identifies four roles within the one-party system, namely, the technocrat, the mobilizer, the Malay vote-getter, and the Chinese-educated intellectual.

274 **Singapore.**
Chang Heng Chee. In: *Military-civilian relations in Southeast Asia*. Edited by Zakaria Haji Ahmad, H. Crouch. Singapore: Oxford University Press, 1985, p. 136-56.
Centres on the Singapore armed forces and describes the organization, structure, and ideological aspects as well as the principle of civilian control of the armed forces in Singapore.

275 **The PAP and the nineties: the politics of anticipation.**
Chan Heng Chee. In: *ASEAN in the regional and global context*. Edited by Karl Jackson (et al.). Berkeley: University of California Press, 1986, p. 163-82.
Based on the political development of Singapore under People's Action Party (PAP) rule, Chan discusses the future possibilities, self-renewal, the restructuring of political institutions, and social policies for the future, among other aspects.

276 **Singapore in 1985. Managing political transition and economic recession.**
Chan Heng Chee. *Asian Survey*, vol. 26, no. 2 (Feb. 1986), p. 158-67.
A review of the year's developments in domestic politics, the elected opposition, economic development, and foreign policy.

277 **Legislature and legislators.**
Chan Heng Chee. In: *Government and politics of Singapore*. Edited by Jon S. T. Quah, Chan Heng Chee, Seah Chee Meow. Singapore: Oxford University Press, 1987, rev. ed., p. 71-91.
Focuses on the functions of the legislature in Singapore and looks into its role as 'a goal-setting agency' in the political system, the social background of the legislators, and their political behaviour in parliament.

278 **Political parties.**
Chan Heng Chee. In: *Government and politics of Singapore*. Edited by Jon S. T. Quah, Chan Heng Chee, Seah Chee Meow. Singapore: Oxford University Press, 1987, rev. ed., p. 146-72.
The People's Action Party (PAP) and several opposition parties in Singapore are analysed in the context of the current party system. The author then discusses in detail the PAP, its ideology and organization, and the problems faced by the opposition.

279 **Postscript: politics in Singapore 1984-1986.**
Chan Heng Chee. In: *Government and politics of Singapore.*
Edited by Jon S. T. Quah, Chan Heng Chee, Seah Chee Meow.
Singapore: Oxford University Press, 1987, rev. ed., p. 309-21.

The first edition of this book was completed in 1982 and published in 1985. The purpose of this postscript is to update the information provided in the first edition. The author discusses the 1984 general election and gives an assessment of the changing perspectives of the electorate, among other things.

280 **S. Rajaratnam. The prophetic and the political.**
Edited by Chan Heng Chee, Obaid ul Haq. Singapore: Graham Brash; New York: St Martin's Press, 1987. 540p.

A selection of speeches and writings by S. Rajaratnam, the Senior Minister in the Prime Minister's Office in Singapore. The speeches are organized into five chapters: the party, the Malaysian interlude, nation-building, restructuring society, and international and regional politics. The final chapter presents three personal interviews of Rajaratnam by the editors.

281 **Nation-building in Singapore.**
David W. Chang. *Asian Survey*, vol. 8, no. 9 (Sept. 1968), p. 761-73.

Assesses the nation-building effort in Singapore in 1968, three years after the attainment of independence. Chang provides the relevant data 'to demonstrate the efficiency and success of the People's Action Party government in several areas of nation-building.' He contends that other countries can learn a great deal from Singapore's experience in nation-building.

282 **Singapore: threat perception and defence spending in a city-state.**
Chin Kin Wah. In: *Defence spending in Southeast Asia.* Edited by Chin Kin Wah. Singapore: Institute of Southeast Asian Studies, 1987, p. 194-223.

Describes the strategic environment and threat perception in Singapore as well as the corresponding responses and defence strategy adopted. Identifies the trends and turning points in defence spending and discusses the interrelationship between the latter and economic development. Concludes that defence spending in Singapore is related to the city-state's psychological insecurity and perceptions of external threats.

283 **Singapore. The PAP and the problem of political succession.**
Carolyn Choo. Kuala Lumpur: Pelanduk Publications, 1985. 225p.

The reader is warned in the publisher's preface that 'this book is not intended to be a profound academic study of its subject.' It is, instead, a presentation of the author's perspective on the changes taking place in the political scene. Choo deals with five topics, namely, the struggle for political power, the opposition, political self-renewal, Lee Hsien Loong (the Prime Minister's eldest son), and a changing Singapore.

284  **Conflict and violence in Singapore and Malaysia 1945-1983.**
Richard Clutterbuck.  Singapore: Graham Brash, 1984. rev.,
updated, and enlarged ed. 412p. maps. bibliog.
As a recognized expert on terrorist movements, the author addresses the
communist threat from a historical perspective and covers themes such as urban
revolution in Singapore during the 1950s, rural guerrilla warfare in Malaysia, and
the aftermath and prospects for Malaysia and Singapore. There are diagrams and
an index.

285  **Lee Kuan Yew and Singapore: a profile.**
Peggy Durdin.  *Asian Affairs: an American Review*, vol. 3 (Jan.-
Feb. 1974), p. 151-69.
A positive assessment of Singapore and its Prime Minister, Lee Kuan Yew,
during the first nine years of independence. Durdin attributes Singapore's success
in improving its standard of living to Lee's efforts in integrating the various races.

286  **The PAP story: the pioneering years (November 1954-April 1968).**
Fong Sip Chee.  Singapore: Times Periodicals, 1979. 270p.
Written by a cadre member of the People's Action Party (PAP), who insists that
it is not a history of the PAP but a record of events during the PAP's first
fourteen years of existence. It contains thirty-eight pages of photographs and has
five appendixes on the PAP's electoral performance, its activities, its manifesto,
and other important party documents.

287  **Lee Kuan Yew's Singapore.**
T. J. S. George.  London: André Deutsch, 1973. 222p. bibliog.
An unauthorized and highly critical biography of Prime Minister Lee Kuan Yew
of Singapore. The author discusses the man and political events in eleven
chapters. There is an index.

288  **The spectator political culture: a refinement of the Almond and
Verba model.**
David S. Gibbons.  *Journal of Commonwealth Political Studies*,
vol. 9, no. 1 (Mar. 1971), p. 19-35.
On the basis of his research on the political attitudes of 209 Chinese farmers in
Singapore, Gibbons has coined the concept of the 'spectator political culture' to
describe the political attitudes of those farmers who were aware of the political
system as a whole, its output objects, and its input objects, but did not consider
themselves as active participants in the political process.

289  **Political tutelage in rural Singapore: the measurement and analysis
of the cognitive political culture of some Chinese farmers.**
David S. Gibbons, Chan Heng Chee.  *Journal of Southeast Asian
Studies*, vol. 2, no. 2 (1971), p. 100-14.
One of several published analyses of the findings from a survey of 209 Chinese
farmers in Singapore to study their socioeconomic conditions and their awareness
of politics.

Politics

290  **How to win a clean sweep in free elections.**
Willard A. Hanna.  *American Universities Field Staff Southeast Asia Series*, vol. 20, no. 11 (Singapore, Nov. 1972), p. 1-10.
An American correspondent explains how the People's Action Party repeated its feat of winning all the parliamentary seats in the 1972 general election in Singapore.

291  **Culture, yellow culture, counterculture, and polyculture in culture-poor Singapore.**
Willard A. Hanna.  *American Universities Field Staff Southeast Asia Series*, vol. 21, no. 2 (Singapore, 1973), p. 1-12.
Discusses Singapore government's multiple concern with polluting Western influences (yellow culture); the need to overcome the problems of drug addiction, promiscuity, and other side products of affluence; the desire to stimulate the indigenous Asian traditions; and the goal of improving the cultural life of Singaporeans.

292  **Relatively speaking.**
Joan Hon.  Singapore: Times Books International, 1984. 270p.
A biography of Hon Sui Sen, a former Permanent Secretary to the Prime Minister's Office and Finance Minister from 1970 until the time of his death in 1983. As his daughter, the author presents a very personal, unique account of his life, values, and views.

293  **Lee Kuan Yew.**
Alex Josey.  Singapore: Times Books International, 1968. 630p.
A collection of Lee Kuan Yew's speeches from 1950 to 1971, which serves as a useful reference book for readers interested in the political ideas of the Prime Minister of Singapore.

294  **Lee Kuan Yew.**
Alex Josey.  Singapore: Times Books International, 1980. vol. 2. 582p.
A continuation of the book by the same title that Josey published in 1968 (q.v.). Volume 2 presents the speeches by Lee Kuan Yew from 1971 to 1978 or, more specifically, quotations from Lee's speeches in Josey's narration of relevant political events throughout that period. There is an index.

295  **The Singapore general election 1972.**
Alex Josey.  Singapore: Eastern Universities Press, 1972. 176p.
A detailed analysis of the 1972 general election in terms of the prelude to the election itself, the electoral campaign, and the election results and their implications.

296 **Lee Kuan Yew. The struggle for Singapore.**
Alex Josey. Singapore: Angus & Robertson, 1974. 334p.
Attempts to present both the positive and the negative sides of the portrait of Singapore's Prime Minister, discussing, in the process, the major political events in Singapore. See other studies on the same theme by Josey in this section.

297 **Singapore and political stability.**
Lau Teik Soon. *Pacific Community*, vol. 3, no. 2 (1972),
p. 378-88.
Discusses Singapore's efforts at maintaining political stability within the framework of democratic socialism, development-oriented policies, a concern for general welfare, and the presence of a legitimate government.

298 **National threat perceptions of Singapore.**
Lau Teik Soon. In: *Threats to security in East Asia-Pacific: national and regional perspectives*. Edited by Charles E. Morrison. Lexington, Massachusetts: D. C. Heath, 1983, p. 113-24.
Discusses those aspects of the Singapore context which are vulnerable to such threats to national security as the communists, racial extremists, and other antinational elements. The government's response to these threats is discussed. Singapore's perception of regional security and external threats also receive attention.

299 **Singapore and ASEAN.**
Lau Teik Soon. In: *Singapore taking stock*. Edited by C. W. Ng. Singapore: Federal Publications, 1986, p. 97-107.
Describes and discusses the pattern and style of Singapore's foreign policy with the members of ASEAN (Association of Southeast Asian Nations), emphasizing the close links among these countries, particularly between Singapore and Malaysia, and their interdependence in international politics, security and economics.

300 **Non-constituency MPs – a place for the opposition in Singapore?**
Lee Boon Hiok. *Parliamentarian*, vol. 66, no. 3 (1985),
p. 121-25.
A discussion of this particular change in the electoral system and how it was not possible to implement it after the 1984 general election.

301 **Singapore in 1984: a time for reflection and a time for change.**
Lee Boon Hiok. In: *Southeast Asian affairs 1985*. Singapore: Institute of Southeast Asian Studies, 1985, p. 297-305.
A review of the political and economic events during the year, particularly the general elections.

**Politics**

### 302 Political institutionalization in Singapore.
Lee Boon Hiok. In: *Asian political institutionalization*. Edited by Robert A. Scalapino (et al). Berkeley: Institute of East Asian Studies, 1986, p. 202-20.

Discusses the political process in Singapore under the leadership of the People's Action Party, which has become a national institution. Also deals with the growth of the Civil Service, political succession, self-renewal, and demography.

### 303 Singapore's continuous search for quality.
Lee Lai-to. In: *Southeast Asian affairs 1984*. Edited by Pushpa Thambipillai. Singapore: Institute of Southeast Asian Studies, 1984, p. 279-93.

A survey of the significant developments in Singapore concerning politics, economics, and foreign affairs during 1983. One of the main points discussed is the role and performance of the younger generation of political leaders.

### 304 The communist organization in Singapore: its techniques of manpower mobilization and management, 1948-66.
Lee Ting Hui. Singapore: Institute of Southeast Asian Studies, 1976. 151p. bibliog. (Field Report Series, no. 12).

Presents the most important methods used by the communist organization: exploiting personal ties and cultivating friendships, absorption into the movement, deployment of manpower resources, and training. There are two appendixes.

### 305 Politics in Singapore. The first term of the People's Action Party 1959-1963.
Michael Leifer. *Journal of Commonwealth Political Studies*, vol. 2 (1964), p. 102-19.

A historical description of the political events of this period and an analysis of their significance for the future political development of Singapore.

### 306 Singapore in Malaysia: the politics of federation.
Michael Leifer. *Journal of Southeast Asian History*, vol. 6, no. 2 (1965), p. 54-70.

An interesting political analysis of the events of this historical phase. Today, this article has a special historical value, as the author gives details of the political events leading to the separation of Singapore from Malaysia.

### 307 Reflections.
Lim Yew Hock. Kuala Lumpur: Pustaka Antara, 1986. 137p.

Lim Yew Hock was a Chief Minister of Singapore in the late 1940s and participated actively in Singapore politics during the struggle for independence. This is his autobiography, which the author presents in eight chapters: a prologue,

74

the Japanese occupation, the British, the Americans, his role in Singapore politics, his time as Malaysia's ambassador to Australia, and his conversion to Islam and his life as a Muslim.

308 **No man is an island. A study of Singapore's Lee Kuan Yew.**
James Minchin. Sydney: Allen & Unwin, 1986. 375p. bibliog.
Like most other studies on Lee Kuan Yew, this one claims to be 'even-handed'. Thirteen chapters follow, in chronological order, the political developments and personal events involving Lee and Singapore. The author includes brief biographies of the leaders he interviewed. There is an index.

309 **Singapore's People's Action Party. Its history, organization and leadership.**
Pang Cheng Lian. Singapore: Oxford University Press, 1971. 87p. bibliog.
A concise history in five sections: the historical background proper, organization and finance, membership, and conclusion. There is an index.

310 **The political thought of Lee Kuan Yew (1963-1965).**
Jon. S. T. Quah. *Journal of the Historical Society* (University of Singapore) (July 1970), p. 48-54.
Lee's political thought from 1963 to 1965 can be summarized thus: Malaysia was plagued by many problems – nation-building, problems of leadership, confrontation, and economic problems – which could be solved only by the adoption of the democratic, socialist, non-communal approach of the ruling party rather than the conservative policies of the Alliance. However, the secession of Singapore from Malaysia has denied the People's Action Party the chance of applying its democratic, socialist, non-communal approach in solving the problems of Malaysia.

311 **Singapore in 1983: the continuing search for talent.**
Jon S. T. Quah. *Asian Survey*, vol. 24, no. 2 (1984), p. 178-86.
Reviews the political, economic, and foreign policy developments in Singapore during 1983. Among the major developments was the search for educated Singaporeans to increase the size of the local talent pool through marriage and child-bearing.

312 **Singapore in 1984: leadership transition in an election year.**
Jon S. T. Quah. *Asian Survey*, vol. 25, no. 2 (1985), p. 220-31.
Discusses the major political, economic, and foreign relations developments of the year and concentrates on the significance of the general elections and the process of power transfer to the younger People's Action Party leaders.

313 **Meeting the twin threats of communism and communalism: the Singapore response.**
Jon S. T. Quah. In: *Governments and rebellions in Southeast Asia*. Edited by Chandran Jeshrun. Singapore: Institute of Southeast Asian Studies, 1985, p. 186-217.

Describes and evaluates the People's Action Party (PAP) government's strategies for dealing with the threats posed by the communists and communalists in Singapore by using a policy approach. Concludes that what is needed for success in dealing with the communist and communal threats is an effective government which takes these threats seriously and employs a comprehensive strategy for tackling them. The Singapore case during the 1959-84 period under the PAP government illustrates this contention very clearly.

314 **Singapore's security concerns and responses.**
Jon S. T. Quah. In: *Proceedings of the Conference on Western Pacific Security reexamined: problems and prospects*. Edited by K. Y. Chang, K. Glaser. Taipei: Freedom Council, 1985, p. 85-111.

The domestic context not only determines Singapore's security concerns but also shapes its responses to these concerns. The government's response to the three threats posed by the communists, racial riots, and the possibility of external attack is to adopt an integrated strategy with the following components: enforcing the internal security laws to counter the communist threat, nurturing the growth of a Singaporean national identity among the population to minimize if not eliminate the threat of racial riots, and pursuing a policy of total defence to meet and discourage the threat of external aggression.

315 **Political science in Singapore.**
Jon S. T. Quah. In: *Singapore studies: critical surveys of the humanities and social sciences*. Edited by Basant K. Kapur. Singapore: Singapore University Press, 1986, p. 83-145.

Describes the origins and evolution of the study of political science in Singapore and provides a comprehensive review of the research literature on the subject in terms of its subfields. These are: national politics, public administration and public policy; and foreign policy. The chapter concludes by recommending an agenda for further research on nineteen research gaps in the three subfields.

316 **Singapore.**
Jon S. T. Quah. In: *The local political system in Asia. A comparative perspective*. Edited by Chung-Si Ahn. Seoul: Seoul National University Press, 1987, p. 224-48.

Describes the local political system in Singapore. Provides first a description of the Singapore context and then discusses management committees, Citizens' Consultative Committees, and Residents' Committees.

317 **Government and politics of Singapore.**
Edited by Jon S. T. Quah, Chan Heng Chee, Seah Chee Meow.
Singapore: Oxford University Press, 1987. rev. ed. 338p. bibliog.
The first university textbook on the government and politics of Singapore, which is written by a team of eight local scholars. This revised edition contains the twelve chapters, which were originally published in 1985, and a postscript on 'Politics in Singapore 1984-1986', written by Chan Heng Chee to provide an update on recent political developments. The twelve chapters are organized into three parts. Part I has three chapters, which describe the foundations of Singapore politics in terms of the evolution of the political system, the economy, and the social-cultural framework. The five chapters in Part II cover the contemporary political system and deal in turn with the legislature, civil service, statutory boards, political parties, and parapolitical institutions. Part III of the book is devoted to an analysis of four contemporary problems and issues, namely, education, public housing, public transportation, and foreign policy. There is a useful select bibliography of 130 books and articles.

318 **Lee Kuan Yew.**
Jon S. T. Quah. In: *Encyclopedia of world biography*. New York: McGraw-Hill, 1987, p. 379-81.
A short biography of Lee Kuan Yew, who has been Prime Minister of Singapore since June 1959. Lee's family background, education, entry into politics, and his achievements as a capable Prime Minister are discussed.

319 **Dyason Memorial Lectures 1973.**
S. Rajaratnam. *Australian Outlook* (Dec. 1973), p. 243-60.
The Dyason Memorial Lectures were organized by the Australian Institute of International Affairs of Melbourne and published in the institute's journal above. S. Rajaratnam was Singapore's Minister of Foreign Affairs when he delivered these lectures in November 1973. He covered three topics: new themes for Asia, Southeast Asia in transition, and the Singapore solution.

320 **The rise and fall of Singapore's 'second industrial revolution.'**
Garry Rodan. In: *Southeast Asia in the 1980s. The politics of economic crisis*. Edited by Richard Robison, Kevin Hewison, Richard Higgott. London: Allen & Unwin, 1987, p. 149-76.
Discusses the politics of economic planning by first presenting the historical background to the 'second' industrial revolution, the government policy underlying the second industrial revolution, and the progress, problems, and policy revisions of this revolution.

321 **Singapore politics 1945-63: the myth of the 'leftward drift.'**
Seah Chee Meow. *Review of Southeast Asian Studies*, vol. 1, no. 4 (1971), p. 21-32.
Discusses the assumption that Singapore was facing a serious challenge from the political left during the struggle for independence and during the early years of consolidation.

Politics

322  **Community centres in Singapore. Their political involvement.**
Seah Chee Meow.   Singapore: Singapore University Press, 1973.
142p. bibliog.

The first systematic study of community centres as grassroots organizations in
Singapore. The author presents the historical background of the political system
in the introduction and proceeds to discuss the development and political
involvement of the community centres, their functions and personnel, leadership,
and the organizational evolution of the People's Association. There is an index.

323  **Political change and continuity in Singapore.**
Seah Chee Meow.   In: *Singapore: twenty-five years of
development.* Edited by You Poh Seng, Lim Chong Yah.
Singapore: Nan Yang Xing Zhou Lianhe Zaobao, 1984, p. 235-52.

Discusses constitutional and political developments in Singapore, 1959-84,
examines the People's Action Party's (PAP) political philosophy, and discusses
the question of political succession. The final section evaluates the results of the
PAP rule on system maintenance in Singapore.

324  **Singapore.**
Seah Chee Meow.   In: *Politics in the ASEAN States.* Edited by
Diane K. Mauzy. Kuala Lumpur: Maricans Academic Series, 1984,
p. 186-224.

A description of Singapore's political structure from the colonial period under
British rule to the mid-1980s. The final section discusses future developments.

325  **The civil service.**
Seah Chee Meow.   In: *Government and politics of Singapore.*
Edited by Jon S. T. Quah, Chan Heng Chee, Seah Chee Meow.
Singapore: Oxford University Press, 1987, rev. ed., p. 92-119.

The civil service is analysed in terms of its origins and evolution and its
organizational structure. The discussion covers other aspects of the role and
responsiveness of the civil service.

326  **Parapolitical institutions.**
Seah Chee Meow.   In: *Government and politics of Singapore.*
Edited by Jon S. T. Quah, Chan Heng Chee, Seah Chee Meow.
Singapore: Oxford University Press, 1987, rev. ed., p. 173-94.

Discusses the organization and roles of three major parapolitical institutions as
instruments of the government's political consolidation. These institutions are the
Community Centres, the Citizens' Consultative Committees, and the Residents'
Committees.

327 **Singapore – the technocratic state.**
Robert Shaplen. In: *A turning wheel.* Robert Shaplen. London:
André Deutsch, 1979, p. 175-200.
In the only chapter in which Shaplen discusses Singapore, he presents his personal
interpretation of Singapore's political structure and the leadership style of its
Prime Minister, Lee Kuan Yew.

328 **Malay participation in the national development of Singapore.**
Edited by Sharom Ahmat, James Wong. Singapore: Central
Council of Malay Cultural Organizations Singapore, 1971. 25p.
The report of a seminar organized by the Council of Malay Cultural
Organizations in Singapore in 1971. It includes the opening address by a
prominent Malay political leader and member of the government and three
papers on the following subjects: Malay education and national development,
employment opportunities, and the impact of public housing on Malay family life.
There is a final section on 'areas of action'.

329 **The developmental élite in Singapore.**
K. E. Shaw, P. M. Chang. In: *Elites and national development in
Singapore.* Edited by K. E. Shaw (et al.). Tokyo: Institute of
Developing Economies, 1977, p. 27-60.
A description and discussion of the power position of the bureaucratic élite in the
context of national development. The authors first present a brief outline of
concepts in the study of élites and then focus on Singapore following a historical
perspective.

330 **Political parties in Singapore.**
Shee Poon Kim. In: *Political parties of Asia and the Pacific.*
Edited by Haruship Fukui. London: Greenwood Press, 1985,
p. 971-97.
Traces the history of party politics and focuses on the People's Action Party, the
formation of which, in the author's view, marked the entry of Singapore into 'an
era of mass politics.'

331 **Singapore's one party system: its relationship to democracy and
political stability.**
Tae Yul Nam. *Pacific Affairs* (Dec. 1969), p. 465-80.
A description and discussion of the political features of the young nation which
had attained independence just four years before the author wrote this paper. He
argues that the dominance of the People's Action Party reflects the people's will
in the elections.

332 **Governing Singapore. Interviews with the new leaders.**
Raj Vasil.  Singapore: Times Books International, 1988. rev. ed.
247p.

The first edition of this book appeared in 1984 and was published by Eastern
Universities Press. This edition differs only slightly from the first edition. The
author discusses in the first of six chapters decolonization and independence. The
other chapters are on the People's Action Party; the creation of social, economic
and educational foundations of a democracy; the aspect of multiracialism: the
nature and role of government; and preparing for the future. There are two
appendixes: 'Conversations with First Deputy Prime Minister Goh Chok Tong'
and 'Conversations with Prime Minister Lee Kuan Yew.'

333 **The future of Singapore – the global city.**
Edited by Wee Teong Boo.  Singapore: University Education
Press, 1977. 220p.

A collection of papers and proceedings of a seminar on political and economic
trends in Singapore held in Singapore, 13-14 December 1975, by the Democratic
Socialist Club. Among the themes discussed are the politics of the global city, the
role of a political opposition, and the role of intellectuals.

# Legal System

### 334 Family law in Malaysia and Singapore.
Ahmad Ibrahim. Singapore: Singapore Malayan Law Journal,
1984. 2nd ed. 359p. bibliog.

Currently, this is the most complete study of legislation concerning the family in
Malaysia and Singapore. The first edition of this book appeared in 1978. Professor
Ahmad Ibrahim is a well-known authority on the subject and has the advantage of
being equally expert in both Islamic and non-Islamic systems of law in Singapore
and Malaysia. The most important contribution of his book is precisely the
discussion of both legal systems. English-speaking readers will not find a better
presentation of Islamic family law as practised in these two countries. Numerous
court cases are presented to illustrate the application of the Islamic and non-
Islamic legislations. The book is divided into eleven chapters. The first chapter
provides a historical description of the various forms of marriage. The other
chapters deal with non-Muslim family law, effects of marriage on status and
property, divorce and matrimonial proceedings, parent and child, inheritance
rights, Muslim marriage, effect of marriage on the legal status of women under
Islamic law, dissolution of Muslim marriage, parent and child under Islamic law,
and inheritance rights. There is an appendix containing the 1983 Islamic Family
Law Enactment in Kelantan, Malaysia, and an index.

### 335 An introduction to the Singapore legal system.
Helena H. M. Chan. Singapore: Malayan Law Journal, 1986.
140p.

The book is addressed to 'the law student, foreign lawyer or interested layman'
and thus the reader will find that the usual legal references to court cases and
legal terms add details for the experts without obstructing the flow of information
for laymen. There are six chapters covering the historical background of the legal
system, sources of law, the structure of government, legal institutions, legal
procedure, and a conclusion on the legal culture and the future. There is also an
index.

## Legal System

336  **Index to Singapore/Malaysia legal periodicals 1932-1984.**
Edited by Molly Cheang, Sng Yok Fong, Carolyn Wee.
Singapore: Malayan Law Journal, 1986. 431p.

As the editors explain, this index is based on a larger periodicals computerization project undertaken by the National University of Singapore Library. It covers the articles published in the Malayan Law Journal from its first volume in 1932 until December 1984. It also includes legal articles on Singapore and Malaysia published in the following eight periodicals: *INSAF Journal of the Malaysian Bar* (1967-84), *Journal of Malaysian and Comparative Law* (1974-84); *Law Times* (1965-83), *Malaya Law Review* (1959-84), *Malaysian Current Law Journal* (1981-84), *Me Judice* (1958-68), *Singapore Association of Women Lawyers News* (1980-84), and *Singapore Law Review* (1969-84). The entries are presented under a subject index and an author and title index. Each entry provides information on authorship, title, journal, and date of publication.

337  **Common law in Singapore and Malaysia. A volume of essays marking the 25th anniversary of the *Malaya Law Review*.**
Edited by A. J. Harding.   Singapore: Butterworths, 1985. 371p.

Eleven chapters written by twelve contributors, eleven of whom were teaching staff at the Faculty of Law of the National University of Singapore when the book was in preparation. Chapter 1 deals with the application of English law in this region and was written by G. W. Bartholomew. Chapter 2 by Soon Choo Hock and Andrew Phang Boon Leong is on reception of English commercial law in Singapore. Chapter 3 by Helena Chan Hui Meng is on the privy council as court of last resort. Chapter 4 by Walter Woon is on judicial precedent. Chapter 5 by Stanley Yeo Meng Hong deals with the application of common law defences to the penal code. Chapter 6 written by Leong Wai Kum focuses on common law and Chinese marriage custom. Chapter 7 by the editor A. J. Harding deals with the use of the maxim *res ipsa loquitur* (or 'the facts speak for themselves'). Chapter 8 by W. J. M. Ricquier is on land law and common law. Chapter 9 by C. M. Chinkin discusses abuse of discretion. Chapter 10 by T. K. K. Iyer is on *certiorari*. The final chapter by V. S. Winslow is dedicated to the discussion of the first pillar of justice. The book includes also a table of cases, a table of statutes, and a subject index.

338  **Parent-child law in Singapore.**
Khoo Oon Soo.   Singapore: Butterworths, 1984. 223p.

Reviews and discusses the relevant legislation in five parts. Part 1 deals with legitimacy, illegitimacy, and legitimation according to customary Chinese and Indian marriages, Muslim law, and common law and the relevant law reforms. Part 2 is dedicated to the maintenance of children according to the Women's Charter and under Muslim law. Part 3 focuses on guardianship of infants as seen in common law and in Singapore's Children and Young Persons Act. Part 4 is on adoption of children in England and in Singapore. Part 4 discusses the Women's Charter (Amendment) Act of 1980, particularly concerning legitimacy, maintenance, welfare of children and wife, and child abuse. There are eight appendixes showing samples of summonses, a table of statutes, a table of cases, and an index.

339    **The law of partnership in Singapore and Malaysia.**
Peter Koh Soon Kwang.    Singapore: Professional Publications,
1984. 2nd ed. 95p.

The first edition of this book was published in 1979. The author indicates that he
wrote this edition for businessmen and other laymen. The subject is presented in
seven brief chapters dealing with sources of law, the nature of partnership,
formation and duration, relations between partners and third parties, reciprocal
relation of partners, and dissolution and its consequences. The book includes a
table of statutes, a list of cases, and an index.

340    **The duty to maintain spouse and children during marriage.**
Leong Wai Kum.    *Malaya Law Review*, vol. 29 (1987), p. 56-79.

A discussion of relevant statutory provisions in Singapore concerning the
maintenance rights of wives and children and the corresponding obligations on the
part of husbands and parents.

341    **Companies and securities handbook. Singapore and Malaysia.**
Compiled by Philip N. Pillai.    Singapore: Butterworths, 1984.
1,410p.

An annotated compilation of the legislation pertaining to companies and
securities. Pillai has put together all the relevant Acts of Parliament, the Stock
Exchange rules, bylaws, corporate disclosure policy, takeover codes and practice
notes, and other material on the subject, which businessmen and other interested
readers will find rather informative.

342    **Law contract in Malaysia and Singapore. Cases and commentary.**
Visu Sinnadurai.    Singapore: Butterworths, 1987. 2nd ed. 847p.

The first edition of this book appeared in 1979. The author presents in this second
edition the current situation and the changes that have taken place since 1979.
There are fourteen chapters organized into six parts. Part 1 is an introduction to
the law of contract in Malaysia and Singapore, covering its historical background
and a description of the present law. Part 2 deals with the formation of a contract,
including the process of an agreement and consideration, and the privity of
contract. Part 3 focuses on the contents of a contract. Part 4 has five chapters
dealing with void and voidable contracts. Part 5 is on performance and discharge.
Part 6 discusses damages and remedies. There is a table of cases and an index.

343    **Principles of Singapore law (including business law).**
Myint Soe.    Singapore: The Institute of Banking and Finance,
1987. 534p. bibliog.

Written primarily for bankers and law students, the book has sixteen chapters
arranged in two parts. The first part, consisting of eight chapters, deals with
general aspects of Singapore law. The second part is on business law and covers,
among other topics, law of contract, agency, sale of goods, hire purchase,
negotiable instruments and banking, and insurance. There is an index, a table of
statutes, and a table of cases.

344 **The legal system of Singapore.**
Walter C. M. Woon. In: *The modern legal systems cyclopedia.*
Edited by Kenneth Redden. New York: William S. Hein, 1985,
p. 677-743.
Presents a succinct description of the legal system arranged into six sections:
historical background, the sources of law, the constitution, statutes and other
legislation, the judicial system, and the legal profession. Two appendixes provide
data on the judicial tribunals and the evolution of the courts of appeal. For a
more detailed presentation of the Singapore legal system see Helena Chan's book
in this section.

345 **Commercial law of Singapore. An introduction.**
Walter C. M. Woon. Cambridge, England: Woodhead-Faulkner,
1986. 301p. bibliog.
The book is addressed to 'the intelligent layman'. The discussion is presented in
four parts. Part 1 has a chapter on the history and sources of law in Singapore.
Part 2 deals with business organizations in three chapters, namely: sole
proprietorships, partnerships, and companies. Part 3 focuses on commercial law
and has five chapters on sale of goods, negotiable instrument insurance, corporate
finance and securities regulation, and trade marks. Part 4 has only one chapter
and it deals with taxation. These appendixes provide further details. There is an
index and a table of statutes.

346 **The Singapore lawyer. The structure of the legal profession in
Singapore.**
Walter C. M. Woon. *Law Society's Journal*, vol. 3, no. 1 (Mar.
1986), p. 8-14.
A succinct description of the legal profession, including entry into the profession,
practising as an advocate and solicitor, regulation and discipline, and ethics.

347 **Legal protection of shareholders.**
Walter C. M. Woon. *Securities Industry Review*, vol. 12, no. 2
(Oct. 1986), p. 1-10.
A brief but informative description of the protection given in Singapore to
shareholders by the Companies Act. The presentation is divided into two sections
according to the author's idea that 'share holders need to be protected' from 'two
groups of people': the company directors and the other shareholders.

348 **Judicial management in Singapore.**
Walter C. M. Woon. *Singapore Accountant* (Jan. 1988),
p. 13-17.
Explains the 1987 amendment to the Companies Act, whereby a company that
cannot pay its debts is allowed 'a breathing space in which to effect a rescue
operation' through the appointment of a judicial manager by the Court.

# Public Administration

### 349 Bureaucracy and development in Singapore.
Thomas J. Bellows. *Asian Journal of Public Administration*, vol. 7, no. 1 (June 1985), p. 55-69.

Describes the political and economic context in Singapore and provides an overview of the Singapore Civil Service and the statutory boards. Discusses the issue of institutional coordination and control and speculates on future directions.

### 350 Public services.
G. E. Bogaars. In: *Towards tomorrow: essays on development and social transformation in Singapore*. Singapore: National Trades Union Congress, 1973, p. 73-83.

A description of the development of the Singapore Civil Service, 1946-73, by a former senior civil servant who was then Permanent Secretary in the Ministry of Foreign Affairs. The various constitutional changes affecting the civil service and the latter's response to such changes are discussed.

### 351 In the service of the nation.
John Drysdale. Singapore: Federal Publications, 1985. 219p.

The history of the police force in Singapore in seventeen chapters covering aspects such as the colonial period with problems of various kinds including the secret societies; the 'new horizon' with a force of volunteers, then the police national service; reorganization; public relations; civil defence; boys' clubs; the Neighbourhood Police Post; crime prevention and detection; controlling drugs; disaster management; computerized operations; and other aspects of police work.

352 **The public personnel system in Singapore.**
Lee Boon Hiok.   In: *Asian civil services: development and trends.* Edited by Amara Raksasataya, Heinrich Siedentopf. Kuala Lumpur: Asian and Pacific Development Centre, 1980, p. 431-79.

This detailed analysis of the public personnel system in Singapore focuses on the legal framework of the Singapore Civil Service, the central personnel agencies, and issues related to the management of the public personnel system. The concluding section assesses the changes and developments in the public personnel system in Singapore from 1960 to 1980 and makes recommendations about future policies and trends.

353 **Ministry of Labour annual report 1986.**
Ministry of Labour.   Singapore: Ministry of Labour, Public Relations Section, 1987. 46p.

A brief overview of the activities of the Ministry of Labour covering the following areas: highlights of 1986, a description of the ministry, employment, terms of employment and working conditions, industrial relations, industrial safety, industrial health, social security, ASEAN (Association of Southeast Asian Nations) and international labour affairs, and laws administered by the ministry.

354 **999 true cases from the CID.**
Nicky Moey.   Singapore: Times Books International, 1987. 143p.

The purpose of this book is to educate the public concerning crime prevention. The book provides a detailed account of ten real-life crimes and the efforts by the Criminal Investigations Department (CID) of the police force to solve these crimes and bring the criminals to justice.

355 **Singapore.**
Ow Chin Hock.   In: *The role of public enterprise in national development in Southeast Asia: problems and prospects.* Edited by Nguyen-Truong. Singapore: Regional Institute of Higher Education and Development, 1976, p. 153-256. bibliog.

A detailed description of the historical background; the types, features, and scope of public enterprises; and an evaluation of their performance, problem areas, and prospects for success. Useful data are provided.

356 **Budget innovation in Singapore.**
Cedric Pugh.   *Asia Pacific Journal of Management*, vol. 3, no. 3 (May 1986), p. 157-75.

Discusses the implementation of programme budgeting by the Singapore government and the relationship between budget changes and political and administrative goals.

Public Administration

357 **Origin of Public Service Commissions in Singapore.**
Jon S. T. Quah. *Indian Journal of Public Administration*,
vol. 18, no. 4 (1973), p. 563-70.
The idea of establishing Public Service Commissions (PSCs) in the British
colonies was first introduced by the British government in 1946. The author
describes and discusses the process that followed the setting up of Singapore's
PSC.

358 **Administrative and legal measures for combating bureaucratic**
**corruption in Singapore.**
Jon S. T. Quah. Singapore: Department of Political Science,
University of Singapore, 1978. 23p. (Occasional Paper no. 34).
A description and evaluation of the two major anti-corruption measures in
Singapore: the Prevention of Corruption Act (POCA) and the Corrupt Practices
Investigation Bureau (CPIB), in addition to other non-specific measures. The
POCA and CPIB are the most important and effective measures, given the
comprehensive nature of POCA and the wide powers given to the CPIB.

359 **Police corruption in Singapore: an analysis of its forms, extent and**
**causes.**
Jon S. T. Quah. *Singapore Police Journal*, vol. 10, no. 1 (Jan.
1979), p. 7-43.
Identifies the forms of police corruption in Singapore on the basis of reported
cases of such corruption during 1845-1921 and 1965-77. An attempt is also made
to ascertain the extent and causes of police corruption in Singapore during these
two periods.

360 **The public bureaucracy and national development in Singapore.**
Jon S. T. Quah. In: *Administrative systems abroad.* Edited by
Krishna K. Tummala. Lanham, Maryland: University Press of
America, 1982, rev. ed., p. 42-75.
Describes and explains how the public bureaucracy has contributed to national
development in Singapore. Within the constraints imposed by the Singapore
environment, the public bureaucracy has contributed to the attainment of national
development goals by performing three tasks: (1) ensuring quality control of its
personnel through the Public Service Commission, (2) preventing and controlling
corrupt behaviour among its employees by means of the Corrupt Practices
Investigation Bureau and the Prevention of Corruption Act, and (3) implementing socioeconomic programmes (such as family planning and public housing)
which have significantly transformed the way of life of most Singaporeans.

361 **Public bureaucracy, social change and national development.**
Jon S. T. Quah. In: *Singapore: development policies and trends.*
Edited by Peter S. J. Chen. Singapore: Oxford University Press,
1983, p. 197-223.

Describes how the public bureaucracy contributes to national development by
bringing about desired social change in Singapore. Focusing on three innovations
introduced by the public bureaucracy during the post-1959 period, namely, public
housing, family planning, and traffic management, this chapter concludes that the
public bureaucracy has transformed the way of life of Singaporeans in three areas:
where and how they live, when and how they limit their families, and when and
how they go to work.

362 **Productivity in the Singapore police force: some suggestions for
improvement.**
Jon S. T. Quah. *Asian Journal of Public Administration*, vol. 6,
no. 1 (June 1984), p. 2-17.

The Singapore Police Force (SPF) has a very high output as a result of its
increased workload. It is difficult to measure the SPF's productivity at this stage,
however, as the corresponding input data are not available. Therefore, to
improve the SPF's productivity, the following measures must be adopted:
productivity measurement, implementation of a productivity programme, improving the quality of supervision, increasing manpower in the SPF by recruiting more
women officers, and nurturing the development of the productivity ethic among
members of the SPF.

363 **The public policy-making process in Singapore.**
Jon S. T. Quah. *Asian Journal of Public Administration*, vol. 6,
no. 2 (Dec. 1984), p. 108-26.

After defining public policy and describing the policy context in Singapore, the
process of formulating, implementing, and evaluating public policies is described.
The public policy-making process in Singapore is characterized by three features:
(1) policy formulation is élitist, with Prime Minister Lee Kuan Yew and his cabinet
colleagues playing pre-eminent roles; (2) policy implementation is highly efficient
because of governmental support for policies formulated, efficient and effective
public bureaucracy, low level of bureaucratic corruption, reliance on national
campaigns, social discipline of the population, and the small size of Singapore;
and (3) policy evaluation is weak because it is still in its infancy in Singapore.

364 **Public administration in a city-state: the Singapore case.**
Jon S. T. Quah. In: *Comparative study on the local public
administration in Asian and Pacific countries.* Edited by Keiso
Hanaoka. Tokyo: EROPA Local Government Centre, 1984,
p. 206-16.

Describes the nature of public administration in Singapore in terms of eight
features: product of local and foreign influences, search for talent, emphasis on
efficiency, low level of formalism, the dominance of the People's Action Party

(PAP) over the public bureaucracy, reliance on administrative reform, the public bureaucracy's role as an agent of social change, and the urban nature of public administration. The public bureaucracy's success in contributing towards national development can be attributed not only to Singapore's assets, but also to the PAP leaders' commitment to development, their intolerant attitude towards corruption, and the high standards of discipline within the civil service and statutory boards.

365   **The public bureaucracy in Singapore, 1959-1984.**
Jon S. T. Quah.   In: *Singapore: twenty-five years of development.*
Edited by You Poh Seng, Lim Chong Yah. Singapore: Nan Yang
Xing Zhou Lianhe Zaobao, 1984, p. 288-314.

Describes the following eight changes in the public bureaucracy in Singapore from 1959 to 1984: increase in the size of the civil service, the increasing number of statutory boards, the role of the public bureaucracy as an agent of social change, focus on administrative reform, minimizing corruption, change in the budgeting system, improving personnel management, and reliance on national campaigns. In terms of strengths, the public bureaucracy was found to be relatively incorrupt, highly efficient in policy implementation, and willing to learn from the experiences of public bureaucracies in other countries. On the other hand, the public bureaucracy is deficient in terms of job analysis, its reliance on traditional methods of performance appraisal, inadequate emphasis on training, and its over-reliance on national campaigns.

366   **Towards productivity and excellence: a comparative study of the**
**public personnel systems in the ASEAN countries.**
Jon S. T. Quah.   *Asian Journal of Public Administration*, vol. 8,
no. 1 (June 1986), p. 64-99.

Describes and compares the public personnel systems in Indonesia, Malaysia, the Philippines, Singapore, and Thailand in terms of such personnel functions as recruitment and selection, classification, compensation, promotion, training, performance evaluation, and disciplinary control. Among the five countries, only Singapore and Malaysia appear to be likely to meet the goals of productivity and excellence.

367   **Statutory boards.**
Jon S. T. Quah.   In: *Government and politics of Singapore.*
Edited by Jon S. T. Quah, Chan Heng Chee, Seah Chee Meow.
Singapore: Oxford University Press, 1987, rev. ed., p. 120-45.

A detailed analysis of the origins, evolution, role, and performance of statutory boards in Singapore from 1959 to 1981. The chapter is divided into four sections, the first of which defines a statutory board and identifies its major characteristics. The reasons for the formation of the statutory boards and their evolution are discussed in the second section. The third section describes the eight functions performed by the statutory boards in Singapore. The final section deals with the performance of the major statutory boards and assesses their contribution to national development in Singapore.

368   **The budgetary process in the Singapore bureaucracy: some observations.**
Seah Chee Meow.   *Singapore Manager*, vol. 7, no. 1 (1973), p. 25-29.
A description of Singapore's process of 'relating expenditure of funds to accomplishment of planned objectives.' Discussion covers the formulation stage, legislative authorization, execution, audit phase, and strengths and weaknesses of the process.

369   **Public relations in the Singapore bureaucracy. A neglected aspect in administration.**
Seah Chee Meow.   *Indian Journal of Public Administration*, vol. 19, no. 4 (1973), p. 612-26.
Examines the importance given to public relations 'as a function of bureaucracy', the main established channels for 'rectifying grievances,' and suggestions for improving the system.

370   **The Singapore bureaucracy and issues of transition.**
Seah Chee Meow:   In: *Singapore society in transition*. Edited by Riaz Hassan. Kuala Lumpur: Oxford University Press, 1976, p. 52-66.
Describes the process of adjustment of the Singapore bureaucracy to political and constitutional changes and identifies its strengths and strains. In particular, two sources of strain are identified: 'the practice of appointing senior bureaucrats to serve on the board of management in parastatal bodies or as directors in ventures in which the government has a vested interest' and 'the task of retaining skilled or trained manpower' in the Singapore bureaucracy.

371   **A survey of personnel practices in Singapore.**
James B. Shaw, Cynthia D. Fisher, Irene Chow.   Singapore: Singapore Institute of Personnel Management, 1987. 35p.
The authors, all academics from the National University of Singapore School of Management, identify 'the types of personnel and human resource management practices used in Singapore.'

# Foreign Relations

372  **Singapore's perspective on the Soviet-Vietnamese alliance and the security of Southeast Asia.**
Bilveer Singh.   In: *The Soviet-Vietnamese alliance and the security of Southeast Asia.* New York: International Security Council, 1986, p. 61-82.
Describes the main aspects of Singapore's 'hardline' foreign policy concerning the Soviet-Vietnamese alliance and discusses its implications.

373  **Singapore: a foreign policy of survival.**
Les Buszynski.   *Asian Thought and Society. An International Review*, vol. 10 (1985), p. 128-37.
Discusses the role of Singapore in the balancing of regional security and harmonious relations with its neighbours. New leaders in the nations of the region will determine the path of regional foreign policy.

374  **Singapore's foreign policy. 1965-1968.**
Chan Heng Chee.   *Journal of Southeast Asian History*, vol. 10. no. 1 (Mar. 1969), p. 177-91.
Describes Singapore's foreign policy during its first three years of independence and concludes that during this period the major concern of the People's Action Party government was to establish a firm economic and defence base.

375 **The defence of Malaysia and Singapore. The transformation of a security system 1957-1971.**
Chin Kin Wah. Cambridge, England: Cambridge University Press, 1983, 219p. bibliog.

Focuses on the origins, development, and changes of the Anglo-Malaysian Defense Agreement (AMDA), and discusses the pre-treaty defence relations of the participating nations (Britain, Australia, and New Zealand) in the agreement to defend the Malayan-Singapore region; the decolonization and institution of AMDA; its extension, external testing, and problems faced; and the transition into a new five-power defence system. There is an index.

376 **Foreign policy.**
Obaid Ul Haq. In: *Government and politics of Singapore.*
Edited by Jon S. T. Quah, Chan Heng Chee, Seah Chee Meow.
Singapore: Oxford University Press, 1987, rev. ed., p. 276-308.

Describes Singapore's foreign policy as a small state's search for security and survival. In spite of being small and resource-poor, Singapore has 'carved for itself a significant niche in regional international relations.' Even though the objectives of Singapore's foreign policy have been achieved. Haq cautions that in pursuing a pragmatic foreign policy, Singapore's political leaders should never forget that Singapore is a small and militarily weak country.

377 **Singapore and state succession: international relations and internal law.**
S. Jayakumar. *International and Comparative Law Quarterly* (July 1970), p. 398-423.

A detailed discussion of two sets of relevant 'international rights and obligations', namely, those with the United Kingdom when it relinquished sovereignty over Singapore and those with Malaysia after Singapore separated from the Federation.

378 **Malaysia-Singapore relations: crisis of adjustment, 1965-1968.**
Lau Teik Soon. *Journal of Southeast Asian History*, vol. 10, no. 1 (Mar. 1969), p. 155-76.

Deals with the relations between Singapore and Malaysia in four areas: economics, defence, politics, and immigration and labour during the period 1965-68.

379 **Singapore's perceptions of ASEAN's role.**
Lau Teik Soon. In: *Political and social change in Singapore.*
Edited by Wu Teh-yao. Singapore: Institute of Southeast Asian Studies, 1975, p. 155-70.

Singapore's views on ASEAN (Association of Southeast Asian Nations) have focused on three aspects: economic cooperation, the need to maintain a nonaligned posture, and the necessity for developing countries to assist the organization.

380    **The role of Singapore in Southeast Asia.**
Lau Teik Soon.    *World Review*, vol. 1, no. 3 (Aug. 1980),
p. 34-44.
Stresses the importance of enhancing regional economic cooperation and developing a regional identity. Singapore is moving closer to its ASEAN (Association of Southeast Asian Nations) neighbours in regional cooperation and security, and this trend will continue so long as its national interests are not at stake.

381    **Singapore and ASEAN.**
Lau Teik Soon.    In: *Singapore: development policies and trends.*
Edited by Peter S. J. Chen. Singapore: Oxford University Press,
1983, p. 285-300.
Discusses Singapore's role in the development of ASEAN (Association of Southeast Asian Nations) and focuses on such aspects as Singapore's views on ASEAN's development in the political and security fields, Singapore's attitudes towards the Kampuchean problem, and the development of ASEAN into a diplomatic bloc and security organization.

382    **Constraints on Singapore's foreign policy.**
Lee Boon Hiok.    *Asian Survey*, vol. 22, no. 6 (1982), p. 524-35.
The small size of Singapore both in terms of land and population is seen as an important constraint in the nation's foreign policy. Economic, social, and political aspects of foreign policy constraints on Singapore are also discussed.

383    **China's changing attitudes towards Singapore, 1965-75.**
Lee Lai-to.    In: *Political and social change in Singapore.* Edited
by Wu Teh-yao. Singapore: Institute of Southeast Asian Studies,
1975, p. 155-70. (Southeast Asian Perspectives, no. 3).
A detailed discussion of the four phases in China's policies towards Singapore, 1965-75, namely: (1) the early years of Singapore's independence, 1965-69; (2) the Bank of China incident and its aftermath, 1969-71; (3) people-to-people diplomacy, 1971-74; and (4) the overtures to formal ties, 1974-75.

384    **Singapore and East Asia.**
Lee Lai-to.    In: *Singapore: development policies and trends.*
Edited by Peter S. J. Chen. Singapore: Oxford University Press,
1983, p. 335-66.
Analyses the place of East Asian countries in Singapore's foreign policy by using statistics of Singapore's foreign trade and its communications with these countries. East Asian countries will be of considerable importance to Singapore.

385 **The Singapore Foreign Service.**
Ministry of Foreign Affairs. Singapore: Ministry of Foreign
Affairs, 1987. 27p.

Intended for people who want to join the Foreign Service, this booklet presents a
clear and systematic description of the organization of the service, the work of a
Foreign Service officer, the Foreign Service grade structure, overseas allowances
and benefits, training, requirements for application, and instructions on how to
apply.

386 **Strategies of survival: the foreign policy dilemmas of smaller Asian
states.**
Charles E. Morrison, Astri Suhrke. St. Lucia, Australia:
University of Queensland, 1978. 346p.

An analysis of the foreign policy dilemmas of seven Asian countries. In the
chapter on Singapore, the nature of the domestic setting, the linkages between
domestic and foreign policy, regional threats and external support, and the role of
Singapore in Southeast Asia are discussed. 'There is a very close connection
between Singapore's domestic and foreign policies,' and the domestic context
imposes 'relatively narrow limits on Singaporean foreign policies.'

387 **Singapore's foreign policy in Southeast Asia: options for national
survival.**
Seah Chee Meow. *Pacific Community*, vol. 4 (July 1973),
p. 535-51.

For the People's Action Party, government national survival depends on the
successful implementation of a three-pronged foreign policy: (1) the cultivation of
political ties with friendly big powers, (2) the transformation of the economy from
an entrepôt to a manufacturing base, and (3) the building of a sufficient defence
credibility. Singapore's foreign policy will continue to be 'dictated by its
considerations of national interest and how it can maximize and consolidate its
options for national survival.'

388 **Southeast Asia and the enemy beyond. ASEAN perceptions of
external threats.**
Robert O. Tilman. Boulder, Colorado: Westview Press, 1987.
184p. bibliog.

Discusses the countries in the Association of Southeast Asian Nations (ASEAN),
namely, Indonesia, Malaysia, Singapore, the Philippines, and Thailand. The
reader interested in Singapore will find the comparison of Singapore with the
other ASEAN partners interesting and informative. There are eight chapters: an
introduction presenting the framework of analysis, a description of ASEAN and
the main features of the region, the variations found in policy formulation, the
USSR and Vietnam as perceived by ASEAN, China, Japan, the United States,
and a final chapter on the main perceptions of internal and external threats. There
is an index.

389 **Singapore's foreign policy.**
Kawin Wilairat.   Singapore: Institute of Southeast Asian Studies,
1975. 105p. (Field Report Series no. 10).
The first of four chapters describes foreign policy and foreign relations prior to
independence, that is, from 1959 to 1965. Chapter 2 looks at the first decade,
1965-75, characterizing foreign policy then as a 'policy of survival'. Chapter 3
deals with regional policy, and the final chapter is a brief conclusion.

# Economy

390 **Measuring the overall budget balance in Singapore.**
Mukul G. Asher. *ASEAN Economic Bulletin*, vol. 3, no. 2 (1986), p. 275-80.

Discusses the problems inherent in the official measure of the national budget balance, identifies two specific limitations, and proposes a solution.

391 **Patterns and impact of foreign investment in Singapore.**
Chia Siow Yue. In: *Patterns and impact of foreign investment in the ESCAP region*. Edited by the Economic and Social Commission for Asia and the Pacific (ESCAP). Bangkok: Economic and Social Commission for Asia and the Pacific, 1985, p. 195-223.

Discusses the degree, nature, and sources of foreign investment in the Singapore economy and analyses the presence of multinational corporations, the American and Japanese influences, and relevant policy measures. A similar discussion by the same author may be found in *Foreign trade and investment: economic development in the newly industrialising Asian countries*, edited by W. Galenson and published in 1985 in Madison, Wisconsin, by the University of Wisconsin Press, p. 259-97.

392 **The economic development of Singapore: a selective survey of the literature.**
Chia Siow Yue. In: *Singapore studies: critical surveys of the humanities and social sciences*. Edited by Basant K. Kapur. Singapore: Singapore University Press, 1986, p. 183-242.

Covers publications dealing with the performance of the Singapore economy after Singapore's independence in 1959 and published within the period 1960 to the first half of 1982. Aspects discussed include economic growth, employment, human resources, income distribution, industrialization, foreign investment, banking, and external trade.

### 393 Singapore in the world economy.
Chng Meng Kng. In: *New Zealand in the world economy*. Edited by Hyam Gold. Dunedin, New Zealand: University of Otago, 1985, p. 61-66.

A discussion of the most important features of Singapore's economic development since independence. This succinct article is a useful summary. For a related theme see also the chapter by the same author, entitled 'The promotion and coordination of Singapore's trading relations' on pages 96-99 of the same book.

### 394 Report of the Public Sector Divestment Committee.
Michael Y. O. Fam. Singapore: Ministry of Finance, 21 February 1987. 120p.

The Public Sector Divestment Committee was appointed by the Minister for Finance in January 1986 to formulate a programme of divestment of government-linked companies. This report, presented by the chairman and the other five members of the committee, describes its terms of reference and objectives, the scope and approach used, principles and guidelines of divestment, recommendations on companies, privatization of statutory boards, and absorbtive capacity and funds flow. There are twelve appendixes with further information.

### 395 The practice of economic growth.
Goh Keng Swee. Singapore: Federal Publications, 1977. 265p.

A collection of thirty speeches and essays of Goh Keng Swee from 1972 to 1977, when he was Deputy Prime Minister and Minister of Defence in Singapore. An economist by training, Goh stressed in his preface that he was writing as a practitioner rather than a theoretician. Nearly two-thirds of the book is devoted to economics and industrial relations. The remaining chapters deal with sociological topics (Chapters 20 to 25), defence (Chapters 26 to 28), university education (Chapter 29) and transportation (Chapter 30).

### 396 A theoretical model of 'Singapore-type' financial and foreign-exchange systems.
Basant K. Kapur. *Singapore Economic Review*, vol. 30, no. 2 (1985), p. 91-102.

Addresses economics experts in this discussion of the particular Singaporean approach to the coordination and monitoring of the financial and foreign exchange systems. The experience of Singapore may be found useful in other countries.

## Economy

397 **The Singapore economy: new directions. Report of the Economic Committee.**
Lee Hsien Loong (et al.). Singapore: Ministry of Trade and Industry, 1986. 234p.

The Minister for Trade and Industry appointed the Economic Committee in April 1985 'to review the progress of the Singapore economy and to identify new directions for its future growth.' The committee consisted of its chairman, Lee Hsien Loong, who was the Minister of State in the same ministry, and eleven members. This book is the outcome of their deliberations. After the executive summary, the discussion is divided into five parts. Part 1 deals with a review of the nation's economic performance from 1980 to 1984 and the causes of recession. Part 2 discusses policy changes. Part 3 presents future strategies and prospects. Part 4 discusses policies for economic growth. Part 5 focuses on specific sectors of the economy, namely, manufacturing, banking and financial services, other services, tourism, construction, commerce, and international trade. Three appendixes provide more information on the interim report of July 1985, a list of subcommittee members, and the secretariat.

398 **Expatriate living costs in Singapore.**
Compiled by Lee Ju Song. Singapore: Singapore International Chamber of Commerce, 1987. 24th ed. 30p.

This slim booklet should be required reading for foreigners planning to live in Singapore for any period of time. It presents first a concise description of basic terms and concepts and then deals with specific aspects such as: inflation and living conditions, food, housing, utilities, domestic servants, transport, medical expenses, clothing, entertainment and leisure, education, labour costs, personal income tax, and other relevant topics.

399 **Industrialization in Singapore.**
Lee Soo Ann. Victoria, Australia: Longman, 1973. 132p.

Eight chapters dealing with the state of the political economy, planning for industrialization, the state development plan, the Economic Development Board, the pattern of industrial growth, developments, assessment, and conclusions. This study's findings provide the reader with a historical account of the industrialization efforts in the late 1960s and early 1970s.

400 **Economic restructuring in Singapore.**
Lim Chong-Yah. Singapore: Federal Publications, 1984. 117p. bibliog.

A collection of fourteen papers previously presented by the author at various meetings or published elsewhere. Among the topics of these papers are wage policy, economic policy, the role of government in wage policy, skills development, and other related aspects. There are some appendixes.

401 **Report of the Central Provident Fund Study Group.**
Lim Chong Yah, Vincent C. H. Chua, K. P. Kalirajan (et al.).
*Singapore Economic Review*, Special Issue, vol. 31, no. 1 (Apr.
1986), 108p.

The Central Provident Fund is a system of compulsory savings representing an integrated social security scheme for Singapore workers. All twelve Central Provident Fund (CPF) Study Group members teach at the Department of Economics and Statistics of the National University of Singapore. The chairman of the CPF Study Group indicates in the preface that this was an independent study because the group was not a government-appointed committee and it had access only to published statistics. The report consists of nine chapters dealing with the following themes: the evolution and operation of the CPF; state welfarism and the CPF; portfolio management of the CPF; home ownership and the CPF; Medisave; the CPF and inflation; the CPF and company welfarism through employers' contributions; old-age security financing, annuities, and life insurance; and a final summary of recommendations.

402 **Singapore: resources and growth.**
Edited by Lim Chong Yah, P. J. Lloyd. Singapore: Oxford
University Press, 1986. 279p.

The objective of this book is to document both the economic growth of Singapore and the causes of its rapid pace. The eleven contributors are academics. The topics discussed cover basic aspects of the Singapore economy and are presented in eight chapters.

403 **Policy options for the Singapore economy.**
Lim Chong Yah (et al.). Singapore: McGraw-Hill, 1988. 499p.

Addresses some important issues of economic policy. The first chapter is a 'retrospective overview', and the other fifteen chapters focus on recession and economic recovery; the role of the government; land utilization policy; population policy; manpower policy; wage policy; savings policy; foreign investment policy; foreign trade policy; exchange rate policy; monetary policy; fiscal policy; poverty, income distribution, and the less privileged; limits to growth; and modelling of the Singapore economy. There is an index.

404 **Economic survey of Singapore 1984.**
Ministry of Trade and Industry. Singapore: Ministry of Trade
and Industry, 1985. 139p.

An annual publication providing useful and factual information on ten main areas: a general review of Singapore in the world economy, economic growth, manufacturing, external trade, balance of payments, public finance, manpower and productivity, prices, energy, and monetary developments. There is a statistical appendix with detailed tables on the aspects mentioned.

405  **Multinationals and the growth of the Singapore economy.**
Hafiz Mirza.   New York: St Martin's, 1986. 297p. maps. bibliog.

Mirza's book is part of the Croom Helm series on the growth economies of
Southeast Asia. The author discusses in six chapters the role of multinational
corporations in Singapore, covering the historical background of economic
development in Singapore; the role of multinationals in the manufacturing,
banking, and financial sectors; and the place and the future of Singapore in the
international economy. The author has a preference for technical language and
displays an abundance of figures (there are seventy-four tables). The reader may
disagree, however, with Mirza's interpretation of the figures.

406  **The Singapore economy.**
Edited by You Poh Seng, Lim Chong Yah.   Singapore: Eastern
Universities Press, 1971. 421p.

A joint effort by eighteen economists from the former University of Singapore.
The first attempt to document the economic transformation of Singapore from
1959 to 1970, it begins with an overview of Singapore's economic development in
the 1960s and beyond and concludes with a chapter on statistical materials on
Singapore. The other fifteen chapters deal with such topics as population growth,
industrialization, entrepôt trade, banking structure, investment in human capital,
ASEAN (Association of Southeast Asian Nations) in perspective, the Vietnam
war's impact on the Singapore economy, and trends and issues in social
development.

# Finance and Banking

407 **Singapore.**
Mukul G. Asher.   In: *Tax reform in the Asian-Pacific countries.*
Edited by Asian-Pacific Tax and Investment Research Centre.
Singapore: Asian-Pacific Tax and Investment Research Centre,
1986, p. 74-103.
An analysis of recent tax reform initiatives in Singapore, their implications for investors, and some relevant issues on the future tax structure in Singapore. The author discusses first the salient features of Singapore's revenue system, then explains the reasons for tax reforms and the major objectives of such reforms.

408 **Issues in public finance in Singapore.**
Edited by Mukul G. Asher, Susan Osborne.   Singapore:
Singapore University Press, 1980. 244p.
Presents the proceedings of a symposium on public finance organized in Singapore in 1979 by the Economic Society of Singapore. The introductory chapter provides a brief background on the Singapore economy. The first of three parts deals with papers on taxation. Part 2 presents a discussion of non-tax issues and the government role. Part 3 deals with policy questions on government expenditure, stabilization, and consumption and income-based taxes.

409 **Taxation of non-residents.**
Laurence Chan.   In: *Proceedings of the intensive course on principles and practice of Singapore taxation.* Asian-Pacific Tax and Investment Centre and National University of Singapore.
Singapore: Asian-Pacific Tax and Investment Centre; National University of Singapore, 1986. 36p.
Deals with ten aspects of the topic: the concept of residence, dual residence,

101

residence in double taxation agreements, the concept of non-residence, tax implications for non-residents, the basis of tax charge, deduction and payment of tax on income paid to non-residents, persons chargeable, collection of tax through appointed agents, and sections in the Income Tax Act affecting non-resident persons.

### 410 Who audits Singapore.
Sebastian Chong, Ho Hin Dong, Tan Mui Siang, Tan Teck Meng, M. C. Wells.   Singapore: Singapore University Press, 1986. 68p.

A brief description of the audit fees paid by companies listed on the Singapore Stock Exchange, the change in fees over the previous two years, the relation between fees on the one hand and company sales and total assets on the other hand, the size of the audit services market, and a list of audit firms ranked by their audit fees and their number of clients.

### 411 Singapore: a guide to the structure, development and regulation of financial services.
Edited by the *Economist*.   London: Economist Publications, 1987. 176p.

This is the second of a series of guides prepared by the *Economist* to provide an informative description of the trade environment and the regulations of the financial sector.

### 412 Tax incentives for the economic expansion and development of Singapore.
Margaret Fordham.   In: *Proceedings of the intensive course on principles and practice of Singapore taxation*. Asian-Pacific Tax and Investment Centre and National University of Singapore. Singapore: Asian-Pacific Tax and Investment Centre; National University of Singapore, 1986, 15p.

Focuses on the Economic Expansion Incentives (Relief from Income Tax) Act 2, which specifies the available tax incentives.

### 413 Capital allowance and losses.
Michael R. J. Grover.   In: *Proceedings of the intensive course on principles and practice of Singapore taxation*. Asian-Pacific Tax and Investment Centre and National University of Singapore. Singapore: Asian-Pacific Tax and Investment Centre; National University of Singapore, 1986, 49p.

Deals with the principles and practice of Singapore taxation in relation to capital allowance and losses. It covers four main aspects: plant and machinery, industrial building allowance, investment allowances, and losses proper.

414 **Taxation of corporate distributions.**
Richard J. Hay. In: *Proceedings of the intensive course on principles and practice of Singapore taxation*. Asian-Pacific Tax and Investment Centre and National University of Singapore. Singapore: Asian-Pacific Tax and Investment Centre; National University of Singapore, 1986, 11p.

A brief review of the taxation of sole proprietorships and partnerships in Singapore and the taxation of corporations.

415 **Double tax agreements.**
Peter J. Knight. In: *Proceedings of the intensive course on principles and practice of Singapore taxation*. Asian-Pacific Tax and Investment Centre and National University of Singapore. Singapore: Asian-Pacific Tax and Investment Centre; National University of Singapore, 1986, 30p.

There are three main parts to this paper: an introduction to the aspects of double taxation in Singapore and the existing role of tax treaties, an examination of selected double tax treaty provisions, and particular items of interest under Singapore tax treaties, including the case of the treaty with Malaysia.

416 **The monetary and banking development of Singapore and Malaysia.**
Lee Sheng-Yi. Singapore: Singapore University Press, 1986, rev. ed. 298p. bibliog.

Discusses in the first of five parts of the book the historical development of the Singapore Currency Board system, the commercial banks and the merchant banks. Part 2 deals with monetary and exchange rate issues. Part 3 discusses financial structures. Part 4 is dedicated to monetary policies, and Part 5 to monetary analysis. There are fifteen appendixes (with a table each, providing detailed information) and an index.

417 **The financing process in the public sector in Singapore.**
Linda Low. *Bulletin for International Fiscal Documentation*, vol. 39, no. 4 (1985), p. 148-65.

The public sector is defined as the government sector and major statutory boards. The author analyses the approach employed by the Singapore government since 1965 to finance economic development and focuses on non-tax revenue as the main financial resource for economic development.

418 **Papers on monetary economics.**
Edited by the Monetary Authority of Singapore. Singapore: Monetary Authority of Singapore; Singapore: Singapore University Press, 1981. 212p.

Commemorates the tenth anniversary of the Monetary Authority of Singapore. There are nine chapters written by economics experts. The papers dealing specifically with Singapore are: 'The evolution of money in Singapore since 1819' by P. J. Drake; 'The dynamics of money demand and monetary policy in Singapore' by Mohsin S. Kahn; 'Monetary stability and exchange rate objectives in Singapore' by W. H. Branson; and 'Offshore markets in foreign currencies and monetary control: Britain, Singapore and the United States' by R. I. McKinnon.

419 **Stock market investment in Malaysia and Singapore.**
Neoh Soon Kean.   Kuala Lumpur: Berita Publishing, 1986. 312p.
An informative volume covering the subject matter in seven sections. The first section deals with speculation, section two points out the professionals in the field, section three is on learning from the professionals, section four covers the fundamentals of investment, section five discusses shares and securities, section six is on more advanced topics on investment, and the last section is on 'putting all that you have learnt together.'

420 **Banking in Singapore.**
Peat, Marwick, Mitchell & Company.   Singapore: Peat Marwick International, 1983. 3rd ed. 187p.
This book was written for the clients of Peat Marwick International, a multinational accounting and auditing firm with clients in ninety-three countries. It is informative, acquainting the reader with the banking system in Singapore. The first section provides a brief background on Singapore's history, geography, government, the economy, and other basic aspects. The second section covers the banking system and main financial institutions. Section 3 gives guidelines for the establishment of companies in Singapore, including laws, living arrangements, staff, operating costs, and other relevant information. There are fourteen appendixes with further details.

421 **State enterprise in Singapore: legal importation and development.**
Philip N. Pillai.   Singapore: Singapore University Press, 1983. 223p.
The first chapter is on state enterprise and legal importation and development; Chapter 2 is on the process of legal importation; Chapter 3 discusses comparative theory, context, and experience of state enterprise law in Britain and Singapore; some case studies are discussed in Chapter 4, and the conclusions are presented in Chapter 5. There is an index.

422 **Doing business in Singapore.**
Price Waterhouse.   Singapore: Price Waterhouse, 1984. 98p.
A detailed and systematic description of the investment climate in Singapore, aspects of doing business, accounting, and taxation. Ten appendixes provide further information.

423 **Structure of the Income Tax Act.**
Sidney C. Rolt.   In: *Proceedings of the intensive course on principles and practice of Singapore taxation.* Asian-Pacific Tax and Investment Centre and National University of Singapore.
Singapore: Asian-Pacific Tax and Investment Centre; National University of Singapore, 1986, 29p.

This paper is addressed to businessmen and presents a brief but clear explanation of the Income Tax Act. It also includes references to the similarities and differences in taxation law between Singapore and other countries.

424 **Securities market in Singapore.**
Saw Swee Hock.   Singapore: Singapore Securities Research Institute, 1985. 2nd ed. 120p.

The first edition was published in 1980. The author discusses in five chapters the background to securities industry, security market regulations, the stock exchange of Singapore, share price indexes; investment information, investment education and research, and growth and structure of the market. There are two appendixes.

425 **Investment analysis in Singapore.**
Edited by Saw Swee Hock, Lim Choo Peng.   Singapore: Singapore Securities Research Institute; Singapore University Press, 1985. 550p.

A selection of seventy-five papers on a wide variety of aspects of the securities market and of the Singapore Stock Exchange. The papers were taken from two local trade journals, namely, the *Singapore Stock Exchange Journal* and the *Securities Industry Review.*

426 **Deduction.**
Brij S. Soin.   In: *Proceedings of the intensive course on principles and practice of Singapore taxation.* Asian-Pacific Tax and Investment Centre and National University of Singapore. Singapore: Asian-Pacific Tax and Investment Centre; National University of Singapore, 1986, 67p.

A detailed analysis of income tax deductions under the Singapore legislation. The paper discusses allowable deductions, conditions of allowance, specific provisions of the Act, and other relevant aspects, including a section comparing Singapore with Malaysia, India, Australia, South Africa, and England.

427 **Administration of the [Income Tax] Act.**
Sum Yee Loong. In: *Proceedings of the intensive course on principles and practice of Singapore taxation*, Asian-Pacific Tax and Investment Centre and National University of Singapore. Singapore: Asian-Pacific Tax and Investment Centre; National University of Singapore, 1986, 8p.

A summary of the basic steps and procedures in the administration of the Income Tax Act in Singapore.

428 **Financial markets and institutions in Singapore.**
Tan Chwee Huat. Singapore: Singapore University Press, 1987. 5th ed. 372p. bibliog.

A detailed and informative description of the financial sector in Singapore. In five chapters, the author discusses the role of Singapore as an international financial centre, the various financial institutions in the private sector, financial markets, the government financial institutions, and the characteristics of business and personal finance. The book includes a glossary of terms and an index.

429 **Taxation of partnership income.**
Peter Tosi. In: *Proceedings of the intensive course on principles and practice of Singapore taxation*. Asian-Pacific Tax and Investment Centre and National University of Singapore. Singapore: Asian-Pacific Tax and Investment Centre and National University of Singapore, 1986, 24p.

Deals with fiscal aspects of taxation in Singapore. The discussion is divided into two parts: one deals with the provisions of the Singapore Income Tax Act and the other part discusses the various practical aspects of partnership taxation.

# Trade

**430 Guide to doing business in Singapore.**
Deloitte Haskins & Sells.   Singapore: Singapore National Printers
Publication Division, 1987. 142p.

The authors indicate that 'the objective of this book is to provide background
information to potential investors.' They accomplish this in six chapters dealing
with the business environment, the mechanics of investment, business regulations,
taxation, investment incentives, and other taxes and duties. Thirteen appendixes
provide specific details.

**431 Handbook for businessmen. Doing business in Singapore.**
Compiled and edited by Goh Tianwah.   Singapore: Rank Books,
1987. rev. ed. 144p.

The first edition of this handbook appeared in 1985. There are ten chapters: a
brief but useful description of basic things to do and to avoid when doing business
in Singapore, the Partnership Act, the Business Registration Act of 1973,
procedures for incorporating a company, investment incentives, the Factory Act,
the Employment Act, the workmen's compensation guide, Central Provident
Fund, and a simple guide to taxation in Singapore. Eight appendixes provide
further relevant details.

**432 Trade, employment and industrialisation in Singapore.**
Linda Lim, Pang Eng Fong.   Geneva: International Labour
Organisation, 1986. 110p.

This is one in a series of country studies sponsored by the International Labour
Organisation. The book explains Singapore's successful approach to industrialization in five chapters. The first chapter provides a description of the social and
economic characteristics of Singapore, including its economic performance from
1960 to 1983 and with relevant institutions involved. The other chapters deal with

economic development strategies and experiences, the dynamics of development, the case of the electronics and garments industries, and finally some lessons and prospects.

### 433   A study of planned shopping centres in Singapore.

Sim Loo Lee.   Singapore: Singapore University Press, 1985. 138p.

Focuses on retailing patterns in Singapore and discusses changes over time in the form, structure, location, and function of the industry. The analysis also covers consumers' behaviour and shopping patterns as well as the impact of the growth of shopping centres upon the overall retail market and the established shopping districts.

### 434   Trading with Singapore.

Singapore Indian Chamber of Commerce.   Singapore: Singapore Indian Chamber of Commerce, 1986. 478p.

A special 60th-anniversary issue of the *Singapore Indian Chamber of Commerce trade directory*. It includes general information, a profile of the Singapore Indian Chamber of Commerce, a review of the economic survey of Singapore in 1985 and 1986, a summary of the report of the Economic Committee, trade information, trade statistics, and trade procedures and incentives. There are also a list of addresses, a classification of products and services, and an alphabetical list of members.

# Industry

435 **Building and construction news yearbook 1985.**
Al Hilal Publishing.   Singapore: Al Hilal Publishing (Far East),
1986. 372p.

A summary of major events and developments in the building and construction
industry in Singapore and Malaysia. The first chapter presents an overview of the
industry. The others are specialized chapters dealing with the MRT (Mass Rapid
Transit), public works, public housing, urban redevelopment, and public roads.
There are also some sections on professional aspects of the industry.

436 **Productivity survey of Singapore 1987.**
Edited by Chan Hwa Loon, Woon Kin Chung.   Singapore:
National Productivity Board, 1987. 108p.

This well-documented report describes and discusses the development of the
productivity movement in Singapore in the period 1986-87 but provides
comparative figures for the 1980s. In addition to the introduction, there are
seventeen chapters dealing with productivity performance in general and in the
manufacturing and nonmanufacturing sectors, value added analysis at the
company level, assisting companies to improve their efficiency, flexible wage
system, labour-management relations, human resource development, technological progress, productivity promotion, productivity attitudes, the quality
movement, productivity management, productivity movement in companies,
productivity development project, the bottom lines, and conclusion. There is an
appendix with eighteen tables.

437 **Technology and skills in Singapore.**
Chng Meng Kng, Linda Low, Tay Boon Nga, Amina Tyabji.
Singapore: Institute of Southeast Asian Studies, 1986. 108p.
bibliog.

The discussion of the characteristics and problems of technology transfer and skills enhancement in Singapore is presented in six chapters. The specific topics of these chapters are: industrialization strategies and policies, science and technology policies in Singapore, skills enhancement and manpower development, technology enhancement in four industries (namely, machinery except electrical and electronic; instrumentation equipment, photographic, and optical goods; electrical machinery, apparatus, appliances, and supplies; and electronic products and components), and conclusions and recommendations.

438 **National training directory '85/'86.**
Compiled by the National Productivity Board (NPB). Singapore:
National Productivity Board, 1985. 114p.

This directory provides details of management and supervisory training courses offered by various institutions in Singapore, such as the Management Development Institute of Singapore, the Marketing Institute of Singapore, the National Productivity Board, the Ngee Ann Polytechnic, and the National University of Singapore.

439 **National Productivity Board annual report 1986/87.**
National Productivity Board (NPB). Singapore: National Productivity Board, 1987. 40p.

This report includes the chairman's statement on the year's developments, a description of NPB's productivity promotion activities; assistance to companies, measurement of productivity, the Skills Development Fund, the Resource Centre, corporate support services, international cooperation, and the audited statement of accounts.

440 **Industrial restructuring, technological development and implications for manpower planning: the Singapore case.**
G. Shantakumar. In: *Manpower planning in ASEAN countries*.
Edited by the Asian Regional Team for Employment Promotion and the RIHED (Regional Institute of Higher Education and Development). Singapore: Regional Institute of Higher Education and Development, 1985, p. 41-60.

The author focuses on the current economic situation and discusses the role of Singapore in the competitive world market and the need for, and implications of, industrial and technological change.

441 **A comparative guide to collective agreements in the manufacturing sector, 1985.**
Compiled by Singapore National Employers Federation.
Singapore: Singapore National Employers Federation, 1985. 377p.
Provides information on salaries, annual increments, and other terms of employment in 158 collective agreements. The compiler indicates that the guide is useful for designing or reviewing salary structures and fringe benefits.

442 **A guide to jobs and careers. The information processing industry in Singapore.**
Edited by John W. F. Wong (et al.).   Singapore: Jointly published by the National Computer Board, Singapore Federation of the Computer Industry, Singapore Computer Society, Data Processing Managers' Association, and Singapore National Printers, 1987. 2nd ed. 110p.
The first edition of this guidebook was published in 1984. This updated edition has five chapters. The first one explains new developments. The other chapters deal with information technology in Singapore, information processing organizations, jobs and careers in the industry, and education institutes for information processing professionals.

# Transport

**443 The land transport of Singapore. From early times to the present.**
Ministry of Culture, Archives and Oral History Department.
Singapore: Archives and Oral History Department, 1981. 100p.
bibliog.

This charming collection of photographs is arranged in twelve chapters providing the reader with a tour of the historical phases of the development of land transport. In chronological order, it covers jinrickshaws, horse and carriage, bullock-carts, trams, railways, motor cars, trishaws, traffic police, lorries and vans, street vendors, buses, and the most recent Mass Rapid Transit (MRT) system.

**444 Dwell time of buses in Singapore.**
H. C. Chin, Y. Tanaboriboon. In: *Proceedings of the 2nd Conference on Mass Transportation in Asia.* Singapore: Chartered Institute of Transport, 1984, p. 467-77.

A report of the findings from a study of the relationship between dwell time of public transport buses and number of boarding or alighting passengers.

**445 Bus lane in Singapore – its implementation and effect.**
K. K. Chin, Y. Tanaboriboon, H. C. Chin. In: *Proceedings of the Conference on Transport – New Challenges.* Edited by Chartered Institute of Transport (Singapore Chapter). Singapore: Chartered Institute of Transport (Singapore Chapter), 1985, p. 35-44.

This paper argues that bus lanes are an efficient transport management tool, based on the findings of a study of the bus lane system used in Singapore since 1974.

446 **Singapore's transport and urban development options. Final report of the MRT Review team.**
Kenneth R. Hansen. Singapore: Ministry of Finance, September 1980. 236p.

This report is presented in eight chapters describing the scope of the MRT (Mass Rapid Transit) Review group, the bus alternative, the bus rapid transit alternative, fleet and manpower requirements, visual and environmental impacts of the MRT, links between the MRT and travel demands, employment, and other aspects. Eight appendixes provide detailed figures.

447 **Implementation of the Singapore Mass Rapid Transit: some aspects of noise and vibration.**
Raymond B. W. Heng. In: *Planning, design and construction of urban public transportation.* Edited by Maruzen Investment. Singapore: Maruzen Asia; Technology Transfer Institute, 1983, p. 457-70.

Heng, a university lecturer in mechanical engineering, deals with two common technical problems of subway and railroad construction and focuses on the specific aspects that had to be considered in Singapore.

448 **Traffic restraint in Singapore.**
Edward P. Holland, Peter L. Watson. Washington, DC: World Bank, 1978. 9p. (Reprint Series no. 75).

Describes the Area Licence Scheme implemented in Singapore to control traffic congestion. The paper was originally published in *Traffic Engineering and Control*, vol. 19, no. 1 (1978), p. 14-22.

449 **Singapore MRT System.**
Mass Rapid Transit Corporation. Singapore: MRT Corporation, 1985. 28p.

The Mass Rapid Transit (MRT) Corporation was set up by an Act of Parliament in 1983 to acquire land, award contracts, and hire staff from around the world to build the MRT on schedule and within budget. This publication provides information on the organization, its activities, history, the MRT stations, construction, and project implementation.

450 **Singapore tide tables and port facilities 1986.**
Port of Singapore Authority, Hydrographic Department. Singapore: Port of Singapore Authority, 1986. 223p.

Provides specialized information on tidal height and stream predictions for tidal stations in Singapore as well as a detailed description of the available port facilities, including notification of arrival procedures, navigational channels, wharfs, berths, docks and repair berths, and other information useful to mariners planning to sail to Singapore.

451 **Some key issues in Singapore's domestic transportation: who gets where, when, and how.**
Seah Chee Meow:    In: *Political and social change in Singapore.*
Edited by Wu Teh-yao. Singapore: Institute of Southeast Asian
Studies, 1975, p. 70-112. (Southeast Asian Perspectives no. 3).

One of the first serious analyses of the public transport system in Singapore. It deals with the background of transport policies, the nature of the transport problem, the motor car and the transportation controversy, and policy implications.

452 **Government policy choices and public transport operations in Singapore.**
Seah Chee Meow.    *Transport Policy and Decision Making*, vol. 1
(1980), p. 231-51.

A discussion of the government's and transport groups' position concerning the need to upgrade and modernize the public transport services in Singapore. See also in the same publication Seah's paper entitled 'Mass mobility and accessibility: transport planning and traffic management in Singapore' (p. 55-71) and his 1986 work, 'Strategies management', in this section.

453 **The MRT debate in Singapore: to do or not to do?**
Seah Chee Meow.    *Southeast Asian affairs* . Singapore
Institute of Southeast Asian Studies, 1981, p. 290-306.

A clear description and discussion of the complexity of public transport policy, dealing with the arguments presented from various sides for the implementation of the MRT (Mass Rapid Transit) as an alternative solution to public transportation. For details on the current situation see Seah's paper on the 'Strategies management' of public transport in this section.

454 **Strategies management in the delivery of an effective transportation system in Singapore.**
Seah Chee Meow.    In: *Delivery of public services in Asian countries: cases in development administration.* Edited by Suchitra Punyaratabandhu-Bhakdi, Purachai Piumsombun (et al.).
Bangkok: National Institute of Development Administration,
1986, p. 175-201.

This discussion of the background of the transportation problem in Singapore is divided into five sections. Seah first presents the basic premises and definitions in the analysis of the problem; the other sections deal with a historical description, the government's approach and the environmental and social constraints faced, the actual policies taken and their effectiveness, and the case of taxi regulations.

455 **Public transportation.**
Seah Chee Meow. In: *Government and politics of Singapore.*
Edited by Jon S. T. Quah, Chan Heng Chee, Seah Chee Meow.
Singapore: Oxford University Press, 1987. rev. ed., p. 259-75.
The main argument of this chapter is that public transportation is a major political issue in Singapore. Seah provides a brief historical background on urban planning in Singapore before discussing four main dimensions of the transportation problem: adjustment of land-use policy, the search for effective public transport, road pricing and other regulatory measures of traffic restraint, and the search for possible improvements in transport modes.

456 **The MRT handbook '84.**
Singapore Manufacturers' Association. Singapore: Singapore
Manufacturers' Association, 1984. 164p.
A detailed description of the Mass Rapid Transit (MRT) system and the Mass Rapid Transit Corporation addressed to MRT tenders, potential contractors, and workers.

457 **The motorist and the law in Singapore.**
Awther Singh. Singapore: Quins, 1980. 657p.
A detailed and comprehensive presentation of all information needed by motorists driving in Singapore. Its fourteen chapters cover legislation, enforcement, construction and use of vehicles, motor insurance, pedestrian crossing rules, registration and licencing of drivers and driving schools, degree of fault and careless driving, reckless or dangerous driving, drunk driving offences, miscellaneous offences, weaknesses of the law, and legislation and the accident rate. Eleven appendixes with specific details complement the information. There is an index.

458 **National policy towards cars: Singapore.**
Andrew H. Spencer, Chia Lin Sien. *Transport Reviews*, vol. 5,
no. 4 (1985), p. 301-23.
A review of government policies to discourage the use of private cars and to control traffic congestion. Each policy is examined and discussed and its possible effectiveness is considered.

459 **Mass rapid transit in Singapore.**
Tan Chee-Teik. In: *Planning, design and construction of urban public transportation.* Edited by Maruzen Investment. Singapore: Maruzen Asia; Technology Transfer Institute, 1983, p. 1-12.
A general description of the plans to build the Mass Rapid Transit (MRT) system in Singapore. Tan deals with the feasibility studies commissioned before the government decision to implement the system and traffic congestion, labour shortage, technology transfer, consultants, design of stations, and social effects of the MRT.

**Transport**

460 **Focus on transportation.**
Edited by Rex Toh. Singapore: Chartered Institute of Transport (Singapore Division), 1976. 119p.

Thirteen chapters of interest to readers concerned with the development of transportation in Singapore. The papers cover shipping, air transport, trucking and railways problems, urban transport, and legislation on air and sea transportation.

461 **Shipping guide of Singapore.**
USAHA Advertising Corporation. Singapore: USAHA Advertising Corporation, 1980. 8th ed. 375p.

A compilation of articels and information addressed to businessmen in Singapore and overseas. It includes a review of Singapore's shipping industry, lists of main associations and groups in the trade, with addresses, a list of registered vessels, legislation on shipping, and other relevant information.

462 **Relieving traffic congestion: the Singapore Area Licence Scheme.**
Peter L. Watson, Edward P. Holland. Washington, DC: World Bank, 1978. 284p. maps.

This is, in at least two respects, a unique publication. On the one hand, it is the first study of its kind undertaken by the World Bank's Urban Projects Department. On the other hand, the subject of discussion in this book is, according to the authors and other expert observers around the world, 'the world's first use of road pricing to reduce congestion.' The authors present a well-researched report organized into eleven chapters dealing with an overview of the principal findings; the Area Licence Scheme; implementation, utilization, and finances; traffic performance, parking, and accidents; changes in travel behaviour; and the effects of the scheme on pedestrians, air pollution, the business community, and the general public. The final chapter, on designing an area pricing scheme, is addressed to officials in other countries who could learn from Singapore's success. There are 64 tables with relevant statistics and a large number of diagrams, charts, and maps.

463 **Singapore comprehensive traffic study.**
Wilbur Smith & Associates, Mott, Hay & Anderson Overseas, Halcrow International Partnership, London Transport International. Singapore: Ministry of Communications, August 1980. 137p. maps.

This is the report presented to the Ministry of Communications by the authors in their capacity as government-appointed consultants. The report is presented in two volumes. The first volume is the technical proposal with charts (122 pages), detailing the objectives of the study, the terms of reference, methodology, and current and future travel needs. The second volume is a brief (15 pages) financial proposal, describing the proposed budget for the study.

# Employment and Manpower

464 **Singapore Standard Occupational Classification 1978.**
Khoo Chian Kim.   Singapore: Department of Statistics, 1980.
152p.

This publication is useful for the specialist reader interested in the analysis of
the occupations in Singapore. It presents the revised and updated Singapore
Standard Occupational Classification (SSOC), which follows the latest occupational classifications used by the United States and the International Labour
Office. The SSOC was prepared by a special working committee appointed by the
Census Planning Committee in 1978 for the purpose of classifying the occupations
during the 1980 Census of Population and for use in subsequent censuses and
surveys of the Singapore population.

465 **Report on labour-management relations survey 1986.**
Irene Koh.   Singapore: National Productivity Board, 1986. 72p.

Includes a methodological description of the study and discusses the findings in
ten chapters: the state of labour-management relations (LMR) and associated
factors; impact of improved LMR on productivity; state of LMR and resistance to
productivity improvement measures; major outcomes of LMR; areas and scope of
participation by management, workers, and unions; extent of information-sharing
schemes to improve labour-management cooperation; issues of greatest impact
upon LMR; and comparison with Japan. A final chapter presents main
conclusions and recommendations.

**Employment and Manpower**

466 **Towards an information society: changing occupational structure in Singapore.**
Eddie C. Y. Kuo, Chen Huey Tsyh. Singapore: National University of Singapore, Department of Sociology, 1985. 29p. (Sociology Working Paper no. 69).

A brief discussion of the trend towards an increasing number of workers in the 'information' occupations, which the authors define as fields involving most white-collar occupations, including managerial, adminstrative, supervisory, and clerical jobs as well as machine operators and people working in postal and telecommunications (from postmen and sorters to telephone linesmen).

467 **Institutional and policy measures for effective manpower planning: Singapore case study.**
Linda Low. In: *Manpower planning in ASEAN countries*. Edited by the Asian Regional Team for Employment Promotion and the RIHED (Regional Institute for Higher Education and Development). Singapore: Regional Institute for Higher Education and Development, 1985, p. 199-219.

Reviews the basic policies and approaches on manpower and educational planning in Singapore and the government bodies in charge of policy planning and policy implementation.

468 **Report on the labour force survey of Singapore 1985.**
Ministry of Labour, Research and Statistics Division. Singapore: Ministry of Labour, 1985. 139p.

This report is divided into three parts. The first part describes the research methodology used to conduct the labour force survey, the second part is an overview of the main findings of the survey, and the third part is a display of figures on the Singapore labour force characteristics presented in eighty-seven tables. In contrast to the 1980 survey, this report does not include the questionnaire used in the 1985 survey.

469 **Five-foot way traders.**
Edited by Ong Choo Suat, Tan Beng Luat. Singapore: Archives and Oral History Department, 1985. 104p.

The term 'five-foot way' refers to paths for pedestrians which, according to stipulations by the founder of Singapore, had to be provided by adding, to the front of every building, a covered corridor about five-feet wide. These paths were promptly used by small traders, hawkers, and craftsmen who used to make a living by peddling their wares, food, or services and became a common feature of street life in the old Singapore and throughout the best part of this century. This is a collection of about 100 photographs of such traders, each with an explanatory caption in English and Mandarin.

470  **The labour force of Singapore.**
Saw Swee-Hock.   Singapore: Department of Statistics, 1984. 79p.
(Census Monograph no. 3).

This is the third monograph from the series of monographs on specific aspects of
the 1980 Census of Population figures, sponsored and published by the
Department of Statistics (the first monograph is on demographic trends and the
second on language, literacy, and education). Saw presents and analyses labour
force figures in five chapters covering the economic activity of the population, the
labour force participation rates (that is, the proportion of population in the labour
force), the industrial structure of the labour force, the occupational patterns, the
economically active population, and the future labour force.

471  **Labour force projections for Singapore 1980-2070.**
Saw Swee-Hock.   Singapore: Institute of Southeast Asian Studies,
1984. 30p.

An analysis of the current labour force figures and their possible growth pattern.
This brief paper provides data for a study of the implications of dependency on
foreign versus local labour.

472  **New population and labour force projections and policy implications
for Singapore.**
Saw Swee-Hock.   Singapore: Institute of Southeast Asian Studies,
1987. 94p.

A logical sequel to Saw's papers on population projections (see the section on
population) and labour force projections (in this section), this paper presents and
discusses the population figures for 1985 as well as the findings from the 1985
labour force survey.

473  **Human resources development in Singapore.**
G. Shantakumar.   In: *Twenty-five years of development.* Edited
by You Poh Seng, Lim Chong Yah. Singapore: Nam Yang Xing
Zhou Lianhe Zaobao, 1984, p.165-88.

Emphasizes the importance of manpower and training to help the labour force
meet the challenges of the skill-intensive economy in which Singapore is now
engaged. Details on relevant aspects of manpower planning and training are
provided.

474  **Perspective manpower development in Singapore.**
G. Shantakumar.   Cairo: Cairo Demographic Centre, 1986. 23p.
(Research Monograph Series no. 14 [special issue]).

A discussion of the 'unique transformation' that Singapore's economy underwent
from 'a labour-surplus' to 'manpower-shortage' situation during the past two
decades, the implications of such a change within the framework of the world's
economic climate, and possible future strategies on manpower developoment.

475 **Report on the survey of employment of graduates 1980.**
Singapore Inland Revenue Department, Research and Statistics
Unit.   Singapore: Inland Revenue Department, Sept. 1981. 103p.

The first twenty pages of this report describe the survey procedure and a profile of
university graduates and their income. The rest of the report consists of tables and
graphs presenting the details of the survey findings.

476 **'Can survive, la.' Cottage industries in high-rise Singapore.**
Margaret Sullivan.   Singapore: Graham Brash, 1985. 255p.
bibliog.

As the author describes it, this book 'is about the lives of ordinary – yet
extraordinary – contemporary Singaporeans who make things with their hands.'
This is in fact, a photographic and explanatory description of craftsmanship in
Singapore. There are two types of photographs illustrating the craftmen at work
and their surroundings: original photographs taken specifically for this book by
Henry Wong and Michael Neo and photographs provided by the Archives and
Oral History Department of the Singapore Ministry of Culture. The fifteen
chapters deal with the different types of goods produced by these small industries
such as food, medicines, cloth and clothing, footware, furniture, jewellery, wood
carving, religious and ritual paraphernalia, and other items. There is a glossary of
local terms.

477 **National skill standards. Industrial sectors.**
Vocational and Industrial Training Board.   Singapore: Vocational
and Industrial Training Board, 1984. 322p.

This manual describes in detail the skill standards of twenty-eight skilled
occupations that are certificatable at the National Trade Certificate Grade 2 level
in Singapore. As a specialized publication, the information it provides is very
useful to both employers and workers seeking information on the officially
required skills for given occupations. The occupations listed cover a wide range of
industries: air-conditioning and refrigeration, construction, electrical and electronics, garments, hairdressing, heavy duty diesel, hotel food and beverages,
mechanical maintenance, precision engineering, printing, road transport, sheet-
metal fabrication, shipbuilding, and repairing and woodbase industries.

# Labour Movement and Trade Unions

478 **Report of the Executive Council 1979/1980.**
Amalgamated Union of Public Employees (AUPE). Singapore:
Amalgamated Union of Public Employees, 1981. 136p.

Presented to the AUPE's First Triennial Delegates' Conference held in Singapore
on 31 August 1980. Gives a detailed account of AUPE's activities, including
collective agreements, medical benefits, international affairs, and other union
matters.

479 **Amalgamated Union of Public Employees (AUPE).**
Amalgamated Union of Public Employees (AUPE). Singapore:
AUPE, 1982. rev. ed. 71p.

This is the constitution of AUPE. It includes organizational matters such as
membership branches, welfare schemes, and trade disputes. There is an index.

480 **A brief history of the Singapore trade union movement.**
V. R. Balakrishna. Singapore: National Trades Union Congress
(NTUC), 1980. 18p.

This slim handbook provides a succinct description of the key features of
Singapore's labour movement. The author wrote it in his capacity as NTUC's
Secretary for Information and Publicity.

481 **Tomorrow. The peril and the promise.**
C. V. Devan Nair. Singapore: National Trades Union Congress
(NTUC), 1976. 225p.

This is the report by the Secretary-General of NTUC to the Triennial Delegates'
Conference held in Singapore in 1976. The author's main message, 'Tomorrow.

The peril and the promise', is one of the most informative parts in this report. The others are the conference papers dealing with politics, modernization, and the economy.

482  **Inlook and outlook.**
C. V. Devan Nair.   Singapore: National Trades Union Congress, 1977. 208p.
This is the NTUC Secretary-General's report to the Ordinary Delegates Conference held in October 1977. Devan Nair served later on as President of the Republic. In addition to the usual reports from NUTC committees, cooperatives, and economic enterprises, this volume is particularly informative, as it presents Devan Nair's vision of the labour movement in Singapore.

483  **The rules of the Food, Drinks and Allied Workers Union.**
Food, Drinks and Allied Workers Union.   Singapore: Food, Drinks and Allied Workers Union [n.d.]. 46p.
In addition to the constitution, this booklet includes details concerning administration and development of the union.

484  **Organising the unorganised.**
V. Jayakody, V. R. Balakrishna.   Singapore: National Trades Union Congress (NTUC), 1976. 60p.
This slim volume was prepared as part of the NTUC Workers' Education Series with the aim of providing basic concepts, information, and guidelines for trade union organizers to use in their recruitment exercises. The booklet is written in English and Mandarin.

485  **Public sector labour relations in the Singapore context.**
Lee Boon Hiok.   Singapore: University of Singapore, 1979. 26p. (Department of Political Science Occasional Paper no. 37).
An overview of the structure of the Civil Service, describing the historical background of the labour movement in the public sector and relevant aspects of labour-management relations.

486  **Innovative approach in industrial relations: consensus building in the Singapore context.**
Lee Boon Hiok.   In: *Innovative approaches to industrial relations in ASEAN*. Edited by the International Labour Organization. Bangkok: International Labour Organization, 1985, p. 133-67.
A collection of papers presented at the ASEAN (Association of Southeast Asian Nations) Symposium on Innovative Approaches in Industrial Relations, held in Pattaya, Thailand, from 4 to 8 November 1985. In his Singapore paper, Lee presents a brief description of the setting; the relations between the party in power, the People's Action Party, and the National Trades Union Congress; and industrial relations and consensus building.

487 **Trade unions in Singapore: from confrontation to cooperation.**
Lee Boon Hiok. In: *Singapore: taking stock.* Edited by
C. W. Ng. Singapore: Federal Publications, 1985, p. 19-26.
A succinct but informative description of trade unions in terms of their historical
development and role.

488 **NTUC Third Triennial Delegates' Conference 1979.**
Lim Chee Onn. Singapore: National Trades Union Congress
(NTUC), 1980. 195p.
This is the Secretary-General's report, which includes reports from the sectional
organizations, cooperatives, and committees as well as the proceedings of the
ordinary and extraordinary delegates' conferences. See also *Fourth Triennial
Delegates' Conference 29-30 April 1982* (q.v.) and *NTUC Triennial Delegates'
Conference 1-3 April 1985* (q.v.).

489 **Plan of action for the 80's.**
Lim Chee Onn. Singapore: National Trades Union Congress
(NTUC), 1980. 61p.
Lim presented this paper in his capacity as NTUC Secretary-General to the
adjourned Third Triennial Delegates' Conference of the NTUC in 1980. The
paper has six sections dealing with a review of the labour movement in the 1970s,
the NTUC plan of action for the 1980s; organization and administration,
industrial relations, the social role of trade unions, and external relations.

490 **Work and excel for an even better quality of life.**
Lim Chee Onn. Singapore: National Trades Union Congress
(NTUC), 1980. 299p.
This is the report by the NTUC Secretary-General to the Ordinary Delegates'
Conference held in Singapore from 2 to 4 November 1980. It includes the regular
sectional reports from cooperatives and economic enterprises, but the most
informative parts are the 'Secretary-General's preamble' outlining the parameters
of the labour movement in Singapore and the three papers on 'Performance
appraisal', 'Attitudes of the Singapore workforce', and 'Enhancing the
participation of young workers in the work environment and community – the
role of the trade union'.

491 **Fourth Triennial Delegates' Conference 29-30 April 1982.**
Lim Chee Onn. Singapore: National Trades Union Congress,
1982. 143p.
Includes the Secretary-General's report and his perspective of the labour
movement, in addition to the various reports from union committees, cooperatives and economic enterprises. See also *NTUC Third Triennial Delegates'
Conference 1979* (q.v.).

492 **Labour strategies and the high-tech challenge: the case of Singapore.**
Linda Lim, Pang Eng Fong. *Euro-Asia Business Review*. vol. 3, no. 2 (Apr. 1984), p. 27-31.

A brief but informative discussion on official strategies concerning industrial restructuring, foreign labour, and women workers.

493 **Chronology of trade union development in Singapore 1940-1984.**
Compiled by Lim-Ng Bee Eng. Singapore: Singapore National Trades Union Congress (NTUC), 1985. 36p.

Covers the colonial period until 1954; the period of self-government and independence, 1955-56; the post-independence decline, 1966-79; and progress in the 1980s.

494 **Constitution of the National Trades Union Congress (NTUC).**
National Trades Union Congress (NTUC). Singapore: NTUC, 1964. 41p.

The NTUC constitution is presented here in the four official languages, namely, Malay, Mandarin, Tamil, and English.

495 **Progress into the 80's.**
National Trades Union Congress (NTUC). Singapore: National Trades Union Congress, 1980. 216p.

A collection of the papers presented at the NTUC seminar, 'Progress into the 80s', held in Singapore from 6 to 10 November 1979. The sixteen interesting papers by political leaders and other speakers deal with the role, prospects, and evolution of the labour movement in Singapore and the relations between workers and the state.

496 **Teaming up for progress.**
Ong Teng Cheong. Singapore: National Trades Union Congress (NTUC), 1984. 130p.

This is the report by the NTUC Secretary-General to the Ordinary Delegates' Conference held in Singapore from 27 to 29 April 1984. The main paper with the above title was presented by Ong, who is also Minister without Portfolio, and deals with his perspective of the objectives of the labour movement in Singapore.

497 **NTUC Triennial Delegates' Conference, 1-3 April 1985.**
Ong Teng Cheong. Singapore: National Trades Union Congress (NTUC), 1985. 149p.

This volume is the annual report of the NTUC Secretary-General, who is also the second Deputy Prime Minister. In addition to the usual reports from the various committees and union projects, Ong presents his own perspective on the labour movement in Singapore. See also *NTUC Third Triennial Delegates' Conference 1979* (q.v.).

### 498  Public employee magazine December '83.
Edited by Paul Tan.   Singapore: Amalgamated Union of Public Employees (AUPE), 1983. 148P.

In addition to regular sections on AUPE union news, this edition includes discussions on workers' productivity concepts and perspectives applied to the public sector in Singapore.

### 499  Public empoyee magazine 1984.
Edited by Paul Tan.   Singapore: Amalgamated Union of Public Employees (AUPE), 1984. 108p.

This issue of the magazine includes messages from political leaders, AUPE's president, and other union officials as well as an informative 'pictorial recollection' of AUPE during the period 1959-84.

### 500  Human and industrial relations in Singapore: the management of compliance.
Barry Wilkinson, Chris Leggett.   *Euro-Asia Business Review*, vol. 4, no. 3 (July 1985), p. 9-15.

The authors focus on the economic restructuring which took place in 1979 and, in particular, the implementation of a programme of social engineering.

# Statistics

501 **Economic and social statistics. Singapore. 1960-1982.**
Department of Statistics. Singapore: Department of Statistics,
1983. 270p.
Provides useful and reliable data on the following important social and economic
subjects: climate and land use; demography; labour and employment; national
income and balance of payments; agriculture, livestock, and fisheries; industrial
production; electricity, gas, and water supply; building, construction and housing;
external trade; transport and communication; finance and insurance; public
finance; prices; education; health; and culture and recreation.

502 **Singapore Trade Statistics. Imports and Exports.**
Khoo Chian Kim. Singapore: Department of Statistics,
1980- (monthly).
Provides monthly information on domestic exports at commodity item level and
trade by economic and geographic region. Goods in transit through Singapore
between countries other than Malaysia (Peninsular Malaysia) are excluded. A set
of explanatory notes and the classification of goods precede the data tables. There
is also an alphabetical index of commodities by code number.

503 **Census of Population 1980 Singapore. Release no. 1.**
Khoo Chian Kim. Singapore: Department of Statistics,
Dec. 1980. 54p.
The first of nine volumes published by the Department of Statistics on the results
of the 1980 Population Census. This volume under the supervision of the
superintendant of the census, provides statistics on the total population by age
group, ethnic group, sex, marital status, language of literacy, census district,
census division, and residential status. It also includes two maps of the census
division and census districts in 1980.

504   **Census of Population 1980 Singapore. Release no. 2. Demographic characteristics.**
Khoo Chian Kim.   Singapore: Department of Statistics,
Jan. 1981. 89p.

The second census report released under the supervision of the superintendent of the census includes fifty-five census tables on the demographic characteristics of the ethnic groups in Singapore, including age, sex, age group, citizenship, residential status, place of birth, and marital status. Two charts illustrate the population changes between 1970 and 1980.

505   **Census of Population 1980 Singapore. Release no. 3. Literacy and education.**
Khoo Chian Kim.   Singapore: Department of Statistics,
Mar. 1981. 93p.

Fifty-three census tables and six charts produced under the supervision of the superintendent of the census are presented in this volume to provide detailed statistics on the highest educational qualification attained by the total population, by each of the ethnic groups, and by people born in Singapore and outside Singapore, Other statistics provided in this report are the language of literacy, general literacy rates, and information on the educational level and language of literacy of the student population.

506   **Census of Population 1980 Singapore. Release no. 4. Economic characteristics.**
Khoo Chian Kim.   Singapore: Department of Statistics,
Apr. 1981. 303p.

Seventy-seven census tables and thirteen charts produced under the supervision of the superintendent of the census provide information on relevant aspects of the economic activities of the population. These aspects are: economic activity status, occupational status, description of the economically active population, economically inactive populations, working persons aged ten years and over, and unemployed persons aged ten years and over. The figures include the age group, sex, marital status, language of literacy, residential status, industry, and occupation of these groups.

507   **Census of Population 1980 Singapore. Release no. 5. Geographic distribution.**
Khoo Chian Kim.   Singapore: Department of Statistics, May
1981. 247p.

This release, produced under the supervision of the superintendent of the census, contains 46 tables, 10 charts, and detailed maps on the geographic distribution of the Singapore population in terms of census area, census division, and island. The geographic distribution is reported by ethnic group, sex, highest qualification, type of household, type of house, number of persons in house, country of birth, economic activity, marital status, industry, and population density, among others.

508    **Census of Population 1980 Singapore. Release no. 6. Households and houses.**
Khoo Chian Kim.    Singapore: Department of Statistics, June 1981. 129p.

Presents ninety-two census tables and 14 charts produced under the supervision of the superintendent of the census describing the population in terms of type of household, size of household, house occupancy, tenancy of household, persons living in private households, and institutions. All these categories of residence are presented for the various ethnic groups, literacy groups, and other relevant categories of people.

509    **Census of Population 1980 Singapore. Release no. 7. Income and transport.**
Khoo Chian Kim.    Singapore: Department of Statistics, July 1981. 133p.

This volume provides 56 census tables and 22 charts produced under the supervision of the superintendent of the census on the subject of the population's income and modes of transportation. The information is presented in terms of the total population as well as population subgroups determined by occupational, working, and marital status, language of literacy, highest qualifications, sex, type of house, residential status, and other relevant aspects.

510    **Census of Population 1980 Singapore. Release no. 8. Languages spoken at home.**
Khoo Chian Kim.    Singapore: Department of Statistics, Aug. 1981. 147p.

The theme of this volume reflects the importance of bilingualism in Singapore. This release presents 84 census tables and 32 charts produced under the supervision of the superintendent of the census depicting the bilingual or multilingual characteristics of the Singapore population. As in the other volumes, the information on languages spoken at home is presented for the total population as well as population subgroups. The focus of analysis is the principal language spoken at home by individuals to parents and to brothers and sisters.

511    **Census of Population 1980 Singapore. Release no. 9. Religion and fertility.**
Khoo Chian Kim.    Singapore: Department of Statistics, Sept. 1981. 129p.

This is the last census release published by the Department of Statistics under the supervision of the superintendant of the census based on the 1980 census figures. It presents census figures on religion and the number of children born alive. Following the same system of presentation used in the previous census releases, both religion and fertility figures are presented for the total population and for relevant population groups.

512 **Statistics on marriages 1983.**
Khoo Chian Kim.    Singapore: Department of Statistics, 1984.
59p.

This is the fourth annual report on marriage statistics published by the
Department of Statistics. In addition to a description of marriage trends from
1961 to 1983 and of age-specific marriage rates, there are 40 tables and 8 charts
presenting official figures on Singapore's Muslim and non-Muslim marriages.

513 **Yearbook of statistics Singapore 1986/7.**
Khoo Chian Kim.    Singapore: Department of Statistics, 1987.
265p.

The first edition of this annual report was published in 1968. It is a collection of
basic and relevant statistics on key social and economic indicators, climate and
land use, demography, labour and employment, national income and balance of
payments, agriculture, livestock and fisheries, industrial production, electricity
and water supply, building, construction and housing, external trade, transport
and communication, finance (general and public) and insurance, prices,
education, health, culture, and recreation.

514 **Monthly digest of statistics.**
Khoo Chian Kim.    Singapore: Department of Statistics, vol. 26,
no. 4, April 1987.

The *Monthly digest of statistics* provides the most current official figures on the
same aspects of demography, the economy, transport, and some social indicators
that appear in the *Yearbook of statistics* (q.v.).

515 **Annual statistics bulletin 1985.**
Ministry of Health, Research and Evaluation Department.
Singapore: Ministry of Health, 1986. 79p.

This bulletin covers official figures on hospital services; primary health care
services; support services; including laboratory investigations, radiotherapy, and
blood transfusion; and dental health services.

516 **1985 Singapore yearbook of labour statistics.**
Ministry of Labour Research and Statistics Division.    Singapore:
Ministry of Labour, 1986. 145p.

This annual report by the Ministry of Labour presents figures on the labour force,
including establishments (industries, commercial firms, or enterprises) and
factories, weekly earnings and work hours, occupational wages, terms of
employment, and other relevant information. This is the tenth annual report in
the series.

517    **Yearbook of building and real estate statistics 1985.**
       Ministry of National Development, Research Unit.    Singapore:
       Ministry of National Development, 1986. 91p.

The figures in this yearbook deal with projects given planning approval, projects at the building plan approval stage, notices on commencement stage, building completion stage, real estate statistics, building materials and labour statistics, and other construction statistics.

518    **Economic survey of Singapore 1986.**
       Ministry of Trade and Industry.    Singapore: Ministry of Trade
       and Industry, 1986. 139p.

This specialized annual publication provides the reader with detailed figures on the Singapore economy, including an overview of the situation of Singapore in the world economy and statistics on economic growth, manufacturing, external trade, balance of payments, and public finance.

519    **Singapore facts and pictures 1987.**
       Compiled and edited by Ng Poey Siong.    Singapore: Ministry of
       Communications and Information, 1987. 214p. maps.

This is an annual publication presenting a summary of the most relevant information on Singapore covering history, government, the economy, trade and industry, agriculture, finance, employment, education, health, community development, and several other aspects of interest to visitors and residents alike. The first issue of this series was published in 1961 under the title *Singapore facts and figures*. The current title has been in use since 1968. The 1987 edition is an expanded and improved version with more colour photographs and new details included.

520    **Shipping and cargo statistics.**
       Port of Singapore Authority.    Singapore: Port of Singapore
       Authority, 1986. 90p.

This is a monthly publication originally published by the Department of Statistics and, from July 1986, published and distributed by the Port of Singapore Authority. The publication includes movement of vessels (entry and clearance of motorized vessels exceeding seventy-five net registered tons) and data on seaborne cargo discharged and loaded by vessels of all tonnages at all ports of Singapore including private wharfs and anchorages and transhipment cargo. The period covered is the calendar month. The book also includes a summary of shipping and cargo statistics for the current and previous calendar years.

521 **Report on registration of births and deaths, 1984.**
Registrar-General of Births and Deaths. Singapore: Ministry of
Home Affairs, National Registration Department, Registry of
Births and Deaths, 1985. 102p.

The Registry of Births and Deaths publishes this annual report covering five main
areas of information: the natural increase of the population by ethnic group and
sex; a description of live-birth figures by place of occurrence, type of attendant at
birth, ethnicity of father and mother, parental age and occupation, period of
gestation, and birth weight and sex of child; figures on still-births by ethnicity and
age of mother, place of occurrence, attendant at birth, period of gestation, and
birth weight and sex of the child; and a description of figures on deaths by
ethnicity, age, sex, marital status, occupation, place of occurrence, cause, and
type of certification. The report also includes a set of charts conveying the same
information given in tables and five appendixes describing the procedure of
registration, registration centres, and samples of the certificates used to register
births, still-births, and deaths.

522 **A guide to the economic and social statistics of Singapore.**
Saw Swee-Hock. Singapore: Applied Research Corporation,
1981. 103p. bibliog.

This book describes the organization of national official statistics and bodies
dealing in, collecting, and compiling official statistics. There are two parts: the
first, describes the statistical system of Singapore, including the move towards
decentralization, statistical legislation, and bodies involved. Part II is an
annotated bibliography of statistical publications by general topic.

# Environment

523 **A history of Singapore architecture. The making of a city.**
Jane Beamish, Jane Ferguson.   Singapore: Graham Brash, 1985.
180p.

Provides a well-illustrated description of architectural styles and changes in
Singapore from 1819 to 1985. It is not a scholarly study of architectural design.
Instead, the authors address the general public, using a descriptive, simple
approach and abundant illustrations. About two-thirds of the book is made up of
photographs or illustrations of buildings and landscapes.

524 **Effects of slum clearance, urban redevelopment and vector control
on densities of *Aedes* mosquitoes in Singapore.**
Chan Kai Lok, J. J. Counsilman.   *Tropical Biomedicine*, no. 2
(1985), p. 139-47.

A detailed description of the successful multi-pronged and collaborative approach
taken by the Ministry of the Environment, the Housing and Development Board,
and the Urban Redevelopment Authority in Singapore to control the breeding of
the *Aedes* mosquitoes, which transmit dengue haemorragic fever. See also the
section on health.

525 **Ethical dilemmas arising from urban development and environ-
mental change: Singapore.**
Chia Lin Sien.   In: *Ethical dilemmas of development in Asia.*
Edited by Godfrey Gunatilleke, Neelan Tiruchelvam, Radhike
Coomaraswamy. Lexington, Massachusetts: Lexington Books,
1983, p. 223-41.

After describing the history of urban development and renewal in Singapore, the
author discusses several ethical issues concerning traditional values, social justice,
equity, the need to build up national identity, and the need for a clean
environment.

### 526 Higher education and marine food resources in Indonesia, Malaysia, Singapore and Thailand.
Chia Lin Sien. Singapore: Regional Institute of Higher Education and Development, 1984. 109p.

The discussion of marine food resources is presented in three sections. The first section deals with a background of marine resources and their exploitation in these countries; the second section focuses on the managerial, production, and marketing problems of fishery industries in the region; and the third section deals with national policies and the role of higher education and research. The author suggests some guidelines for a better involvement of educational institutions.

### 527 A history of the survey and mapping of Singapore.
Chiang Tao-Chang. In: *Proceedings of the 12th Conference of the International Cartographic Association*. Edited by D. T. Pearce. Perth: International Cartographic Association 12th Conference Committee, vol. 2, 1984, p. 549-66.

A detailed description of the historical background of cartography in Singapore, tracing its roots back to the British tradition.

### 528 Singapore changing landscapes: Geylang, Chinatown, Serangoon.
V. Gopalakrishnan, Ananda Perera. Singapore: FEP International, Singapore Broadcasting Corporation, 1983. 100p.

A good collection of high quality photographs of the architecture, landscape, and people of three historically interesting areas in Singapore: Geylang, a well-known Malay settlement; Serangoon, a traditionally Indian settlement, and Chinatown. Based on the scripts and stills from three documentaries produced by the Singapore Broadcasting Corporation, this book not only illustrates vividly the physical environment of these areas but also provides views and opinions expressed by the residents during the documentary interviews.

### 529 National monuments of Singapore.
Christopher Hooi. Singapore: National Museum, 1982. 49p. maps.

This is an illustrated guide to nineteen buildings that have been officially gazetted by the Preservation of Monuments Board as national monuments. Each monument is depicted in a black-and-white photograph accompanied by relevant details such as a brief description of the location, a map, lot, title, area, owner, status, and short history.

### 530 Proceedings of the 3rd Symposium on Our Environment, March 27-29, 1984.
Edited by Koh Lip Lin, Hew Choy Sin. Singapore: National University of Singapore, Faculty of Science, 1985. 510p.

The symposium papers appearing in this publication of proceedings are based on detailed studies on a wide range of environmental aspects, from restoration of historical buildings to water pollution. Although the papers were written by scientists from various countries, the reader will find relevant chapters dedicated to the Singapore environment.

531 **Emerald Hill. The story of a street in words and pictures.**
Lee Kip Lin.   Singapore: National Museum Singapore, 1984.
88p. maps.

Based on a previous article written by the author and Yeh Ding Shin entitled 'Emerald Hill: its architecture and history relative to the urbanization and development of Singapore's environment' published in the *Institute of Planners Journal* in 1974. This book is an expanded version of that article, including more detailed information on the architectural aspects of this picturesque street in Singapore. The main contribution of this volume is its four appendixes providing specific information on the historical ownership of land in Emerald Hill, the architects who built the houses (pages 35-38), and the fifty-one pages of photographs, maps, and building plans. Lee dedicates only fourteen pages of the book to the history of Emerald Hill and supplements his narration with twenty pages of footnotes.

532 **Code of practice on water services.**
Owen Liu.   Singapore: Public Utilities Board, 1981. 2nd ed. 67p.

This code covers the distribution and storage of water, the use of appliances, work on water sites, and the inspection, testing, and maintenance of the water supply in Singapore.

533 **Revised Master Plan written statement, 1980.**
Ministry of National Development, Planning Department.
Singapore: Ministry of National Development, 1981. 28p. maps.

A description of the contents of the Master Plan for Singapore, its population bases, definitions, proposals, development intensity, and building and preservation areas. It includes a set of tables with relevant figures.

534 **Annual report '86.**
Ministry of the Environment.   Singapore: Ministry of the
Environment, 1986. 41p. maps.

This report is divided into five sections: organizational chart, main annual events, finance and administration, the report from the Environment Engineering Division, and the report from the Environmental Public Health Division. A set of appendixes offers further information. The Ministry of the Environment was set up in September 1972 to take up the functions of environmental public health and pollution control, previously assigned to the ministries of Health and National Development, respectively.

535 **The MRT and property values.**
Philip Motha. *South East Asia Building Annual 1985* (1985), p. 116-28.

Reviews studies of change in land value due to changes in transit systems and land use, presents the case of Hong Kong as an example of the effect of the subway system on land value, and discusses the future impact of the MRT (Mass Rapid Transit) system upon Singapore's property values.

536 **The quality of Singapore drinking water in relation to trihalomethanes.**
W. J. Ng, K. K. Chin. In: *Proceedings of the Interclean 84 Conference*. Edited by K. K. Chin. Singapore: Environmental Engineering Society of Singapore, 1984, p. 50-63.

The term trihalomethanes refers to chemical compounds such as chloroform and bromoform. The study's objective was to determine the nature and total concentration of these chemicals in drinking water. The findings show that the national average concentration was much lower than the recommended maximum established by the World Health Organization and thus was well within the international safety standards for drinking water.

537 **A statistical study of various traffic noise distributions in Singapore.**
P. P. Ong, H. K. Sy, K. L. Tan, S. H. Tang. In: *Proceedings of the 13th International Conference on Noise Control Engineering*. Edited by William W. Lang, New York: Noise Control Foundation, 1984, p. 323-26.

The results from a survey of 300 sites in Singapore are reported in this paper. The authors compare traffic noise fluctuations and distribution in terms of duration and location in different areas in Singapore.

538 **Environmental education and research in Singapore.**
James E. Pakiam. Singapore: Maruzen Asia, 1982. 72p. bibliog. (Regional Institute of Higher Education and Development Occasional Paper Series).

This paper discusses in nine chapters the basic problems of definition and activities concerning environmental issues, the scope and nature of environmental problems, general aspects of environmental research and education, and specific aspects of environmental research and education in Singapore. The paper includes two appendixes.

539 **Conservation and the Singapore River.**
Robert Powell. *Singapore Institute of Architects Journal*, no. 132 (Sept.-Oct. 1985) p. 3-5.

The main contribution of this brief article rests on suggestions for a national conservation policy, using the case of the Singapore River as the main example.

540   **Survival in the city.**
      Robert Powell. *Singapore Institute of Architects Journal*, no. 129
      (Mar.-Apr. 1985), p. 38-42.

Basic concepts of urban design and the conservation of natural resources are
discussed in the context of urban development in Singapore.

541   **Environmental protection in Singapore. A handbook.**
      Science Council of Singapore.   Singapore: Science Council of
      Singapore, 1980. 114p. bibliog.

An editorial committee of nine experts from the Singapore Science Council and
other organizations put together this handbook. In nine chapters, it discusses
various relevant aspects such as environmental planning, air, water and marine
pollution, solid waste disposal, ionizing radiation, noise pollution, and industrial
health and safety. The last chapter provides a brief annotated general
bibliography on environmental protection. There are four appendixes on
environmental legislation and a list of relevant organizations in Singapore.

542   **Recreational facilities in Singapore.**
      Russell A. Smith.   *Journal of the Singapore Professional Centre*,
      vol. 10, no. 1 (1985), p. 28-33.

The short- and medium-term recreational facilities available to Singaporeans in
Singapore and Malaysia are compared and discussed and suggestions for
improvement of Singapore's facilities are given.

543   **Fluoridation of public water supplies in Singapore.**
      C. S. Teo.   *Annals of the Academy of Medicine Singapore*,
      vol. 13, no. 2 (1984), p. 247-51.

The author describes the fluoridation programme first introduced in 1956 in
Singapore and provides figures on school children to demonstrate that the
programme has had positive results by lowering the incidence of dental caries.

544   **Condominium living in Singapore: stock-taking of a decade's effort.**
      Teo Siew Eng.   *International Real Estate Journal*, vol. 9, no. 1
      (1985), p. 40-47.

Discusses the government's efforts to introduce high-rise private housing developments in the early 1970s, describes the development and growth of condominium
living since then, and assesses the success of the government's plans.

545   **Singapore landscape: a historical overview of housing change.**
      Teo Siew Eng, Victor R. Savage.   *Singapore Journal of Tropical
      Geography*, vol. 6, no. 1 (1985), p. 48-63.

An interesting and detailed analysis of the transformation of the physical
landscape in response to political and economic changes that took place since the
formal founding of Singapore in 1819. The main types of housing prevailing in
different historical periods of Singapore are identified.

# Education

546 **University-industry interaction: the Singapore experience in an industrial orientation programme for science students.**
L. H. L. Chia. In: *Proceedings of the Asian Chemical Conference on Priorities in Chemistry in Development of Asia.* Edited by Loke Su Eng, M. Mohinder Singh. Kuala Lumpur: Institiut Kimia Malaysia, 1984, p. 375-81.
Describes the programme, including its historical background, planning, implementation, and development and the role played by the various groups involved, i.e., the science faculty academic staff at the university, university science students, people in the industrial sector, and government and quasi-government bodies. Concludes that the programme has given positive results.

547 **Sociology education in Singapore: its development, problems and prospects.**
John R. Clammer. Singapore: Regional Institute of Higher Education and Development, 1984. 66p.
As a British anthropologist, the author offers his own perspective of the discipline of sociology and his views on how sociology has been and should be taught in Singapore.

548 **Report on university education in Singapore 1979.**
Sir Frederick Dainton. Singapore: University of Singapore, 1979. 8p.
The author was invited by the Prime Minister of Singapore in June 1979 to give his views on university education in Singapore when there were two universities, namely, Nanyang University and the University of Singapore.

549 **Report on the Ministry of Education 1978.**
Goh Keng Swee, Education Study Team.   Singapore: Ministry of Education, 10 Feb. 1979. 102p.

A very important work that served as the basis for the current educational system in Singapore. The Prime Minister appointed Dr Goh Keng Swee (then deputy Prime Minister and Minister for Education) 'to look into the problems of the Ministry of Education with a team of your choice.' This report presents their findings in five chapters: an overview of the problem, existing problems in the educational system, educational policies (including bilingualism), and systems and procedures as contributing factors. The sixth and final chapter presents the team's recommendations. Nearly half of the report's volume is made up of annexes providing graphic and numerical data on various relevant aspects of education.

550 **Towards a national educational system.**
S. Gopinathan.   In: *Singapore: society in transition.* Edited by Riaz Hassan. Kuala Lumpur: Oxford University Press, 1976, p. 67-83. (East Asian Social Science Monographs).

Looks at the educational system over five historical stages of transition, including the aspects of national identity and bilingualism. There is a useful list of references.

551 **Education.**
S. Gopinathan.   In: *Government and politics of Singapore.* Edited by Jon S. T. Quah, Chan Heng Chee, Seah Chee Meow. Singapore: Oxford University Press, 1987. rev. ed., p. 197-232.

Education has been one of the areas undergoing rapid change in Singapore. This chapter describes such changes before 1980. The author deals with the impact of the demographic profile of the population, including ethnic composition, and the influence of politics and ideology before describing the main features of the educational system and the role of the schools in fostering national identity and bilingualism.

552 **Literacy in Singapore, 1970-1980.**
Eddie C. Y. Kuo.   *RELC Journal*, vol. 14, no. 1 (1983), p. 1-17.

The term RELC refers to the Regional English Language Centre. This paper is based on an analysis of the statistics from the 1970 and 1980 population censuses, with particular emphasis on literacy and language of literacy among the main ethnic groups in Singapore and the differences between male and female literacy.

553 **Planning and management of the University of Singapore and Nanyang University prior to merger.**
Lee Boon Hiok.   Singapore: Regional Institute of Higher Education and Development, 1983. 91p. bibliog.

The merger of the two universities took place in 1980. The author describes briefly the historical development of the two institutions; the factors that, in his view, influenced their development; and the different management features characterizing each institution. The final section of this monograph examines the reforms implemented after the merger. Includes seventeen appendixes.

554 **Language and language education.**
Lee Kok Cheong. Singapore: Singapore University Press, 1983. 132p.

Centres on the importance of language proficiency and bilingualism in Singapore and educational policies and specific aspects of the teaching of English in Singapore.

555 **Education and national development.**
Lim Chong-Yah. Singapore: Federal Publications, 1983. 122p.

A collection of thirteen essays written by the author from 1970 to 1980 and presented at various forums and seminars. Several of the essays have been published elsewhere. The main theme throughout the essays is on development of the educational system, particularly of postsecondary education. Some of the essays include relevant statistics for readers interested in the situation prior to 1980.

556 **Confucian ethics and moral education in Singapore.**
Martin Lu. In: *Proceedings of the 1st World Conference in Chinese Philosophy*. Edited by the Chinese Philosophical Association. Taipei: Chinese Philosophical Association, 1985, p. 279-302.

The author presents his views on the moral education programme introduced by the government in 1982 and discusses the implications of such a programme in the context of the possible functions of religion in society.

557 **Education in Singapore.**
Ministry of Education. Singapore: Educational Publications Bureau, 1972. 2nd ed. 99p.

This is a clear and concise description of the educational system in Singapore up to 1972. It is divided into twelve sections covering the historical background of the educational system; policy, administration, and finance; preschool, primary, secondary, and postsecondary education; teachers and teacher training; adult education; special education; planning, research, and statistics; and regional and international cooperation in education. It includes an appendix containing fourteen tables with further figures. The first edition of this study appeared in 1970.

558 **The education system and policies in Singapore. Recent changes and their rationale.**
Ong Teck Hong. *Journal of East and West Education*, vol. 5, no. 2 (1984), p. 21-29.

Reviews educational policies affecting the full spectrum of formal education in Singapore, from primary school to tertiary level, and presents the author's views on the implications of such policies for child development.

559 **Report on moral education 1979.**
Ong Teng Cheong, Moral Education Committee. Singapore: Ministry of Education, 1 June 1979. 57p.

In 1978, the Minister for Education, Goh Keng Swee, requested that the Minister for Communication, Ong Teng Cheong, 'examine the existing moral education programme in schools.' Ong and his team presented this report of their study. It deals with a description of the team, its terms of reference, and the study approach; the background of the teaching of civics and education for living in schools; the shortcomings of the existing programme; and conclusions and recommendations. Four appendixes include further relevant information.

560 **The place of liberal arts in university education.**
Cedric H. C. Pan. *Commentary* [Singapore], vol. 6, nos. 2 & 3 (1985), p. 91-102.

As a philosophy lecturer, the author presents his perspective of the topic and discusses it within the context of Singapore, emphasizing the relevance of liberal arts for the overall development of the nation.

561 **Education, manpower and development in Singapore.**
Pang Eng Fong. Singapore: Singapore University Press, 1982. 242p. bibliog.

The nineteen chapters of this book are organized into three parts. The first part, six chapters on development and the labour market, discusses employment and changing manpower conditions, including two chapters on growth, inequality, and race. The five chapters in the second part focus on education and earnings, including the role of education in occupational mobility. The third part has eight chapters dealing with manpower development and public policy. In addition to an index, there are forty-eight tables with relevant statistics up to 1980.

562 **The university as a catalyst for social change.**
Phoon Wai On. *Moebius* (University of California Press Journal), vol. 5, no. 3 (1985), p. 25-28.

Focuses on the experience of the Department of Social Medicine and Public Health of the Faculty of Medicine, National University of Singapore, to illustrate how a university can trigger social change. A historical description of the department's work in teaching and research is presented.

563  **Towards excellence in schools. A report to the Minister for Education.**
Principals Study Team.   Singapore: Ministry of Education, Feb. 1987. 85p.

A special team of secondary school principals was appointed by the Minister for Education to visit selected schools in the United States and England and 'identify the factors that make a good and effective school.' The visits took place from November to December 1986. In this report, the principals convey their findings to the minister in ten chapters preceded by an outline of key findings and recommendations and an executive summary. The ten chapters deal with the schools in perspective, school philosophy and policy, organization and school structure, the headmaster, the staff, the school community, the curriculum, finance, physical resources, and conclusions and recommendations. Three appendixes provide further details.

564  **Out-of-school biology activities in Singapore. A check list of out-of-school facilities in Singapore.**
A. N. Rao.   In: *Teaching science out-of-school with special reference to biology*. Edited by G. R. Meyer, A. N. Rao. Singapore: UNESCO, 1984, p. 109-26.

Describes the various sources found in Singapore from which school children may broaden their knowledge of biology, for example, the Singapore Science Centre, the Botanic Gardens, the Singapore Zoological Garden, and the Malayan Nature Society, and concludes that students have sufficient learning opportunities in Singapore and do take advantage of them.

565  **Education reform and national integration.**
Seah Chee Meow, Linda Seah.   In: *Singapore development policies and trends*. Edited by Peter S. J. Chen. Singapore: Oxford University Press, 1983, p. 240-67.

A discussion in four sections: the educational system since 1959, issues in education reform, the supply factors in the educational system, and some implications of the new educational system. Two appendixes and a useful list of references and notes complement the discussion. For more details on the new educational system see the 1978 report by Goh Keng Swee in this section.

566  **University-industry interaction: the Singapore experience.**
K. Y. Sim.   In: *Proceedings of the Asian Chemical Conference on Priorities in Chemistry in Development of Asia*. Edited by Loke Su Eng, M. Mohinder Singh. Kuala Lumpur: Institiut Kimia Malaysia, 1984, p. 365-74.

Presents the findings from a study of the main contributions of the programme. The programme enables the university to contribute suitable trained graduates to the industrial sector while the latter contributes financial assistance in the form of research grants, scholarships, and opportunities for the attachment of students to industrial projects. The government has also made its contribution in the form of the Applied Research Corporation, the Science Park, and funding of research and development projects.

567 **Perception and practice in education. An STU report 1980.**
Singapore Teachers Union. Singapore: Singapore Teachers Union, 1980. 207p.

An interesting statement by the Singapore Teachers Union (STU) concerning its professional views and the rationale behind the union's reservations about the government's 1978 blueprint for radical changes in the educational system, particularly the introduction of a streaming system. Its seven chapters deal with the opinions of a random sample of principals, vice-principals, and teachers in Singapore on problems of streaming and evaluation, language teaching and bilingualism, communication, professionalism, staffing, and full day-schools.

568 **Trends in language, literacy and education in Singapore.**
Mary Tay Wan Joo. Singapore: Department of Statistics, 1983. 117p. (Census Monograph no. 2).

This is the second in a series of monographs on a specific theme of the 1980 Census of Population sponsored and published by the Department of Statistics (the first and third monographs are on demographic trends and the labour force). Tay presents in five chapters her analysis of census data on the themes of language, literacy, and education including 47 tables and 2 charts summarizing census data. Three appendixes provide details on sampling errors, concepts and definitions, and references.

569 **Social engineering in Singapore: educational policies and social change, 1819-1972.**
Harold E. Wilson. Singapore: Singapore University Press, 1978. 300p. bibliog.

An interesting and debatable perspective of educational policies. Wilson sees them as a manifestation of the government's use of education as a vehicle of social control and social change from the time Singapore was a British colony until the initiation of its rapid industrialization. The six chapters in this book deal with the emergence of a divided society, the educational policy prior to the Pacific war, the implications of Japanese educational policy in Singapore, education and the state; experiments in democracy, and education for national identity. The book includes six appendixes and an index. For a related historical work see the *Official reports on education* in this section.

570 **Official reports on education in the Straits Settlements and the Federated Malay States 1870-1939.**
Compiled and edited by Francis H. K. Wong, Gwee Yee Hean.
Singapore: Pan Pacific Book Distributors, 1980. 164p.

Twelve official reports from special commissions or committees appointed by the colonial government are included in this publication. The themes of these reports cover, among other things, the state of education in the colony, the system of vernacular and English education, vernacular and industrial education, advice on a scheme for the advancement of education preparatory to the founding of the University of Singapore, technical and industrial education in the Federated Malay States, the system of education grants-in-aid, and a scheme for a school of agriculture. The compilers present a brief historical background and introduce each document with a statement on the year of publication, names of the official committee members who wrote the report, and the terms of reference of the committees.

# Science, Technology and Social Sciences

571  **Science and technology in Singapore.**
Ang How Ghee.   *ASEAN Journal on Science and Technology for Development*, vol. 1, no. 1 (1984), p. 86-113.
An informative and interesting discussion on the role of the state in the dissemination and growth of science and technology in Singapore. This paper was originally presented at the Association of Southeast Asian Nations-European Economic Community (ASEAN-EEC) seminar on science and technology indicators and science policy, held in London from 13 to 17 June 1983. The author was then chairman of the Singapore Science Council.

572  **A small country in the world of big science: a preliminary bibliometric study of science in Singapore.**
S. Arunachalam, K. C. Garg.   *Scientometrics*, vol. 8, nos. 5-6 (1985), p. 301-13.
An interesting discussion of Singapore's efforts to update and improve research and development in science.

573  **Survey of information needs of the Department of Scientific Services.**
Chan Thye Seng, Chan Fook Weng.   Singapore: National Library, 1981. 23p.
A succinct description of information needs based on the Department of Scientific Services' needs and the increasing trend towards the use of high technology.

144

574 **Project LORADS: Singapore's leap into high technology air traffic control.**
Department of Civil Aviation. Singapore: Department of Civil Aviation, 1981. 31p.
A brief but informative article on the acquisition of the Long Range Radar and Display System (LORADS) to upgrade the radar air traffic control system in Singapore.

575 **National University of Singapore Department of Information Systems and Computer Science handbook.**
Department of Computer Science. Singapore: National University of Singapore, 1985. 56p.
A detailed description of the department's philosophy, practices, facilities, curricula, and staff.

576 **New intellectual technology society.**
Goh Seng-kim. *Media Asia*, vol. 8, no. 4 (1981), p. 182-84.
A brief discussion of the link between technology, information services, and the state in Singapore.

577 **Government induced technology upgrading in Asia's NICs: the case of Singapore.**
A. N. Hakam. Singapore: National University of Singapore, Department of Business Administration, 1982. 30p. (Occasional Paper no. 26).
A discussion of the problems and advantages of the government's involvement in technology upgrading and some reference to the situation in other new industrializing countries.

578 **The market potential of CAD technology in the architectural profession.**
Han Swee Teng, Tan Boon Wan. *Singapore Marketing Review*, vol. 8 (Dec. 1984), p. 40-44.
A brief but interesting discussion of the advantages of computer-aided design (CAD) technology for architects in Singapore.

579 **Singapore studies: critical surveys of the humanities and social sciences.**
Edited by Basant K. Kapur. Singapore: Singapore University Press, 1986. 486p.
A collection of reviews covering Singapore, English, Chinese, and Malay literature; historiography of Singapore; economics; political science; physical and human geography; social work; demography; and sociology. There are variations in the time span covered by each author as well as the thoroughness of each review; most chapters present comprehensive surveys while others – the chapter

on sociology for example – cover only some aspects of the research done in a given field. Nevertheless, the book is informative. All the authors are academic staff members of the National University of Singapore. See also *The social sciences in Singapore* by Ong Jin Hui (*Social Science Series*, UNESCO Reports and Papers no. 35 (1977), p. 97–111) for a review of the development of various aspects of the social sciences up to the mid-1970s.

580    **A guide to the Singapore Science Centre Ecogarden.**
Patricia K. P. Kwok.    Singapore: Singapore Science Centre, 1986. 160p.

Describes the Ecogarden, its facilities, and its educational features, particularly concerning botany and zoology.

581    **Technological education in Singapore: a country report.**
Law Song Seng.    Singapore: Vocational and Industrial Training Board, 1984. 24p. (Paper no. 3).

A brief and specific description of the various institutional settings and procedures used in technical education.

582    **The challenge of the information society: implications for Singapore.**
Lee Boon Hiok.    *Social Science and Policy Research*, vol. 8, no. 2 (Dec. 1986), p. 201-15.

An examination of the political and social environments in Singapore which have given rise to the growth of an information society. The impact of the latter on the political system and the relationship of the mass media to politics in Singapore are also discussed.

583    **Gearing up for high-tech, more gracious Singapore.**
Lee Kuan Yew.    *Singapore Business*, vol. 8, no. 11 (Nov. 1984), p. 69-71.

The Singapore Prime Minister's views on the importance of technological development and its relation to the economy of the nation.

584    **Technology choice and employment creation: a case study of three multinational enterprises in Singapore.**
Linda Lim, Pang Eng Fong.    Singapore: Economic Research Centre, 1982. 32p. (Occasional Paper no. 4).

Three electronic industries in Singapore illustrate the link between the choice of technology and the opportunities and constraints in job creation that given technologies bring.

585  **High-tech and high hopes in the Asian NICs: what can be done to secure Singapore's niche in that world.**
Linda Lim, Pang Eng Fong.  *Singapore Business Yearbook* (1985), p. 35-43.
The authors, both economists, discuss the implications of high technology for the Singapore economy in the context of the current strong international competition among the newly industrialized countries.

586  **Mechanical marvels the answer to productivity.**
Lena Loo.  *Management Journal*, vol. 1, no. 6 (1982), p. 44-50.
Describes the trend towards automation in Singapore and discusses the benefits of computer science applications, particularly in the increase in productivity.

587  **Technology transfer and Singapore's restructuring strategy.**
Pang Eng Fong.  *ASEAN Business Quarterly*, vol. 4, no. 2 (1980), p. 26-32.
A brief but informative account of the Singapore experience in industrial restructuring and the features of its approach to technology transfer.

588  **Technology transfer: the Singapore experience.**
Pang Eng Fong.  *Singapore Business Yearbook* (1981), p. 70-89.
An expanded version of the arguments presented by the author in his 1980 article on technology transfer and restructuring (in this section). Pang discusses the difficulties, implications, and advantages of technology transfer in the context of the Singapore economy.

589  **High technology industries: a survey of factory requirements in Singapore.**
Roger W. Parsons.  *Southeast Asia Building* (Sept. 1987), p. 54-57.
Discusses the design and construction guidelines and problems involving the building of factories for high technology industries in Singapore.

590  **Social sciences in Singapore: some emerging trends in research.**
Jon S. T. Quah.  *East Asian Cultural Studies*, vol. 19, nos. 1-4 (1980), p. 85-100.
An overview of the study and teaching of social sciences as well as research themes and gaps. The author identifies six trends and discusses their relevance and implications.

**Science, Technology and Social Sciences**

591  **Singapore Science Park: a centre for creativity.**
Regional Institute for Higher Education and Development
(RIHED).  *RIHED Bulletin*, vol. 10, no. 4 (Oct.-Dec. 1983),
p. 14-17.
An informative description of the Singapore Science Park project and its
development and goals.

592  **Training and development science in Singapore today – an analysis
and an appeal.**
Tan Jing-hee.  *Singapore Management Review*, vol. 3, no. 2 (July
1981), p. 42-47.
Discusses the approaches taken in Singapore towards the specialized training of
employees and the need for further upgrading.

593  **Teaching of computer science at tertiary and professional levels.**
Tan Kok Phuang.  *Singapore Professionals*, vol. 6, nos. 3-4
(1981), p. 29-37.
Emphasizes the relevance of computer science and electronic data processing for
Singapore's development and focuses on the study and teaching of these subjects
in Singapore.

594  **Accounting technology transfer to less developed countries and the
Singapore experience.**
R. Y. W. Tang.  *Columbia Journal of World Business*, vol. 21
(Summer 1986), p. 85-95.
A discussion of the impact of new technology in the practice of the profession in
Singapore and the advantages and problems of technology transfer in this field.

595  **The new information professionals.**
Edited by Ajita Thuraisingham.  Aldershot, England: Gower,
1987. 356p.
The proceedings of the Singapore-Malaysia Congress of Librarians and Information Scientists, held in Singapore from 4 to 6 September 1986. Papers presented
deal with advances in library science, applications of information technology, and
the link between library and information sciences with reference to Singapore and
Malaysia.

596  **A cross-sectional perspective on science performance in Singapore.**
Yeoh Oon Chye, Tan Yap Kwang.  *Singapore Journal of
Education*, vol. 8, no. 1 (1987), p. 23-55.
A survey of findings on schoolchildren's performance in science subjects and a
discussion of their implications for the teaching and study of science in schools.
The same issue of this journal presents three papers by other authors on related
subjects, namely, science skills and cognitive preference styles, the contribution of
enrichment activities towards science achievement, and the assessment of science
practicals in schools.

# Literature

## Literary history and criticism

597  **Straits Chinese literature: a minority literature as a vehicle of identity.**
John R. Clammer.   In: *Literature and society in Southeast Asia. Political and sociological perspectives.* Edited by Tham Seong Chee. Singapore: Singapore University Press, 1981, p. 287-302.
Focuses on the Straits Chinese communities of Singapore and Malaysia and reviews their literary tradition over time and the role of literature in the community's cultural identity.

598  **Singapore: poet, critic, audience.**
Peter Hyland.   *World Literature Written in English*, vol. 23, no. 1 (1984), p. 137-45.
The author argues that the improvement of poetry as literary expression in Singapore is seriously limited by two facts: the circle of critics and poets is rather small, thus compelling critics to be tactful rather than rigorous, and Singapore does not have a large enough audience for poetry which could press for higher standards.

599  **The Singapore experience. Cultural development in the global village.**
Koh Tai Ann.   In: *Southeast Asian affairs 1980.* Edited by Leo Suryadinata. Singapore: Institute of Southeast Asian Studies, 1980, p. 292-307.
A forceful discussion of the problems faced by Singapore in the late 1970s

concerning its cultural and literary life. Koh describes the aims and functions of cultural development, the emphasis on modernization and economic development, the influence of mass culture, and other relevant aspects.

600 **Singapore writing in English: the literary tradition and cultural identity.**
Koh Tai Ann. In: *Literature and society in Southeast Asia. Political and sociological perspectives.* Edited by Tham Seong Chee. Singapore: Singapore University Press, 1981, p. 160-86.

A historical review of literary work, the problems faced by local writers in English, the critical response to their work, the contrasting situation of poetry and prose, and the need to impose literary value over relevance in the criticism of the quality of local English literature.

601 **Singapore literature.**
Liaw Yock Fang. In: *Encyclopaedia of world literature in the 20th century.* Edited by Leonard Klein. New York: Frederick Ungar, 1984, vol. 4, p. 232-34.

A summary of the historical background of literature in Singapore's four official languages – English, Mandarin, Malay, and Tamil – and a brief discussion of current and future trends.

602 **Singapore writing.**
Edited by Chandran Nair. Singapore: Woodrose Publication for the Society of Singapore Writers, 1977. 202p.

This collection provides the reader with a good sample of creative writing in Singapore in the 1970s and thus facilitates the appreciation of Singapore literature in the 1980s. There are five types of literary work in this collection, including a group of poems in English, English translations of some poems originally written in Malay and Chinese, fourteen reprints of short stories in English by eight Singapore writers, four stories originally written in Malay by three Malay writers, and one story each by three Chinese writers, also translated into English. All these materials are preceded by three introductory essays (one written by Nair) on creative writing in Singapore, the role of writers in a multiracial society, and poetry in English in the 1970s.

603 **An approach to Singapore writing in English.**
Kirpal Singh. *ARIEL (A Review of International English Literature)*, vol. 15, no. 2 (1984), p. 5-24. bibliog.

A detailed, academic discussion of the literary work of Singaporean writers and the problems involved in using English as the medium of expression.

604    **The use of localised English in Singapore poetry.**
       John Platt, Kirpal Singh. *English World Wide. A Journal of Varieties of English*, vol. 5, no. 1 (1984), p. 43-54.
The authors discuss the use of local idioms in poetry and argue that localized English enriches Singapore poetry.

605    **Prose fiction.**
       Kirpal Singh. In: *Singapore studies: critical surveys of the humanities and social sciences*. Edited by Basant K. Kapur.
       Singapore: Singapore University Press, 1986, p. 480-86.
Singh describes the development of 'local' prose fiction in English as slower than that of local poetry in English and discusses the possible reasons for this as he reviews briefly the most notable literary efforts of Singaporean writers. He concludes that there are signs that in the future fiction will become 'a thriving or flourishing activity.'

606    **The poetry of Edwin Thumboo: a study in development.**
       Kirpal Singh, B. E. Ooi. *World Literature Written in English*, vol. 24, no. 2 (1985), p. 454-59.
The authors identify three phases of development in the work of Thumboo, one of Singapore's best known and most acclaimed poets. The three stages correspond to three decades of poetry writing since Thumboo's first published collection in the 1950s.

607    **The impact of urbanization on the recent development of Singapore literature in Chinese.**
       Wong Yoon Wah. *Solidarity*, no. 99 (1984), p. 36-41.
Urbanization and the improvement of economic conditions in Singapore have led to the Chinese-educated public's preference for entertainment in detriment to serious literary work in Chinese.

608    **A survey of criticisms on Singapore poetry in English.**
       Arthur Yap. In: *Singapore studies: critical surveys of the humanities and social sciences*. Edited by Basant K. Kapur.
       Singapore: Singapore University Press, 1986, p. 459-78. bibliog.
A comprehensive listing of critical views, most of which centre on the problem of cultural and linguistic identity of the poet and his or her audience and on the standards that should be applied when assessing the quality of Singaporean poets. Perhaps the best contribution of this article is its useful bibliography of poetry and literary criticism in Singapore.

609 **In search of identity: Chinese literature in Malaysia and Singapore, 1919-1983.**
Yeo Song Nian, Leung Yuen Sang. *Asian Culture*, vol. 5 (1985), p. 18-23.
The authors follow a historical perspective, identifying four stages or periods of growth of Chinese literature from the initial search for identity and strong dependency on China's influence before 1926 to the period of clear differentiation from mainland China that began after Singapore's and Malaysia's independence from Britain in 1959.

# Present trends and major authors

610 **As long as rivers flow.**
Chew Yen Fook, Samydorai.   Singapore: The Authors, 1981. 48p.
A collection of twenty-three poems privately published by the two authors. Each poem is accompanied by a photograph or plate of river scenes.

611 **Made in Singapore.**
Corinne Chia, K. K. Seet, Pat M. Wong.   Singapore: Times Books International, 1985. 128p.
Twelve short stories on the daily lives of average Singaporeans. While the same humorous style is found in other literary work (see other entries in this section), the special contribution of this book is the glimpse it provides on the man-in-the-street's views of events and social circumstances.

612 **Army daze. The assorted misadventures of a national serviceman.**
Michael Chiang.   Singapore: Times Books International, 1985. 116p.
Chiang follows the literary style popularized by Sylvia Toh Paik Choo (see her contributions in this section) in a humorous narration of the daily life of a recruit doing his compulsory military service in Singapore. The reader will find a wealth of examples of the popular army 'lingo', which combines English, Malay, and an assortment of Chinese dialects.

613 **Singapore through sunshine and shadow.**
Bertram van Cuylenburg.   Singapore: Heinemann Educational Books (Asia), 1982. 264p.
In the preface of this book, the author indicated that 'this is a true personal narrative of Singapore as experienced by one who was born here and who has lived in this fascinating island almost all his life.' Those words were originally written in December 1961. Van Cuylenburg died in 1973 at the age of 77, but this

interesting autobiography was published only in 1982. The reader will appreciate its colourful and engaging interpretation of the life and mores of Singapore during the first half of this century.

614   **Poets of Singapore: 81 poems by 35 poets.**
    Compiled and edited by George Fernandez.   Singapore: Society
    of Singapore Writers, 1983. 92p.
The editor was President of the Society of Singapore Writers when the book was published. He presents a collection of poems from well-known writers in Singapore, adding a brief but informative introduction. A succinct biography of each poet precedes his or her contribution. This book is an informative introduction to the contemporary state of poetry in Singapore. While the task of selecting contributors is a complex one, a main gap in this book is the absence of Goh Poh Seng's poetry.

615   **If we dream too long.**
    Goh Poh Seng.   Singapore: Donald Moore, 1972. 177p.
Some literary critics consider this the first novel in English by a Singapore writer. The foreign reader may find the ideas of the novel's main character to be an interesting introduction to aspects of everyday life in Singapore.

616   **Bird with one wing: a sequence of poems.**
    Goh Poh Seng.   Singapore: Island Press, 1982. 65p.
One of the well-known literary figures in Singapore, Goh presents in this volume fourteen long poems and a useful glossary of terms and notes.

617   **The inner world of Lee Tzu Pheng's poetry.**
    Lucila Hosillos.   *Solidarity*, vol. 101 (1984), p. 45-51.
Analyses Lee's first book of poems, *Prospect of a Drowning*, published in 1980 (see reference in this section) and concludes that the power of this Singaporean poet is 'in the creation of memorable moments through personal use of language . . . in a poetic voice that invites lyric contemplation and reflection.'

618   **First loves.**
    Philip Jeyaretnam.   Singapore: Times Books International, 1987.
    200p.
A collection of twenty-one short stories by a young Singaporean writer. One of these won second prize in the 1983 National Short Story Writing Competition and another won first prize in the same competition in 1985. The stories are set in contemporary Singapore, and the book has been on the best seller list of fiction books in Singapore for several months.

619   **Oh no, its the Kitchi Boy gang!**
    Kitchi Boy.   Singapore: Times Books International, 1985. 173p.
This publication is a good example of humorous literature 'Singapore style'. It includes fifteen short stories depicting everyday life in Singapore narrated with a generous supply of local expressions common in colloquial Singapore English.

620 **Labour pains. Coming to grips with sexual inequality.**
Lai Ah Eng, Ng Chong Chu, Ngian Lek Choh, Karen Campbell-Nelson.   Singapore: Asiapac Books, 1984. 112p.

An entertaining piece of literary satire describing in a humorous and simple style scenes from the battle of the sexes, with frequent references to the situation in Singapore.

621 **Little ironies. Stories of Singapore.**
Catherine Lim.   Singapore: Heinemann Educational Books, 1978. 97p.

A collection of seventeen short stories about the daily lives of characters taken from the Chinese community in Singapore. While this is a work of fiction, the description of situations and the activities of the characters are realistic and provide an interesting and colourful portrait of life in Singapore.

622 **A bird's eye view of Singapore.**
Macaw.   Singapore: Times Books International, 1985. 144p.

An entertaining example of Singaporean humour in literature. Macaw, (a pen name) is well known as a writer of a column in a major English-language newspaper in Singapore. The non-Singaporean reader will find this small book an enjoyable journey through the by-roads of Singaporean English.

623 **Son of Singapore. The autobiography of a coolie.**
Tan Kok Seng.   Singapore: University Education Press, 1972. 132p.

This is a unique book on the literary scene in Singapore, as it represents the first time that a coolie, or unskilled labourer, has published his own life story. As indicated on the back cover of the book, Tan completed the book in Chinese and then narrated it in English (a language he learned on his own) to Austin Coates, who helped Tan to write the English version.

624 **Eh, Goondu!**
Sylvia Toh Paik Choo.   Singapore: Eastern Universities Press, 1982. 109p.

This slim book marks the entry of Paik Choo (her pen name) onto the best-seller list in Singapore. She is a pioneer of a special Singaporean style of humour in literature.

625 **The pick of Paik Choo.**
Sylvia Toh Paik Choo.   Singapore: Times Books International, 1982. 200p.

A collection of Paik Choo's best short stories written in her characteristic humorous style. See also *Friendship, courtship, hatred, love . . .* and other works by Sylvia Toh Paik Choo (pseud. Paik Choo) in this section.

626 **Friendship, courtship, hatred, love . . .**
Sylvia Toh Paik Choo.   Singapore: Times Books International,
1983. 135p.

A selection of items from the author's former 'Problem page', a section in the local magazine *Her World*, where she offered humorous 'advice' and answers to readers' letters under the pen name Paik Choo.

627 **Lagi Goondu!**
Sylvia Toh Paik Choo.   Singapore: Times Books International,
1986. 122p.

A sequel to the author's 1982 best seller *Eh, Goondu*! The author's style continues in this book, which offers seven pieces or short stories. See other works by Sylvia Toh Paik Choo (pseud. Paik Choo) listed in this section.

628 **The poetry of Singapore. Anthology of ASEAN literatures.**
Edited by Edwin Thumboo, Wong Yoon Wah, Lee Tzu Pheng,
Masuri bin Salikun, V. T. Arasu.   Singapore: The ASEAN
Committee on Culture and Information, 1985. 559p.

A very useful contribution to the dissemination of local literature among the country members of the Association of Southeast Asian Nations (ASEAN). The introduction, providing an overview of the book and of the state of literature in Singapore, is written by Thumboo. The other chapters are organized by language groups. Malay poetry in Singapore is presented and discussed by Masuri bin Salikun, followed by poems from twelve Malay poets. Each poem appears in its original Malay version as well as in English translation. The same system is followed for all the literary work in this book. The Tamil section features an introductory chapter by V. T. Arasu and the work of nine Tamil poets. The section on Chinese poetry is introduced by Wong Yoon Wah and consists of the work from forty Chinese poets. The final section deals with Singapore poetry in English; it is introduced by a chapter written by Lee Tzu Pheng and it covers the work of eighteen poets. There is a section with the biographical data of the poets featured in the book and an index to first lines of the English versions.

629 **Beyond symbols: selected poetry of Wong Yoon Wah.**
Wong Yoon Wah.   Singapore: Singapore Association of Writers,
1984. 72p.

Eighty-three of the author's poems originally published in Mandarin are included in this slim book. All the poems have been translated into English by the author himself.

# The Arts

### 630 The life and times of Singapore English drama. Loosening the chains.
David Birch. *Performing Arts*, no. 3 (1986), p. 28-32.

A discussion of the trials and tribulations of English drama in Singapore. Birch gives a brief background of its growth, focusing on the 1958-63 period and pointing to the continual search for cultural roots as an unresolved problem even today.

### 631 The Peranakan place. A symbol of Singapore's eclectic architectural heritage.
Chang Pai Ling. *Singa*, no. 10 (1985), p. 132-42.

A block of residential houses in the main tourist belt of Singapore has been preserved by the Urban Redevelopment Authority and named Peranakan Place. The author describes the conversion of this site into a museum-cum-entertainment complex, the implications of that move, and the artistic and architectural value of the houses.

### 632 Revived interest in Baba theatre.
Felix Chia. *Performing Arts*, no. 3 (1986), p. 1-5.

Describes and discusses the recent developments in Baba (Straits Chinese) theatre, emphasizing the interest awakened by a series of four plays performed within eighteen months, and the potential of Baba literature. Photographs of scenes from various plays are provided.

156

**633 Singapore's dance festival: achievements and implications.**
Chua Soo Pong. *Singa*, no. 4 (1982), p. 56-63.
The author provides details of the festival and explains briefly each dance, concluding that Singapore is now more prepared to provide an interested audience for a Singaporean form of dance. Colour photographs of some of the dances are included.

**634 Chinese opera in the park.**
Chua Soo Pong. *Performing Arts*, vol. 1 (1984), p. 9-12.
Describes the development and transformation that traditional Chinese opera has undergone in Singapore and the expression of such changes in the Chinese Opera Festival. The author suggests guidelines to preserve this rich cultural expression, which adds to the national culture of Singapore.

**635 Creative process of Chinese theatre dance in Singapore. 1946-1976.**
Chua Soo Pong. *Journal of the South Seas Society*, vol. 39 (1984), p. 79-89.
An anthropological discussion of the nature and development of Chinese theatre dance as a form of expressive culture in Singapore; the organizational structure, creative process, repertoire, and interaction with audiences of amateur dance groups; and the social and political aspects of dance creation.

**636 Impressions of the ballet workshop conducted by Belinda Wright and Yelko Yuresha.**
Cecilia Hon. *Singa*, no. 10 (1985), p. 126-31.
The Ministry of Community Development (formerly the Ministry of Social Affairs) invited dancers Belinda Wright and Yelko Yuresha to conduct a two-week course on all aspects of ballet for ballet students and dance professionals in Singapore from 18 to 29 March 1985. Cecilia Hon gives her views on the contents and usefulness of such a course, considering the previous experience of local dancers.

**637 The English language theatre in Singapore.**
Max Le Blond. In: *A drop of rain. A single flame.* Edited by June Lim, Peh Chon Seang. Singapore: Educational Publications Bureau, 1981, p. 12-15.
A brief description of the situation of English-language theatre, discussing the type of audience available, the government's position concerning the development of this type of local theatre, and providing some suggestions for the future.

**638 Drama.**
Max Le Blond. In: *Singapore studies: critical surveys of the humanities and social sciences.* Edited by Basant K. Kapur. Singapore: Singapore University Press, 1986, p. 478-80.
A brief but strong statement on the development of 'a truly indigenous Singaporean drama in English' by a well-informed writer, director, and university

lecturer. In his opinion, the Singapore theatre 'marks time, trapped between an old world that is dying and a new one awaiting to be born.' References to other critical essays on the Singapore theatre are provided.

### 639 Drama in Singapore: towards an English language theatre.
Max Le Blond.   In: *Discharging the cannon*. Edited by Peter Hyland. Singapore: Singapore University Press, 1986, p. 112-25.

The author firmly states his dismay again (see earlier items by him in this section) at the absence of 'a truly Singaporean theatre' with its own identity and independent of the 'English literary tradition'. The work of Singaporean playwrights up to now is seen by Le Blond as 'the poor relative' of Singaporean poetry and fiction, and he discusses possible reasons for this situation.

### 640 Prize winning plays.
Edited by Max Le Blond.   Singapore: Department of English Language and Literature, National University of Singapore, 1986. 135p. (NUS-Shell Short Plays Series vol. 1).

This first volume includes six short plays by Singaporean writers: *Ash and Shadowless* by Chua Tze Wei, *Reunion Dinner* by Daniel Koh, *In Praise of the Dentist* by Tan Tarn How and Cheam Li Chang, *The Amah – A Portrait in Black and White* by Christine Lim and Ophelia Ooi, *A Lowellian Drama: 'Tramps like Us* by Kelvin Tan and *Two's Company, or Peter's Passionate Pursuit* by Eleanor Wong.

### 641 In step with our nation's progress: 25 years of Chinese music.
Lee Ngoh Wah.   *Performing Arts*, no. 2 (1985), p. 13-15.

A brief but interesting description of the development of Chinese music in Singapore, tracing the historical background of Chinese orchestras and describing some key musical instruments.

### 642 Recent development in the contemporary music scene in Singapore.
Leong Yoon Pin.   *Performing Arts*, no. 2 (1985), p. 50-52.

Focuses on key personalities in music writing and performing in Singapore, describing the main contributions of each one, the environment in which they work, and the problems that they face, particularly the Singapore composers.

### 643 Audience profile of theatre-goers.
Liew Chin Choy.   *Singa*, no. 13 (1986), p. 60-66.

A brief report on the findings from a survey of the patrons of the 1985 Drama Festival held in Singapore and organized by the Ministry of Community Development (formerly the Ministry of Social Affairs).

644 **Prize winning plays.**
Edited by Arthur D. Lindley.   Singapore: Department of English
Language and Literature, National University of Singapore, 1987.
137p. (NUS-Shell Short Plays Series vol. 2).
Six short plays by local writers: *Pistachios and Whipped Cream* by Liew Kim
Siong, *I Do* by Sim Teow Li, *Two Men, Three Struggles* by Tan Tarn How, *The
Last Will and Testament* by Ngin Chiang Heng, and *Dead on Cue* by Ovidia Yu.

645 **Sculpture – the state of the art.**
Joseph McNally.   *Singa*, no. 11 (1985), p. 103-10.
A brief but informative discussion on the public's response to sculpture as an art-
form and its development in Singapore. Main historical aspects are listed, and
colour photographs of significant pieces are provided.

646 **National Theatre Trust annual report 1983/84.**
National Theatre Trust, Board of Directors.   Singapore: National
Theatre Trust, 1984. 29p.
This annual report provides an overview of the cultural activities planned,
organized, or sponsored by the National Theatre Trust in the areas of music,
dance, and theatre. It also gives details on the trust administration, management
personnel, and expenditure.

647 **Waiting in the wings: a critical look at Singapore's playscripts from
the 1960s and 1980.**
Seet Khiam Keong.   In: *Commentary* [Singapore], vol. 5, nos. 3
& 4 (1982), p. 47-55.
Seet explains why local drama in English began to emerge only in the 1960s and
compares its development with the more favourable climate for the development
of poetry in Singapore, a point also made by Arthur Yap and Max Le Blond (see
their contributions in this and the arts sections).

648 **ASEAN Sculpture Symposium. A report.**
Sng Boh Khim.   *Singa*, no. 4 (1982), p. 44-55.
A brief review of the first ASEAN (Association of Southeast Asian Nations)
Sculpture Symposium held in Singapore from March to May 1981. This was the
first of a planned series of five annual symposiums; five sculptors, one each from
the five member countries (there are six members of ASEAN today) met in
Singapore to create works of art under one roof. Sng describes and provides
colour photographs of the five sculptures completed in Singapore.

649 **A look at music in Singapore over the years.**
Patricia Wei.   *Singa*, no. 3 (1981), p. 62-68.
A colloquial and chronological description of changes in the public's taste for
classical music, the teaching of music in schools, and a brief survey of performing
groups in Singapore.

The Arts

650   **Chen Wen Hsi retrospective: 50 years as a painter.**
Arthur Yap.   *Singa*, no. 5 (1982), p. 98-108.

A very brief commentary on the work of Chen, an immigrant artist who arrived in Singapore from China in the early 1940s and decided to stay. Reproductions of thirteen of his paintings are included.

651   **Prize-winning plays. I. Ronald Alcantra, Stella Kon, Tan Sor Poh.**
Edited by Robert Yeo.   Singapore: Federal Publications, 1980.
145p.

Four winning entries to the Play-Writing Competition (English category) organized by the Ministry of Culture in 1977. The editor provides a brief explanatory introduction. The plays included are *The Scholar's Mother* by Stella Kon, *The Broken Image* by Tan Sor Poh, *The Heavens Have Eyes* by Tan Sor Poh, and *An Eclipse Leaves No Shadows* by Ronald Alcantra.

652   **Prize-winning plays. II. Koh Juan Toong, Elizabeth Su, Yeo Soh Choo.**
Edited by Robert Yeo.   Singapore: Federal Publications, 1980.
146p.

As in volume I, the editor has written an explanatory introduction. The three plays included in this volume won prizes in the Play-Writing Competition (English category) organized by the Ministry of Culture in 1977. The plays are *The Bringer of Wonder* by Koh Juan Toong, *After the Dazzle of Day* by Yeo Soh Choo, and *The Clown* by Elizabeth Su Pow Yuk.

653   **Prize-winning plays. III. Dorothy Jones, Stella Kon.**
Edited by Robert Yeo.   Singapore: Federal Publications, 1981.
193p.

As in volumes I and II, the two plays included in this volume won prizes in the Play-Writing Competion (English category) organized by the Ministry of Culture in 1977. The editor has written an explanatory introduction. The plays are *The Bridge* by Stella Kon and *Daring Deeds in Dustvillage* by Dorothy Jones. The first one is a musical drama, while the second is a romantic comedy and the only winning entry by a non-Singaporean.

# Sports and Recreation

654 **Who's who in sports in Malaysia and Singapore.**
Edited by Thomas R. P. Dawson. Petaling Jaya, Malaysia:
Who's Who in Sports, 1975. 724p.
The contribution of this publication rests on its historical value, as it provides a
picture of the sports personalities in Singapore, many of whom have had an
impact upon the sports scene in the 1980s.

655 **Recreation and the community: Regional Congress on Parks and
Recreation, Singapore.**
Edited by Otto Fung Wai Chan, Ng Siew Yin. Singapore:
Institute of Parks and Recreation, 1981. 47p. maps.
A collection of the papers presented at the First Regional Congress on Parks and
Recreation organized by the Institute of Parks and Recreation in Singapore, 10 to
13 July 1981. The congress's main goal was to discuss the provision, usage, and
management of parks and recreational facilities.

656 **Sports medicine in Singapore (1972-1984).**
C. K. Giam, K. C. Teh. *Singapore Family Physician*, vol. 10,
no. 1 (Jan.-Mar. 1984), p. 18-21.
A brief but informative description of the field of sports medicine in general and
its development, successes, and gaps in Singapore.

161

657  **Social integration, alienation and leisure activity among workers in Singapore.**
Mak Lau Fong. *National Taiwan University Journal of Sociology*, vol. 14 (1980), p. 143-65.

A discussion of the link between recreation and leisure time on the one hand and workers attitudes towards the community and their feelings of alienation on the other.

658  **SHELL Sports Club.**
*Singapore Institute of Architects Journal (SIAJ)*, vol. 111 (Mar./ Apr. 1982), p. 22-23.

A brief description of the activities and facilities of the sports club of the SHELL Corporation. The reader will find in the same issue of this journal similar descriptions of other sports clubs and sports and recreational facilities in Singapore such as the Singapore Airlines (SIA) Group sports complex, the Chinese Swimming Club, the St. Wilfrid Road sports complex, the Jurong Country Club, the Tanglin Club, the Squash and Tennis Centre, and the Changi Sailing Club.

659  **Bukit Merah town centre swimming complex.**
*Singapore Institute of Architects Journal (SIAJ)*, vol. 112 (May/June 1982), p. 14-16.

A description of the facilities and adminstration of this neighbourhood recreational centre. The reader will find in the same issue of this journal similar brief descriptions of the Bedok Swimming Complex, the Ang Mo Kio South Swimming Complex, the Kallang Basin Neighbourhood 3 Swimming Complex, the Big Splash sports complex, the Delta Sports and Swimming complex; and the Housing and Development Board swimming complexes.

660  **Singapore Recreational Club 100th anniversary.**
Singapore Recreational Club.   Singapore: Singapore Recreational Club, 1983. 135p.

This is the centennial celebration publication of the Singapore Recreational Club, which opened in 1883. It provides interesting details on sports and recreation during the colonial period in Singapore.

661  **Singapore Sports Council annual report.**
Singapore Sports Council.   Singapore: Singapore Sports Council, 1973.

This is, perhaps, the best and most reliable source of information concerning the government's involvement in the promotion and organization of sports activities in Singapore.

662 **Singapore Sports Council. First ten years.**
Singapore Sports Council. Singapore: Singapore Sports Council,
1983. 104p. maps.
An informative publication describing the accomplishments and work of the
Singapore Sports Council.

663 **The national household sports survey: participation and non-participation among respondents.**
Singapore Sports Council. Singapore: Singapore Sports Council,
July 1984. 29p. (Research Paper 17/84. Release no. 1).
The first national survey on the population's practice of sports and regular
exercise. The findings reported here were obtained from a random sample of
2,015 persons. The report may be obtained from the Singapore Sports Council,
National Stadium, Kallang, Singapore 1439.

664 **Recreational facilities in Singapore.**
Russell A. Smith. *Singapore Professionals*, vol. 10, no. 1 (1985),
p. 28-33.
An overview of the recreational centres and their main characteristics in
Singapore.

665 **Recreation for high-rise residential living in Singapore.**
Russell A. Smith. *Singapore Institute of Architects Journal
(SIAJ)*, vol. 139 (Nov./Dec. 1986), p. 15-23.
Emphasizes the importance of looking after the recreational needs of the
population living in high-rise apartments, considering that over 80 per cent of the
population in Singapore enjoy that type of accommodation. Briefly describes the
facilities available and evaluates their suitability.

# Libraries and Museums

666 **Experiencing and documenting 25 years (1959-1984) of librarianship.**
Chan Thye Seng. *Singapore Libraries*, vol. 14 (1984), p. 3-6.
A brief but informative account of the work of the librarianship profession in Singapore since independence.

667 **A special library takes shape: the Public Works Department Library.**
Lily Chow. *Singapore Libraries*, vol. 16 (1986), p. 35-39.
The plans and implementation of the Public Works Department's library project, giving a summary of its main features and purpose.

668 **A mirror of minds? Libraries and librarianship in Singapore.**
Jim Davies. *Singapore Libraries*, vol. 14 (1984), p. 47-50.
A personal view of the profession and its constraints and growth in Singapore.

669 **Why automate? The impact of automation on library function, administration and staffing in the NUS Library.**
Peggy W. C. Hochstadt. *Singapore Libraries*, vol. 16 (1986), p. 15-28.
Examines the system of evaluation of the computerization of library services at the National University of Singapore (NUS) as ascertained by the author, who is the NUS Chief Librarian.

670  Towards an online integrated system at the National University of
Singapore Library.
Peggy W. C. Hochstadt, Jill Quah, Ong Gim Hong.  *Singapore
Libraries*, vol. 12 (1982), p. 43-54.

A comprehensive discussion of the computerization of library services at the
National University of Singapore; its planning and progressive implementation;
and the specific aspects of automation, information storage, and retrieval systems.

671  Twenty-seven eventful years, a chronicle of LAS activities, 1955-
1982.
Library Association of Singapore (LAS).  *Singapore Libraries*,
vol. 12 (1982), p. 3-13.

A good account of the professional activities of librarians in Singapore, the
growth of libraries, and expansion of library services is obtained in this article on
the Library Association of Singapore (LAS).

672  LAS news.
Library Association of Singapore (LAS).  Singapore: LAS, 1984-
(quarterly).

Provides information on the management, development, and upgrading of library
facilities as well as news pertaining to the association and matters of relevance to
the profession.

673  Access to information in Singapore.
Lim Hong Too.  *Singapore Libraries*, vol. 11 (1981), p. 11-19.

A description of the available library services concerning information distribution
facilities and bibliographical services in the early 1980s.

674  Problems of distribution and marketing of scientific, technical and
medical journals across the Pacific: a view from Singapore.
Lena U. W. Lim.  *Singapore Book World*, vol. 18, no.1 (1987),
p. 17-28.

The author presents her views based on her actual experience as general manager
of a bookstore in Singapore, discussing not only the marketing but also the
publishing aspects of works in the fields of science and medicine. Moreover, Lim's
training as a professional librarian helps her to assess the intricacies of reaching
target groups, including libraries and other institutions.

675  Library services in financial institutions in Singapore.
Lim Yong Yong.  Loughborough, England: Loughborough
University of Technology, 1985. 80p.

An informative description indicating the trend towards an increased awareness of
the need for library and information services in the financial sector.

676 **National Library annual report.**
National Library.   Singapore: Government Printing Office, 1952.
This official account of the Singapore National Library provides useful
information on library facilities in Singapore and the rapid expansion of such
services during the past decade.

677 **Heritage.**
National Museum.   Singapore: National Museum, vol. 8, 1986.
58p.
The first issue of this periodical was launched in January 1977 by the National
Museum Director, Christopher Hooi. This publication contains articles on
ethnology, history, and art as well as information on the current activities of the
National Museum.

678 **National University of Singapore Library rules.**
National University of Singapore Library.   Singapore: National
University of Singapore Library, 1981. 5p.
This booklet is periodically updated as the library expands its facilities and
services.

679 **National University of Singapore staff handbook for administrative
and library staff.**
National University of Singapore (NUS), Personnel Department.
Singapore: NUS, 1986. [not paginated].
A description of the basic guidelines on duties, rules, and regulations applicable
to all NUS administrative and library staff.

680 **NTI library bulletin.**
Nanyang Technological Institute (NTI) Library.   Singapore:
Nanyang Technological Institute Library, 1982- (irregular).
This bulletin includes news on the NTI Library's activities, holdings and its
accessions list.

681 **Planning for the adoption of *AARC 2* at the National University of
Singapore Library with special reference to the Singapore/Malaysia
collection.**
Jill Quah.   *Singapore Libraries*, vol. 10 (1980), p. 30-40.
Describes the plans to adopt the *Anglo-American Cataloguing Rules*, 2nd edition
*(AACR 2)* to the cataloguing of special collections, particularly in university and
college libraries. The discussion focuses on the Singapore/Malaysia collection at
the National University Library to illustrate specific aspects of implementation.

682   **Place for the people. The history of a national library.**
      Seet Khiam Keong.   Singapore: Times Books International, 1983.
      176p.
An informative book on the origins, work, and development of the Singapore
National Library.

683   **Online information retrieval service at the Medical Library,
      National University of Singapore.**
      Seow Nyuk Yin.   *Singapore Libraries*, vol. 16 (1986), p. 53-58.
The computerization of the university library system has benefited all users in
various ways, and the author describes in this article the information services
available to the National University's medical students and faculty.

684   **Mendaki Foundation home library and reading project.**
      Siti Hanifa Mustapha.   *Singapore Libraries*, vol. 13 (1983),
      p. 25-27.
A brief but informative description of the project by the Council for the
Education of Muslim Children (MENDAKI in Malay) to facilitate Muslim
children's access to books and to motivate the reading habit among them.

685   **Directory of libraries in Singapore.**
      Edited by Sng Yok Fong, Lau Siew Kheng, Khoo Guan Fong.
      Singapore: Library Association of Singapore, 1983. 3rd ed. 194p.
The latest edition of a useful reference book which needs to be updated
periodically, given the continuous improvements and expansion of library services
in Singapore.

686   **Towards productivity gains: the role of high technology, abstracting
      and indexing services in national development.**
      Sundusia Rosdi.   *Singapore Libraries*, vol. 16 (1986), p. 63-74.
An interesting discussion on the advantages of incorporating advanced computer
technology into the librarians' work in general and, particularly, in the context of
Singapore's increasing information needs.

687   **Some thoughts on continuing education for library and information
      science.**
      Ajita Thuraisingham.   *Singapore Libraries*, vol. 15 (1985), p. 3-9.
A succinct discussion of the advantages and problems of continuing education in
this field.

# Directories

688  **German business firms and their representatives in Singapore 1982.**
Federal Republic of Germany Embassy.  Singapore: Kompass
Singapore, 1982. 136p.

A directory of West German institutions represented in Singapore, including
business firms or their representatives, products, services, trade marks, and
agencies.

689  **Real estate directory of Singapore.**
Homes International Pte. Ltd.  Singapore: Homes International,
July-Sept. 1987. 128p.

This directory lists residential, commercial, and industrial property real estate
services, and related products. The information provided includes an orientation
map, an area checklist, and a development checklist.

690  **Directory of French businesses in Singapore.**
Kompass/Embassy Information Pte. Ltd.  Singapore:
Kompass/Embassy Information, 1984. 4th ed. 87p.

After describing the main economic and trade bodies in France and Singapore,
this directory lists the French companies, agents, distributors, products and
services in Singapore.

691  **Directory of American businesses in Singapore.**
Kompass South East Asia Ltd.  Singapore: Kompass South East
Asia, 1985. 212p. map. (annual).

Informative descriptions of important representatives of the United States
economy in Singapore and listings of United States companies, principals, their
agents and distributors, products, and services.

168

692 **Directory of British businesses in Singapore.**
Kompass South East Asia Ltd. ' Singapore: Kompass South East
Asia, 1985. 4th ed. 179p.

The publisher includes in this directory some basic information on the British
High Commission and its Commerce Department, other British and Singaporean
economic institutions, and listings of British company agents, distributors,
products, and services.

693 **Directory of Italian businesses in Singapore.**
Kompass South East Asia Ltd. Singapore: Kompass South East
Asia, 1986. 4th ed. 98p.

A description of the Singapore Economic Development Board and the Trade
Development Board and listings of Italian companies, agents, distributors,
products, and services.

694 **Directory of Singapore exporters 1980.**
Compiled by M & L Trade Services Company. Singapore: M & L
Trade Services Company, 1980. 221p.

There are four sections in this directory: an alphabetical list of exporters, a listing
of general merchandise exporters and export-related services, a product
classification, and a classification by industries.

695 **Singapore government directory January 1988.**
Ministry of Communications and Information, Information
Division. Singapore: Ministry of Communications and
Information, 1988. 514p.

A complete and current listing of all government bodies and officers in charge
including name, telex, facsimile, telebox and address of department or section;
and position, name, and telephone numbers of officer(s) in charge. There is an
alphabetical index of names and a table of telex, facsimile, and telebox numbers
of government organizations listed in alphabetical order.

696 **Singapore architects and builders directory 1986.**
Pacific Trade Press. Singapore: Pacific Trade Press, 1986.
1197p.

This directory has four sections: an alphabetical list of companies, a buyer's
guide, a trade names list, and a listing of official government departments and
statutory boards dealing with the building industry. The latter listing is presented
in three categories, namely, professional institutes, trade associations, and
licensed contractors.

697 **The SIET yearbook and directory of members.**
Singapore Institute of Engineering Technologists (SIET).
Singapore: SIET, 1986. 384p.

In addition to the directory of members, this yearbook presents a list of the SIET
executive council and subcommittees, the SIET constitution, by-laws, examinations,

**Directories**

new courses, events of the year, and articles on various professional topics of interest to engineering technologists.

698   **Tradelink 1987/88 SMA directory.**
Singapore Manufacturers' Association.   Singapore: Singapore
Manufacturers' Association, 1987. 470p.

This publication, formerly the Singapore Manufacturers' Association directory, is an information sourcebook on important sectors of the Singapore economy such as manufacturing and trade. It includes guidelines on 'doing business in Singapore', tax and investment incentives, a brief description of the manufacturing sector, and sections dedicated to specific industries such as food and beverages; pharmaceuticals; garments; wood and furniture; printing, publishing and packing; petroleum, chemicals, and oils; building materials; automation equipment and industrial robots; aircraft-related industries; ocean engineering, shipbuilding, shiprepairing, and oil-rig construction; plastics; and electronics and electrical industries. It also includes a product and service listing, a brand/trade name index, and reference addresses.

699   **Directory of EEC businesses in Singapore/Malaysia.**
Harry Tan, Khai Tamin.   Singapore: Kompass/Embassy
Information, 1983. 480p. maps.

This is the first edition of a directory dedicated to the European Economic Community (EEC) business in Singapore. It includes articles on the investment environment of Singapore and Malaysia, key economic institutions, business groups, and business arrangements. There are also listings and indexes of companies, distributors, products, services, and brand and trade names.

700   **Times business directory of Singapore.**
Times Periodicals Pte. Ltd.   Singapore: Times Periodicals, 1984.
302p.

This annual directory lists relevant business information in two sections. The white pages section presents the local and foreign companies index, the personnel index, the product and brand names index, a Singapore general index, a directory of officials and public bodies, a general information section, the postal codes section, and the buildings and locations index. The pink pages section includes, among other relevant information, a classified index of products.

701   **Builders index 1986/87.**
Westin Media Pte. Ltd.   Singapore: Westin Media, 1986. 984p.

The publishers present this index as a directory and buyers' guide for builders, contractors, architects, surveyors, interior designers, government departments, and people interested in the construction industry. It consists of four sections: professional, trade, and government bodies; an alphabetical list of companies; products and services; and trade names.

702 **CIDB directory of registered contractors 1986.**
Yap Neng Chew. Singapore: Construction Industry Development
Board (CIDB), 1986. 360p.

The CIDB was set up in 1984 to oversee the construction industry and to establish
the Registry of Public Sector Contractors. Preceding the list of registered
contractors, the directory includes a description of the CIDB and its organizational structure, information on the registry, instructions on how to apply and
the conditions for registration, and a profile of major contractors.

**Directory of community and social services for senior citizens.**
*See* item no. 256.

**Directory of social services.**
*See* item no. 260.

# Mass Media

703 **Communication policy and planning in relation to socio-cultural development: the Singapore case.**
Chang Chen Tung. In: *Proceedings of the ASEAN Seminar on the Role of Communication in Socio-Cultural Development*.
Bangkok: ASEAN, 1983, 24p. [no consecutive pagination].
A review of official policies on mass communication including the use of official languages in programme broadcasting; the coverage of ethnically or religiously offensive themes or issues; and the description of some specific projects in communications development.

704 **The early Chinese newspapers of Singapore 1881-1912.**
Cheng Mong Hock. Singapore: University of Malaya Press, 1968. 171p.
A detailed and interesting account of the social conditions that served as background to the setting up of the various Chinese newspapers in Singapore. The text is full of references to Chinese names in Chinese characters. There are also detailed footnotes, relevant illustrations and plates of newspaper pages, photographs, a glossary of terms, and the advertising rates of the Chinese newspaper *Nayang Siang Pau* in 1967.

705 **Chinese television drama: a sociological perspective on Chinese values and popular mass entertainment.**
John R. Clammer. *Asian Culture*, vol. 4, no. 1 (1984), p. 63-67.
An analysis of popular Mandarin television dramas in Singapore, the main values presented, and the characterization of women, youth, and the elderly.

706 **Television in Singapore: an analysis of a week's viewing.**
Erhard U. Heidt.   Singapore: Institute of Southeast Asian
Studies, 1984. 71p.
A presentation and discussion of information collected on television viewing and
identity, range of programmes, broadcasting languages, foreign programmes, and
serialization.

707 **Communication policy and national development.**
Eddie C. Y. Kuo.   In: *Singapore: development policies and
trends.* Edited by Peter S. J. Chen. Singapore: Oxford University
Press, 1983, p. 268-81.
The author reports the findings of his study of parliamentary records and political
leaders' speeches from which main guiding principles on communication policy
were identified and discusses the main trends in the development of mass media,
particularly the aspect of responsible journalism.

708 **Communication policy and planning in Singapore.**
Eddie C. Y. Kuo, Peter S. J. Chen.   London: Kegan Paul;
Honolulu: East-West Communication Institute, 1983. 111p.
The discussion is presented in nine chapters and further details are provided in
three appendixes. The first chapter introduces the sources of information for this
study, i.e. official documents, interviews with community and media leaders and
government officials, and data from a mass media survey of 612 Singaporeans.
The second chapter provides a historical background of Singapore. The other
seven chapters deal with the components of the communication system, media
habits and information needs, communication policies and laws, and two cases to
illustrate communication planning.

709 **Mass media and language planning: Singapore's 'Speak Mandarin'
campaign.**
Eddie C. Y. Kuo.   *Journal of Communication*, vol. 34, no.2
(1984), p. 24-35.
An analysis of the campaign to encourage the speaking of Mandarin among
Chinese speakers since its launching in 1979, the role of mass media in the
implementation phase of the campaign, and the salient role played by radio and
television.

710 **Television and language planning in Singapore.**
Eddie C. Y. Kuo.   *International Journal of Sociology of
Language*, vol. 48 (1984), p. 49-64.
Television has played a very important role in supporting and reinforcing official
language policies in Singapore. This has been made possible through coordination
of efforts between the government-owned Singapore Broadcasting Corporation
and other government bodies.

711 **Communications in Singapore.**
Tham Seong Chee, H. C. Wong. Singapore: Singapore
Association for the Advancement of Science, Singapore Science
Centre, and The United Nations Association of Singapore, 1985.
58p.

A collection of papers presented at a seminar on communications in Singapore
organized by the above groups in 1984. The papers deal with various modes of
communication and communication services in the context of Singapore's aim to
become the communications centre of the region.

# Professional
# Periodicals

712  **Annals of the Academy of Medicine Singapore.**
Singapore: Academy of Medicine, 1972- (quarterly).
This is the official organ of the Academy of Medicine of Singapore. Its articles are on the practice of medicine and occasionally on multidisciplinary themes of importance to physicians.

713  **ARTS Diary.**
Cultural Affairs Division, Ministry of Community Development.
Singapore: Ministry of Community Development, 1986- (monthly).
This is a newsletter with a difference. While its main objective is to provide detailed information on cultural events in Singapore on a monthly basis, a lot of effort has been put into its presentation and contents. There are brief but educational articles on theatre, music, and the arts in general, and it includes colour and black-and-white photographs enhancing the already attractive format.

714  **ASEAN Economic Bulletin.**
Singapore: Institute of Southeast Asian Studies, 1984- (thrice annually).
The *ASEAN Economic Bulletin* appears in July, November, and March. It focuses on economic events and economic relations affecting ASEAN (Association of Southeast Asian Nations, which has currently six country members, namely, Brunei, Indonesia, Malaysia, Philippines, Singapore and Thailand), including economic aspects of ASEAN relations to other individual nations and to international and regional organizations.

## Professional Periodicals

715 **ASEAN Journal of Clinical Sciences.**
Edited by Wong Hock Boon. Singapore: Melirwin Enterprises, 1981- (quarterly).

The aim of this publication is to promote exchanges among clinicians, pharmacists, and scientists working in all aspects of clinical sciences in the ASEAN (Association of Southeast Asian Nations) and Pacific region. Papers published cover the fields of biochemistry, microbiology, immunology, haematology, pathology, cytology, pharmacology, and pharmaceutical sciences in relation to medicine and surgery.

716 **Asia-Pacific International and Strategic Studies Newsletter.**
Singapore: Institute of Southeast Asian Studies, 1984- (thrice annually).

This newsletter deals with experts' views in the fields of international relations and politics.

717 **Contemporary Southeast Asia.**
Singapore: Institute of Southeast Asian Studies, 1979- (quarterly).

Appears in March, June, September, and December and deals mostly with political and economic aspects of international relations in the region.

718 **Gardens' Bulletin Singapore.**
Singapore: Botanic Gardens and Park and Recreation Department, Ministry of National Development, 1948- (semi-annual).

Presents professional articles in the fields of botany, horticulture, and allied subjects.

719 **Institution of Engineers Singapore Yearbook.**
Singapore: Institution of Engineers Singapore (IES), 1971- (annual).

Contains relevant information on the profession, including the IES council members, IES committees, the IES president's annual report, the IES chairman's report on graduates and students, income and expenditure, membership statistics, the National Day honours, and a historical background of IES, its constitution, and other matters.

720 **Journal of Southeast Asian Studies.**
Singapore: History Department, National University of Singapore and Singapore University Press, 1970- (semi-annual).

This journal includes articles on social, political, and economic aspects of the nations and communities in the region of Southeast Asia. Contributors are usually scholars in the social sciences and humanities, such as history, economics, political science, sociology, anthropology, and literature. Its predecessor was the *Journal of Southeast Asian History.*

176

721 **Journal of the Singapore National Academy of Science.**
Edited by A. N. Rao.   Singapore: Singapore National Academy
of Science, 1972- (irregular, annually or semi-annually).
The objective of this journal is to disseminate scholarly and scientific papers on
the biological, chemical, and physical sciences from Singapore or the region.

722 **Journal of the Singapore Paediatric Society.**
Edited by Wong Hock Boon.   Singapore: The Singapore
Paediatric Society, 1959- (semi-annual).
This is the official publication of the Singapore Paediatric Society. It contains
articles on specific aspects of the practice of paediatrics as well as more general
medical papers, a section on letters to the editor, and an author and subject
index.

723 **Performing Arts.**
Singapore: National Theatre Dance Circle, 1984- (annual).
A journal intended to stimulate interest in the arts and to serve as a forum for
views, comments, news, and discussions on the arts in Singapore and the region.
With *Singa*, this is the second vehicle of expression for serious artists, critics, and
other experts in the arts. (See item on *Singa* elsewhere in this section).

724 **Public Employee Magazine.**
Edited by Paul Tan.   Singapore: Amalgamated Union of Public
Employees (AUPE), 1982- (annual).
This is the AUPE's annual publication covering a review of the union's activities
during the year, a message from AUPE's president, a few articles on union
matters by officials and regular members, and other aspects of general interest.

725 **Science and Technology Quarterly**
Singapore: Science Council of Singapore, 1980- (quarterly).
The first issue appeared in July 1980. The main objective of this periodical is
twofold: to disseminate information on technological developments in a clear and
concise manner to planners and decision-makers, and to collate data on the role
and application of technology in Singapore's economic and industrial
development.

726 **Seafarer.**
Singapore: National Maritine Board, 1976- (bi-monthly).
The National Maritine Board (NMB) is a statutory body incorporated in 1973 and
amalgamating five bodies, i.e., the Seamen's Registry Board, the Seafarers'
Welfare Board, the Singapore Mariners' Club, the Singapore Sailors' Institute,
and the Seamen's Lodging Houses Authority. The NMB develops, promotes and
regulates employment among members of the merchant marine and provides,
promotes, and administers training schemes. This is the official newsletter of the
NMB and its objective is to improve communication among seafarers, shipping

employers, and the NMB. It publishes news and brief articles on the trade, relevant legislation, main events of the NMB, safety, jobs, training courses, and others news. Articles are written in English, Malay, and Mandarin.

727 **Singa. Literature and the Arts in Singapore.**
Singapore: Ministery of Culture, Cultural Affairs Division, 1980- (bi-annual).

The Cultural Affairs Division is now under the new Ministry of Community Development. The journal's objective is to disseminate original creative writing by Singaporeans either in English or translations of their original Malay, Mandarin, or Tamil literary work. It also includes papers, reviews, and surveys of music, painting, dance, drama, and other art expressions.

728 **Singapore Business.**
Edited by Mano Sabnani. Singapore: Times Periodicals, 1976- (monthly).

Covers articles on various regular aspects of business in Singapore such as real estate, banking, the national budget, multinationals, legislation relevant to the business community, international trade, business law, new companies and products, investment, key business indicators, new appointments in the executive ranks of the business community, a few features articles, and a special interest essay every month.

729 **Singapore Business Yearbook.**
Singapore: Times Periodicals, 1978- (annual).

Covers articles on the Singapore economy as well as on relevant aspects of the regional and international economic situation, the national budget statement, the top companies, and other aspects of interest to the business community in Singapore.

730 **Singapore Community Health Bulletin.**
Singapore: Ministry of Health and Ministry of the Environment, 1958- (annual).

This bulletin has published brief papers and notes on public health themes such as health education, prevention programmes, school health activities, care of the elderly, and the like. There was no issue for 1985; issue no. 26 covers the years 1986-87, and was released in late 1987. The bulletin has been discontinued after that issue.

731 **Singapore Dental Journal.**
Edited by Keng Siong Beng. Singapore: Singapore Dental Association, 1976- (bi-annual).

This is the official journal of the Singapore Dental Association. It publishes articles on the medical and pharmacological aspects of dentistry as well as news on professional activities, congresses, conventions, and matters pertaining to the running of the Dental Association.

732 **Singapore Economic Review (formerly the Malayan Economic Review).**
Singapore: Economic Society of Singapore and the Department of Economics and Statistics, National University of Singapore, 1956- (bi-annual).

The official journal of the Economic Society of Singapore and the Department of Economics and Statistics, National University of Singapore. It publishes scholarly papers in the field of economics and related subjects in Singapore and the region.

733 **Singapore Family Physician.**
Singapore: College of General Practitioners, Singapore, 1975- (quarterly).

This is the official journal of the College of General Practitioners. Its regular features are an editorial, a section on original papers on general aspects of medical practice, a 'home study' section on scientific discussions and quizzes, and a section on news and notes from the college's council.

734 **Singapore Handicaps' Digest.**
Edited by Gerald Pereira. Singapore: Handicaps Welfare Association, 1975- (bi-monthly).

This is the official publication of the Handicaps Welfare Association and formerly published under the title *Handicaps' Monthly*. It includes articles of special interest to the handicapped such as new developments in mechanical aids, procedures or tips to increase self-reliance in daily living, job opportunities, training, recreation, communication among members, and mutual assistance schemes.

735 **Singapore Journal of Obstetrics and Gynaecology.**
Edited by D. K. Sen. Singapore: Obstetrical and Gynaecological Society of Singapore, 1970- (thrice yearly).

Official journal of the Obstetrical and Gynaecological Society, the publication regularly includes an editorial statement, review articles, special feature articles, original articles, and case reports. While most of the articles deal exclusively with medical topics in obstetrics and gynaecology, some articles discuss wider (but related) issues such as adolescent sexuality.

736 **Singapore Journal of Physics.**
Edited by Tan Kuang Lee. Singapore: Institute of Physics, 1984- (annual).

The predecessor of this journal was the *Institute of Physics Singapore Bulletin*, which was expanded and renamed with the above title in 1984. It now includes scientific papers from physicists in Singapore and the Asia Pacific region on completed research, theoretical discussions, and notes on research in progress.

**Professional Periodicals**

737  **Singapore Journal of Primary Industries.**
Primary Production Department.  Singapore: Primary Production
Department, 1973- (semi-annual).

This journal is published twice a year (January and July). It presents articles on original research findings and reviews of research in progress in the fields of fisheries, horticulture, animal husbandry, veterinary science, and related subjects.

738  **Singapore Journal of Tropical Geography.**
Singapore: Department of Geography, National University of
Singapore, 1980- (semi-annual).

This professional journal is published in June and December. It deals with subjects relevant to geographers such as biogeography, economic, political, social, and urban geography, climate, energy and natural resources, geomorphology, hydrology, land utilization, population and settlement, regional planning, transport, and communication. Articles published in this journal cover various regions in the world such as African, Arab, American, Asian, and Pacific tropical areas in addition to articles dealing specifically with Malaysia and Singapore. The history of this journal goes back to 1953, when the first issue of its predecessor, the *Malayan Journal of Tropical Geography*, was published. The name was changed later to *Journal of Tropical Geography*. The last volume under that name was volume 49, completed in December 1979. The current title was adopted in 1980, with volume 1 appearing in January of that year.

739  **Singapore Medical Journal.**
Singapore: Singapore Medical Association, 1960- (bimestrial).

This is the official journal of the Singapore Medical Association. It appears in February, April, June, August, October, and December and covers articles on medicine and related disciplines and on other aspects of interest to the medical profession.

740  **Singapore Paraplegics.**
Singapore: Society for Aid to the Paralysed, 1976- (monthly).

This magazine is the official publication of the Society for Aid to the Paralysed. It publishes brief articles on new developments in physical aids to help mobility, mutual-help projects and ideas, communication notes among the members, foreign and local news relevant to the handicapped, and sports and social events.

741  **Singapore Portworker.**
Singapore: Singapore Port Workers Union, 1981- (irregular, four
to five times a year).

The official publication of the Singapore Port Workers Union. It covers articles on pension rules, safety, workers' welfare, union elections, social activities and administrative matters, and educational and informative pieces such as those on the world economic crisis and international affairs.

742 **Singapore Safety News.**
Edited by Woo Yuen Hoong.    Singapore: National Productivity
Board, 1982- (bimestrial).

This is a publication on health and safety on the job, including brief articles on industrial safety, health education, legislation on labour and safety, reviews of books or publications on matters relevant to workers' health, quality circles, industrial diseases, and other matters. While originally it was published every two months, it has been a monthly magazine since 1985.

743 **Singapore Scientist.**
Edited by Woo Yuen Hoong.    Singapore: Singapore Science
Centre, 1974- (quarterly).

Addresses school children and aims at providing further information and promoting interest in their science courses by dealing with various topics found in the schools' science curriculum in Singapore. The articles are brief, written in clear language, and well illustrated with colour photographs and graphs. It also includes a question and answer section, letters from readers, and science contests.

744 **Singapore Standards Yearbook.**
Singapore Institute of Standards and Industrial Research
(SISIR).    Singapore: SISIR, 1977- (annual).

A reference to all published Singapore manufacturing standards, including material specifications, codes of practice, glossary of terms, list of preferred sizes, and a list of publications useful to both industrialists and consumers. From 1986, the yearbook will be published once every two years and an addendum will be released in the interim year.

745 **Singapore Veterinary Journal.**
Edited by T. T. Ngiam.    Singapore: Singapore Veterinarian
Association, 1977- (annual).

This is the official journal of the Singapore Veterinary Association. It includes scholarly and scientific papers on practical as well as theoretical aspects in the field, reviews of relevant publications, letters from readers, and professional discussions.

746 **Singaporean News.**
Singapore: National Trade Union Congress (NTUC), 1980- (twice
monthly).

The NTUC's official and bilingual (English and Mandarin) newspaper, covering various aspects of interest to Singapore workers such as labour legislation, skills upgrading programmes, recreation, sports, competitions, union official activities, highlights of events from different member unions, and other articles of national interest.

747    **Sojourn. Social Issues in Southeast Asia.**
Singapore: Institute of Southeast Asian Studies, 1986- (semi-annual).

One of the most recent professional journals, this periodical publishes papers on ethnicity, religion, urbanism, demography, and other social issues. It has a regional advisory board and editorial committee.

748    **Southeast Asian Affairs.**
Singapore: Institute of Southeast Asian Studies, 1974- (annual).

A review of current and relevant political, economic, and social events in Southeast Asia. Every annual issue contains chapters dedicated to specific countries and, commonly, the invited authors are writers, analysts, or scholars native of the country on which they write. The 1987 issue contains twenty papers on the progress of the regional organization ASEAN, Indonesia under Suharto, the latest parliamentary elections in Malaysia, the Singapore economy, and the military in Thailand's political scene, among other topics.

749    **Southeast Asian Journal of Social Science.**
Singapore: Department of Sociology, National University of Singapore and Singapore University Press, 1973- (semi-annual).

A multi-disciplinary journal covering papers on the social sciences. It appears in May and October and it regularly includes an issue covering papers on one theme.

750    **Speeches. A Bi-monthly Selection of Ministerial Speeches.**
Singapore: Information Division, Ministry of Communications and Information, 1977- (six times a year).

A useful publication providing the full text of speeches given by ministers and ministers of state, with a final caption concerning the place and date of every speech. The table of contents lists the speech titles, the names of the ministers, and their portfolios.

# Bibliographies

751 **Singapore national bibliography 1985.**
Edited by Chang Soh Choo. Singapore: Singapore National
Library, 1986. 351p.

Lists all works published in Singapore during the year and deposited at the
National Library under the Printers and Publishers Act of 1970. The material
included covers books and pamphlets whether for sale or not; government
publications; serials; maps; music; and any other material that may reflect the
social, cultural, and other aspects of the country. It excludes university theses, as
these can be found in the National University of Singapore *Publications and
theses* (see item elsewhere in this section). Items are classified by subject and
alphabetically by author. There is an author and title index in English, Mandarin,
and Tamil and a list of publishers.

752 **Singapore books in print 1986.**
Festival of Books Singapore Pte. Ltd. Singapore: Festival of
Books Singapore, 1986. 383p.

A bibliography of titles published in English in Singapore, excluding school
textbooks, workbooks, and books or serials not for sale or which are for limited
distribution only. There are four sections – authors, titles, subject, and series –
and two lists on abbreviations and publishers. Each entry includes author, editor,
title, publisher, year of publication, number of pages, price, and the International
Standard Book Number (ISBN). The time span covered is 1968 to 1985, and there
are approximately 1,950 entries.

753 **Family planning and population, Singapore. A bibliography with selected annotations.**
Compiled by J. Heng, A. J. Chen.   Singapore: Singapore Family Planning and Population Board, 1981. 239p.

There are two parts in this bibliography. Part I lists entries alphabetically by author. Part II is a list by subject with annotations, covering fourteen themes such as contraception policies, sociocultural factors, and other aspects of population control.

754 **A select bibliography on social issues, social services and social work in Singapore and Malaysia: based on publications of staff and graduates of the Department of Social Work, National University of Singapore, 1984.**
Edited by Lim Bee Lum, Ngiam Tee Liang.   Singapore: National University of Singapore, Department of Social Work, 1985. 82p.

Covers the period 1955 to 1984 and includes published and unpublished material such as dissertations and theses. All entries include authors' names, title, publisher, and other information.

755 **Books about Singapore 1984.**
Edited by Lim Kek Hwa.   Singapore: National Library, References Service Division, 1984. 97p.

As the editor acknowledges, this is not a comprehensive bibliography. It covers only English-language books available at the National Library. Entries are arranged alphabetically under subject headings. There is an index.

756 **Catalogue of government department/statutory board publications 1986.**
Ministry of Communications and Information, Information Division.   Singapore: Ministry of Communications and Information, 4th ed. 1986.

A useful list of official publications from all government bodies in Singapore. Each entry provides title, date of publication, pages, price, and place where the publication may be purchased. The catalogue also includes the list of Singapore Overseas Missions, Singapore Trade Development Board Offices, and the names, addresses, and telephone numbers of government departments and statutory boards.

757 **Publications and theses.**
National University of Singapore, University Liasion Office. Singapore: National University of Singapore, 1967- (annual).

A bibliography of the academic staff's publications and the theses completed during the academic year. It includes for each entry, the author's name, title of publication, place of publication, publisher, year of publication, and an abstract of the contents written by the author.

Bibliographies

**758  Index to periodical articles relating to Singapore, Malaysia, Brunei, ASEAN: humanities and social sciences supplement.**
Compiled by the National University of Singapore Central Library, Reference and Information Services. Singapore: National University of Singapore Library, 1985- (quarterly, with annual cumulations).
The printed version of a computerized data base of nearly 14,000 journal articles. This is the first quarterly issue. There are two previous volumes: one in 1984 covering the period 1980 to 1982, and the other in 1985 covering the period 1983 to 1984. In addition to the citations arranged by subject, the index provides the list of core journals from which the articles were taken, a list of common Malay and Arabic names, a list of subject headings, book reviews, and the author index. The limitation of this index is that of the 131 base journals used, only ten are from countries outside Asia, a feature which narrows the scope of the index considerably. On the other hand, by focusing on Asian journals, the index provides non-Asian readers with a useful guide to journals they may not find otherwise.

**759  The making of the National University of Singapore. A selected bibliography.**
Compiled by the National University of Singapore Library, Humanities/Social Sciences/Management Reference Department. Singapore: National University of Singapore, 1984. 157p.
Includes selected studies dealing with the historical background and development of the university as an institution, its faculties, programmes, schools, and departments.

**760  A bibliography of the demography of Singapore.**
Saw Swee-Hock, Cheng Siok-Hwa. Singapore: University Education Press, 1975. 120p.
An annotated bibliography covering population laws, housing, urban renewal, migration, racial composition, labour force, family planning, mortality, nuptiality, and other relevant aspects.

**761  Information resources on women in Singapore. Survey and bibliography.**
Marion Southerwood. Singapore: Ministry of Social Affairs, 1983. 130p.
As indicated in its inner cover, this is a survey of facilities and resources in libraries and other information centres dealing with 'women in development' in Singapore. The author describes in the first forty-seven pages the general scope of publications and reference sources on women and development in Singapore. The actual bibliography occupies another eighty-one pages and covers education, employment, childcare, family planning, legal status, marriage, divorce, political and trade union participation, socioeconomic status, welfare, and a useful list of bibliographies, directories, and statistical sources available before 1980 on the

subject of women. This report is available at the Ministry of Community Development (formerly Ministry of Social Affairs), MCD Building, 512 Thomson Road, Singapore 1129.

762 **Singapore heritage. A booklist.**
Compiled by Fatimah Sulaiman.  Singapore: National Library, 1986. 29p.

This is a rather brief selected bibliography of publications dealing with aspects of Singapore culture, landscapes, customs, religions, arts, language, architecture, biographies, and history.

763 **Social development in Singapore.**
Edited by Gottfried Voelker, Tai Chin Ling.  Bangkok: Clearing House for Social Development, 1975. vol. 1. no. 2. 131p.

Provides, among other things, a directory of institutions dealing with social development in Singapore and a bibliography of book reviews, selected abstracts of publications, periodicals, and research in progress at the time of publication. It is useful for readers interested in a general view of the research situation in Singapore in the mid-1970s.

764 **Annotated urban bibliography of Singapore.**
Compiled by Stephen H. K. Yeh, Margaret W. N. Leong.
Singapore: National University of Singapore, Statistics and Research Department, Housing and Development Board and Economic Research Centre, 1972. 94p.

An informative example of the importance given to research on housing in Singapore during the 1960s and early 1970s. This bibliography is divided into two parts dealing with public sector and private sector publications, respectively. The topics covered are social and economic issues, land-use planning, housing needs and development, and periodicals dealing with housing.

# Indexes

There follow three separate indexes: authors (personal and corporate); titles; and subjects. Title entries are italicized and refer either to the main titles (books), or to other works cited in the annotations. The numbers refer to bibliographic entry rather than page numbers. Individual index entries are arranged in alphabetical sequence.

# Index of Authors

# Index of Titles

199

205

206

# Index of Subjects

212

215

# H

Haematology 715
Hairdressing
  skills 477
Handicapped
  government services
    257
  legislation 262
  services 257
  social policy 262
  voluntary welfare
    organizations 257
  *see also* Society for
    Aid to the
    Paralysed
Handicaps Welfare
  Association
  employment issues
    734
  mechanical aid
    developments 734
  mutual assistance
    schemes 734
  periodical 734
  recreation 734
Hanyu pinyin
  teaching of 123
Health and welfare 3,
  163, 182-237,
  250-64
  economic
    development and
    improvements 250
  estimated household
    expenditure 192
  periodical 730
  preventive
    programmes 730
  primary care 515
  school health
    activities 730
  socioeconomic
    factors 220
  statistics 501, 513,
    515, 519
  support services 515
  *see also* Abortions;
    Amalgamated
    Union of Public
    Employees
    (AUPE); Central

Provident Fund
  (CPF); Child care;
  Child welfare;
  Chinese
  community;
  Cigarette smoking;
  Community work;
  Cooperative
  societies; Elderly;
  Family planning;
  Handicapped;
  Handicaps Welfare
  Association;
  Industry; Medicine
  and, e.g.
  Obstetrics; Mental
  health; Ministry of
  the Environment;
  Ministry of Health;
  Nutrition;
  Occupational
  health and safety;
  Political stability;
  Singapore Cancer
  Society; Singapore
  General Hospital;
  Society for Aid to
  the Handicapped;
  Teban Gardens
  health fair;
  Telephones; World
  Health
  Organization
  (WHO)
Health education 171-
  73, 191, 212, 216-
  17, 222, 236, 730
  *see also* Cigarette
  smoking; Drugs;
  Family counselling;
  Occupational
  health and safety;
  Singapore
  Anti-Narcotics
  Association; Teban
  Gardens health fair
Heart disease
  and alcohol 198
  and blood pressure
    198
  and cholesterol 198
  ischaemic 198

Hepatitis
  B 187, 218
  viral 193, 218
  *see also* Obstetrics
    and gynaecology
*Her World* (magazine)
  problem page 626
Heroin
  abuse 166
High technology
  industry
  factory construction
    589
Hinduism
  deities 134
  festivals 134
  temples 134
  terminology 134
  *see also* History;
    Thaipusam
Historiography 56, 579
  administrative 56
  diplomatic 56
  economic 56
  military 56
  political 56
  social 56
History 6, 9, 12, 19, 47-
  71, 420, 677, 720,
  762
  ancient 62
  and political
    development 305
  architecture 523
  background to
    success 58
  Botanic Gardens 38
  British Empire 54, 68
  British intervention
    93
  caste 97
  Chinese 70, 82, 111
  Chinese (clan
    associations) 95,
    111
  Chinese (communal
    group leadership)
    96
  Chinese (culture) 111
  Chinese (dialect) 111
  Chinese (dialect
    group

flats 141, 238, 242, 248
high-density 238
high-rise 238, 242, 246, 544
infrastructure 247
internal space 238
lifestyles 247-48
low-income families 242
maintenance 238
management 238, 241
management (contracts) 247
management (estate) 247-48
microcosmos concept 238
needs 248, 764
neighbourhoods and precincts 246, 248, 263
periodical 764
planning and design 238, 246-47
planning (land use) 764
policies 238, 247, 544
prefabrication 238
price trends 239-40
prices (high-rise) 239
prices (low-rise) 240
private apartments (cost) 239
problems 241, 317
progress 249
resettlement 141, 242, 247
residents' organizations 238
resource planning 247
safety 247
example to other Nations 244
social issues 764
social situation of high-rise dwellers 242
statistics 501, 513
technology 247
urban community 238

urban planning 249
urban renewal 248
see also Central Provident Fund; Community organizations; Cooperative societies; Expatriates; History; Housing and Development Board; International convention on high-rise, high-density living; Land; Public housing; Recreation (for high-rise dwellers); Residents' committees; Singapore Improvement Trust (SIT), Singapore Professional Centre (SPC)
Housing and Development Board 247, 524
economic analysis 248
government financial assistance 245
government legislation 245
implementation problems 245
reasons for success 244-45
swimming complexes 659
Systems and Research Department 246
see also Lin Thai Ker
Howe Yoon Chong (Minister for Health) 251
Howe Yoon Chong Report (problems

of the aged) 251
Human geography 579
economic 739
political 738
social 738
urban 738
Human resources 13
and economy 392, 406
development 436, 473
see also Manpower
Humanities
bibliography 758
Hypnotics
abuse 166

# I

IARC see International Agency for Research on Cancer
Identity see Ethnic groups (national and ethnic identity), and ethnic groups by name
Ideology 177
dominant 126
political 146
see also Education; Islam; Malay community; Military; People's Action Party; Women
IES see Institution of Engineers
Immigration see Migrants and migration
Immunization see Paediatrics
Immunology 715
Imports
statistics 502

Malaysia *contd.*
political relations 378
relations 299, 377
secession from (1965)
67, 94, 306, 310,
377
*see also* Association
of Southeast Asian
Nations (ASEAN);
Rajaratnam, S.;
Tax treaties
Management
of compliance 500
training courses 438
*see also* Information
technology;
Labour-
management
relations; National
University of
Singapore; Public
personnel
Management
Development
Institute of
Singapore 438
Mandarin language
469, 484, 494, 726,
746, 751
and radio 709
and television 709
promotion 124, 126
Singaporean features
114
'Speak Mandarin'
campaign 709
*see also* Baptist
church; Hanyu
pinyin
Mandarin literature
background 601
creative writing 727
Mandarin poetry 629
Mandarin television
drama 705
Mangrove forests
development 39
ecosystem 39
urban threat 39
Manpower and
manpower
planning 440,
464-77

and development
437, 474, 561
and economic
development 474
and government
institutions 467
and high technology
492
and productivity 404,
498
capital-intensive
production 474
changing conditions
561
future strategies 474
industrial
restructuring
strategies 492
industrialization 474
labour (foreign) 492
labour surplus 474
policies 403, 467, 561
shortage 474
statistics 404, 506,
561
wages 474
*see also*
Management;
Mass Rapid
Transit (MRT);
Mass Rapid
Transit
Corporation;
Skills; Women
(and employment)
Manufacturing 387,
397, 404, 698
codes of practice 744
collective agreements
441
material
specifications 744
periodical 744
product listing 698
productivity 436
publications 744
service listing 698
standards 744
statistics 404, 518
terminology 744
trade names and
brands 698

*see also* Industry and
industries by name,
e.g.
Pharmaceuticals;
Multinational
corporations;
Singapore
Manufacturers'
Association (SMA)
Maps and mapping 20,
58-59, 64, 462, 503,
507, 527, 531, 689,
751
British tradition 527
*see also* History;
Regions by name,
e.g. Emerald Hill
Marijuana
abuse 166
Marine resources
background 526
fisheries (research)
737
fisheries (statistics)
501, 513
fishing industry
(organizational
problems) 526
policies 526
research 526
role of education 526
Marine transport
legislation 460
navigational channels
450
procedures 450
tide tables 450
*see also* National
Maritime Board;
Ports; Shipping
industry
Marital law 334
child maintenance
340
forms of marriage
334
maintenance of
spouse 340
status and property
334
*see also* Divorce;
Wife abuse

(Secretary-General's report, 1984; 1985)
Opera *see* Chinese opera
Opiates
  abuse 166
Opposition (political)
  elected in 1985 276
  non-constituency politicians 300
  political party system 266, 278
  problems 278
  role of 333
  *see also* People's Action Party
Oral history *see* History
Oral History Department 100
Overseas missions 756

## P

Pacific region 738
Paediatrics
  childhood obesity (classification scheme) 197
  childhood obesity (epidemiology) 197
  hospital admissions 231
  hospital mortality 231
  immunization 193, 234, 237
  meningitis 210
  statistics 197
  *see also* Child care; National University of Singapore; Singapore Paediatric Society
PAP *see* People's Action Party
Parapolitical institutions 317
  and government consolidation 326
  *see also* Citizens'

Consultative Committees; Community Centres; Community organizations; Residents' Committees
Parastatal bodies
  management by senior bureaucrats 370
Parenthood *see* Family
Parks
  management 655
  provision 655
  usage 655
  *see also* Institute of Parks and Recreation; Parks by name, e.g. Jurong Bird Park; Regional Congress on Parks and Recreation
Parliament
  members 3, 105
Parties *see* Political party system and names of individual parties
Partnership
  taxation 414, 429
Partnership Act 431
Partnership law 345
  dissolution of partnership 339
  for laymen 339
  formation and duration of partnership 339
  nature of partnership 339
  partners and third parties 339
  reciprocal relations 339
  table of cases 339
  table of statutes 339
Pathology 715
Pattaya 486
Peat Marwick

International (accounting and auditing firm) 420
People's Action Party (PAP) 51, 280, 332
  activities 286
  and change 283
  and development 364
  and 'mass politics' 330
  and non-party institutions 270
  and opposition 270, 283
  and system maintenance 323
  as institution 302
  associations and activities in constituencies 270
  communist alliance 267
  communalist threat (policies against) 313
  electoral performance 286
  future of 275
  future social policies 275
  general election 1968 267
  general election success 1972 290
  grassroots activities 270
  ideology 267, 278
  inception, November 1954 267
  intolerance of corruption 364
  leadership 309
  local issues in constituencies 270
  manifesto 286
  membership 309
  nation-building 281
  organization and finance 267, 278, 309
  organization in constituencies 270

243

245

Singapore Standard
Occupational
Classification
(SSOC) 464
Census Planning
Committee 464
Singapore Teachers
Union
attitude to education
reform 567
report (1980) 567
Singapore Trade
Development
Board
Offices 756
Singapore Veterinary
Association
periodical 545
Singapore Zoological
Garden 564
SIT see Singapore
Improvement
Trust
Skills
enhancement 437
national standards
477
National Trade
Certificate 477
redistribution 474
see also Economy;
Industries and
occupations by
name, e.g.
Construction;
Hairdressing
Skills Development
Fund 439
SMA see Singapore
Manufacturers'
Association
Smoking see Cigarette
smoking; Medicine
(epidemiology)
SNIS see Singapore
National Identity
Survey
Social change 283
see also Bureaucracy;
Crime; crime
prevention;
Education policies;

Malay community;
Singapore Council
of Social Service
(and
socioeconomic
change)
Social conditions 13,
141-81
see also Child care
(effects of
socioeconomic
conditions);
Chinese
newspapers;
Obstetrics (effects
of socioeconomic
conditions)
Social control see
Education policies
Social development 13,
49, 406
bibliography 763
directory of
institutions 763
periodical 763
research 763
Social discipline 179-80
and democracy 180
and public policy 363
and social problems
180
see also Family
planning; Housing;
Language
Social history see
Historiography;
History (social)
and, e.g. (growth
and development)
Social mobility see
English language;
Languages and
dialects
Social policy 3, 184
see also Subjects by
name, e.g. Health
and Welfare
Social problems 162-74
products of affluence
291
promiscuity 291
yellow culture

(western
influences) 291
see also Chinese
secret societies;
Crime; Drugs and
drug abuse;
Education;
Elderly; Homicide;
Social discipline;
Suicide
Social sciences 395, 720
bibliography 758
development 579
periodical 749
research 590
teaching 590
trends 590
see also Crime;
Family; Malay
community
(socioeconomic
motivation);
Methodology
Social security see
Central Provident
Fund (CPF);
Ministry of Labour
Social services 150, 182-
265
classification by
recipients 260
community centres
260
directory 260
government bodies
260
see also Child
welfare;
Community
organizations;
Community work;
Handicapped;
Health and
welfare; Singapore
Association of
Social Workers;
Singapore Council
of Social Service;
Voluntary
organizations;
Housing; Medical
and health services

256

257

1  28' 30" N.

JOHOR BARU

MALAYSIA

Government Copyright Reserved. The approval of the Chief Surveyor
and the publisher is necessary before this map or part thereof may be
copied. SDS 113/88(5)

# Map of Singapore

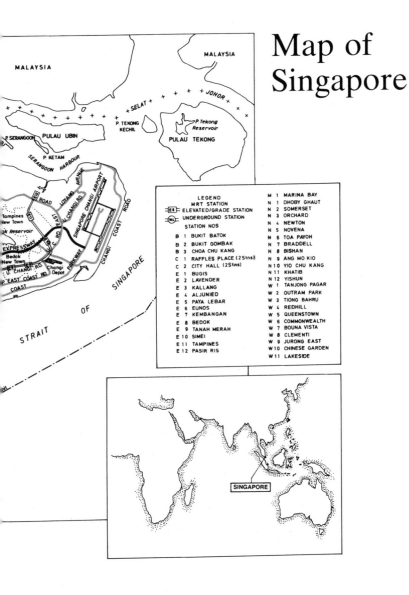

**LEGEND**

**MRT STATION**
- E6 ELEVATED/GRADE STATION
- W1 UNDERGROUND STATION

**STATION NOS**

| | |
|---|---|
| B 1 | BUKIT BATOK |
| B 2 | BUKIT GOMBAK |
| B 3 | CHOA CHU KANG |
| C 1 | RAFFLES PLACE (2 Stns) |
| C 2 | CITY HALL (2 Stns) |
| E 1 | BUGIS |
| E 2 | LAVENDER |
| E 3 | KALLANG |
| E 4 | ALJUNIED |
| E 5 | PAYA LEBAR |
| E 6 | EUNOS |
| E 7 | KEMBANGAN |
| E 8 | BEDOK |
| E 9 | TANAH MERAH |
| E 10 | SIMEI |
| E 11 | TAMPINES |
| E 12 | PASIR RIS |

| | |
|---|---|
| M 1 | MARINA BAY |
| N 1 | DHOBY GHAUT |
| N 2 | SOMERSET |
| N 3 | ORCHARD |
| N 4 | NEWTON |
| N 5 | NOVENA |
| N 6 | TOA PAYOH |
| N 7 | BRADDELL |
| N 8 | BISHAN |
| N 9 | ANG MO KIO |
| N 10 | YIO CHU KANG |
| N 11 | KHATIB |
| N 12 | YISHUN |
| W 1 | TANJONG PAGAR |
| W 2 | OUTRAM PARK |
| W 3 | TIONG BAHRU |
| W 4 | REDHILL |
| W 5 | QUEENSTOWN |
| W 6 | COMMONWEALTH |
| W 7 | BOUNA VISTA |
| W 8 | CLEMENTI |
| W 9 | JURONG EAST |
| W 10 | CHINESE GARDEN |
| W 11 | LAKESIDE |